SYSTEMS THAT SUPPORT DECISION MAKERS

John Wiley
INFORMATION SYSTEMS SERIES

Editors

Richard Boland
Case Western Reserve University

Rudy Hirschheim
University of Houston

Hirschheim: *Office Automation: A Social and Organizational Perspective*
Jarke: *Managers, Micros and Mainframes: Integrating Systems for End-Users*
Boland & Hirschheim: *Critical Issues in Information Systems Research*
Baskerville: *Designing Information Systems Security*
Schäfer: *Functional Analysis of Office Requirements: A Multiperspective Approach*
Mumford & MacDonald: *XSEL's Progress: The Continuing Journey of an Expert System*
Swanson & Beath: *Maintaining Information Systems in Organizations*
Friedman: *Computer Systems Development: History, Organization and Implementation*
Huws, Korte & Robinson: *Telework: Towards the Elusive Office*
Lincoln: *Managing Information Systems for Profit*
Ward, Griffiths & Whitmore: *Strategic Planning for Information Systems*
Irving: *Office Information Systems: Management Issues and Methods*
Silver: *Systems That Support Decision Makers: Description and Analysis*

SYSTEMS THAT SUPPORT DECISION MAKERS
Description and Analysis

Mark S. Silver

Anderson Graduate School of Management
University of California, Los Angeles

John Wiley
INFORMATION SYSTEMS SERIES

JOHN WILEY & SONS
Chichester · New York · Brisbane · Toronto · Singapore

Other Wiley Editorial Offices

John Wiley & Sons, Inc., 605 Third Avenue,
New York, NY 10158–0012, USA

Jacaranda Wiley Ltd, G.P.O. Box 859, Brisbane,
Queensland 4001, Australia

John Wiley & Sons (Canada) Ltd, 22 Worcester Road,
Rexdale, Ontario M9W 1L1, Canada

John Wiley & Sons (SEA) Pte Ltd, 37 Jalan Pemimpin #05-04,
Block B, Union Industrial Building, Singapore 2057

Library of Congress Cataloging-in-Publication Data:

Silver, Mark S., *1956-*
　　Systems that support decision makers : description and analysis / Mark S. Silver.
　　　　p.　　cm.—(John Wiley information systems series)
　　Includes bibliographical references (p.　　) and index.
　　ISBN 0-471-91968-3
　　1. Decision support systems.　I. Title.　II. Series.
　　T58.62.S54　1991　　　　　　　　　　　　　　　90–25321
　　658.4'03—dc20　　　　　　　　　　　　　　　　　CIP

British Library Cataloguing in Publication Data:

Silver, Mark S.
　Systems that support decision makers.
　1. Management. Decision making, use of computers
　I. Title　II. Series.
　658.4030285

　ISBN 0-471-91968-3

Phototypeset in 10/12 pt Baskerville by Dobbie Typesetting Limited, Tavistock, Devon
Printed and bound in Great Britain by Biddles Ltd, Guildford, Surrey

To my wife,
Candace,
and to my parents,
Evelyn and Samuel Silver

CONTENTS

SERIES FOREWORD

In order for all types of organisations to succeed, they need to be able to process data and use information effectively. This has become especially true in today's rapidly changing environment. In conducting their day-to-day operations, organisations use information for functions such as planning, controlling, organising, and decision making. Information, therefore, is unquestionably a critical resource in the operation of all organisations. Any means, mechanical or otherwise, which can help organisations process and manage information presents an opportunity they can ill afford to ignore.

The arrival of the computer and its use in data processing has been one of the most important organisational innovations in the past thirty years. The advent of computer-based data processing and information systems has led to organisations being able to cope with the vast quantities of information which they need to process and manage to survive. The field which has emerged to study this development is *information systems* (IS). It is a combination of two primary fields, computer science and management, with a host of supporting disciplines, e.g. psychology, sociology, statistics, political science, economics, philosophy, and mathematics. IS is concerned not only with the development of new information technologies but also with questions such as: how they can best be applied, how they should be managed, and what their wider implications are.

Partly because of the dynamic world in which we live (and the concomitant need to process more information), and partly because of the dramatic recent developments in information technology, e.g. personal computers, fourth-generation languages, relational databases, knowledge-based systems, and office automation, the relevance and importance of the field of information systems, and office automation, the relevance and importance of the field of information systems has become apparent. End users, who previously had little potential of becoming seriously involved and knowledgeable in information technology and systems, are now much more aware of and interested in the new technology. Individuals working in today's and tomorrow's organisations will be expected to have some understanding of and the ability to use the rapidly developing information technologies and systems. The dramatic increase in the availability and use of information technology, however, raises fundamental questions on the guiding of technological innovation, measuring organisational and managerial productivity, augmenting human intelligence, ensuring data integrity, and establishing strategic advantage. The expanded use of information systems also raises major challenges to the traditional forms of administration and authority, the right to privacy, the nature and form of work, and the limits of calculative rationality in modern organisations and society.

The Wiley Series on Information Systems has emerged to address these questions and challenges. It hopes to stimulate thought and discussion on the key role information systems play in the functioning of organisations and society, and how their role is likely to change in the future. This historical or evolutionary theme of the Series is important because considerable insight can be gained by attempting to understand the past. The Series will attempt to integrate both description—what has been done—with prescription—how best to develop and implement information systems.

The descriptive and historical aspect is considered vital because information systems of the past have not necessarily met with the success that was envisaged. Numerous writers postulate that a high proportion of systems are failures in one sense or another. Given their high cost of development and their importance to the day-to-day running of organisations, this situation must surely be unacceptable. Research into IS failure has concluded that the primary cause of failure is the lack of consideration given to the social and behavioural dimensions of IS. Far too much emphasis has been placed on their technical side. The result has been something of a shift in emphasis from a strictly technical conception of IS to one where it is recognised that information systems have behavioural consequences. But even this misses the mark. A growing number of researchers suggest that information systems are more appropriately conceived as social systems which rely, to a greater and greater extent, on new technology for their operation. It is this social orientation which is lacking in much of what is written about IS. The current volume, *Systems that Support Decision Makers: Description and Analysis*, provides a new perspective on decision making and decision support systems. Silver offers the reader much which is new as he reconceptualises the field of DSS, showing how too much of the work in this area has been misguided and where future research should be directed.

The Series seeks to promote a forum for the serious discussion of IS. Although the primary perspective is a more social and behavioural one, alternative perspectives will also be included. This is based on the belief that no one perspective can be totally complete; added insight is possible through the adoption of multiple views. Relevant areas to be addressed in the Series include (but are not limited to): the theoretical development of information systems, their practical application, the foundations and evolution of information systems, and IS innovation. Subjects such as systems design, systems analysis methodologies, information systems planning and management, office automation, project management, decision support systems, end-user computing, and information systems and society are key concerns of the Series.

Rudy Hirschheim
Richard Boland

PREFACE

When, in the mid-1980s, I began the project that led to this book, my objective was to examine critically the research literature in the emerging field of Decision Support Systems (DSS), investigating where the field had been, where it was, and where it might be headed. Among my many impressions of this exciting young field, which was generating a great deal of enthusiasm among researchers and practitioners, two stood out: (1) the early literature emphasized the processes of developing and implementing DSS rather than such substantive issues as the content of DSS and the effects they have on the processes through which people reach decisions and (2) the early literature consisted more of prescription than of description. These observations were certainly understandable. After all, the literature in a young, growing field cannot cover all possible topics. And clearly, the early DSS researchers believed strongly that the nature of the processes for building and implementing DSS was an important distinguishing characteristic of these systems and that prescription was necessary to "transfer" these processes to the practitioner community. Nonetheless, these observations troubled me, because good prescription depends on good description, and because knowing whether an approach to developing and implementing systems is good depends, in part, on studying the systems and effects it produces.

This book emerged from these observations, and from the conclusion that studying how computer-based systems affect people's decision-making processes must be a central issue in DSS research. The book concentrates, therefore, on systematically describing DSS and differentiating them one from another, a prerequisite for examining systematically how systems affect decision-making behavior.

In Chapter 1, I lay the groundwork for the subject, beginning with an historical tour and an intuitive characterization of DSS. Most importantly, in this chapter I discuss the difficulty of defining DSS formally, and introduce the definition I will use throughout the book. I also introduce the analytic perspective I will adopt—the view of DSS as interventions into decision-making processes—and give the reader a quick overview of those aspects of human decision-making processes that I will draw upon later in the book.

In Chapter 2, I present the broader context for the subject of describing DSS. Looking at the big picture, I present a framework for understanding DSS research and practice. After presenting my framework, I review 15 early and widely cited DSS contributions in terms of the framework. For the reader new to the subject of DSS this chapter serves as an overview of the field as a whole and as a survey of some of its more widely read books and papers. For the experienced DSS reader the chapter presents a new way of looking at the subject and these traditional readings.

At the beginning of Chapter 3, I make the case for description, arguing that a systematic approach to describing and differentiating DSS is necessary for many purposes, among them designing DSS and studying their effects. In the remainder of the book I present a three-tiered approach for describing and differentiating DSS.

I must offer a word of caution, especially to those readers new to the subject: the points of view I adopt are often not the traditional ones. For instance, while numerous DSS definitions abound, mine differs markedly from almost all of them. Similarly, while much of the DSS literature touts the importance of flexibility, I present both pros and cons of restrictiveness in a DSS.

This book represents a first step toward systematically describing and differentiating Decision Support Systems. Each of the subjects presented here requires further examination. My hope is that the book will stimulate further research on this subject, as well as serve as a foundation for examining how DSS affect the decision-making processes of their users.

ACKNOWLEDGMENTS

This book extends the work I began in my doctoral dissertation at the Wharton School. My thanks go to the many people who assisted me in the process of preparing that dissertation. In particular I owe a great debt to my advisor, Jim Emery, and to my committee members, Bob Zemsky, Gerry Hurst, Louis (Kip) Miller, and Lynn Oppenheim, not only for their guidance while I was developing the dissertation, but especially for their insight in encouraging me to revise the dissertation for publication as a book.

Jim Emery introduced me to Decision Sciences—both to the field and to the department—nearly two decades ago when I was an undergraduate. Jim's view of the role that computer-based information systems can play in supporting management has significantly influenced my own. And the ''decision-process'' perspective reflected in the department at Wharton has become central to how I approach computer-based decision support.

Jim also introduced me to Bob Zemsky, Director of the Institute for Research on Higher Education at Penn, with whom I had the pleasure to work for many years. Bob contributed significantly to the intellectual development of the concepts presented here, and the Institute provided valuable opportunities for applying and testing those concepts in practice. The Institute and its staff members provided, as well, a warm and productive working environment.

Since my arrival in Los Angeles, my colleagues in the Information Systems area at UCLA's Anderson Graduate School of Management have been terrific. Eph McLean, before leaving for Georgia State, and Clay Sprowls, before retiring, each urged me to extend my dissertation into a book. Lynne Markus and Burt Swanson were invaluable throughout the process, from discussing my ideas as they emerged through commenting on my drafts as they were written. Lynne demonstrated a unique ability to listen to what I had said or to read what I had written, to grasp its essence, to examine it critically, and then to elevate it to a higher plain. Her office was also a haven for me when I needed to escape from the book for a few minutes of good and revitalizing conversation. Burt methodically tested the logic and completeness of my arguments, ensuring their consistency and persuasiveness. Drawing on his experience, he also gave me sound advice to solve the various practical problems one encounters while writing a book. Both gave willingly of their time to provide me with timely feedback. I have no doubt that the quality of the book improved immeasurably thanks to their efforts.

Sidne Ward served as an able and dedicated research assistant throughout the duration of this project, helping with the full range of substantive and administrative tasks required to produce the manuscript. Neil Ramiller gave me expert editorial advice, and Bi-Chin Lee provided helpful bibliographic support. Virtually all the doctoral students who passed through the Information Systems area at UCLA during these past few years contributed in some way to this effort, either through their participation in class discussions, their feedback on drafts of the manuscript, or their responses when I cornered them in the hallway for their assessment of one passage or another. To all of them, I am grateful.

I have been fortunate to work with a very responsive publisher and editors. Dick Boland and Rudy Hirschheim, the editors of the John Wiley Series on Information Systems, provided valuable suggestions for converting the dissertation into a book and offered constant encouragement throughout the process of doing so. Diane Taylor, Wiley's editor for Management Science, was always ready and able to anticipate my needs, to respond to my inquiries, and to keep the project moving along.

I am thankful to Gerry DeSanctis, Chris Tang, and Ron Goodstein for reading passages from the book in the areas of their specialties and for offering valuable suggestions. Knowing they had reviewed these passages was very reassuring.

I have published some of the material in this book previously in journals and conference proceedings. Chapter 3 updates and develops concepts I introduced in "Descriptive analysis for computer-based decision support," *Operations Research*, vol. 36, no. 6, November–December 1988, pp. 904–916. Chapter 4 is a much-updated and significantly expanded version of "On the restrictiveness of decision support systems," in Ronald M. Lee, Andrew M. McCosh, and Piero Migliarese (eds), *Organizational Decision Support Systems, Proceedings of the IFIP WG 8.3 Working Conference*, Elsevier Science Publishers BV (North-Holland), Como, Italy, June 1988, pp. 259–270. Chapter 5 extends "Decisional guidance for computer-based decision support," *Management Information Systems Quarterly*, **15**(1), March 1991. And, with minor differences, Chapter 6's section "DSS as change agents: designing with system attributes" is contained in "Decision support systems: directed and nondirected change," *Information Systems Research*, vol. 1, no. 1, January–March 1990, pp. 47–70. I appreciate the assistance of the various editors and reviewers whose comments improved the quality of those papers and, therefore, this book.

While I am thankful to all those who contributed to the quality of this book, responsibility for any of its shortcomings and for the opinions expressed herein, of course, rests with me.

In addition to my professional associates I also appreciate the roles played by my family and friends. In particular, my parents have taught me to embrace challenges and pursue excellence, qualities that served me well while working on this project.

I have been engaged in writing this book almost since the day I married my wife, Candy. She has contributed greatly to bringing this project to fruition in many ways, among them by understanding my seemingly endless work schedule and my being generally unavailable to enjoy the California sunshine, by providing constant support and encouragement, and by helping to produce the final manuscript in her characteristically competent manner. For all her devotion, I am most grateful.

Chapter 1
INTRODUCTION

This book is about computer-based information systems that affect, or are intended to affect, the way people make decisions. Its purpose is to foster a better understanding of how these systems do what they do. More specifically, it aims to describe and differentiate systems, concentrating on those features that contribute to a system's effect on the decision-making behavior of its users.

In this introductory chapter I present the subject from several perspectives. It would be nice if I could begin with a definition of the object being studied, but in the field of computer-based decision support, widely accepted definitions have been elusive. Consequently, I start by establishing an historical context for the subject, and then I discuss the topic from an intuitive perspective. Only following these discussions do I confront the problem of formal definitions. After establishing the formal definition I will use throughout the book, I present one more perspective, the process view of decision making, which plays a central role in the study and which leads directly to an overview of decision-making processes. I conclude the chapter with an overview of the book.

AN HISTORICAL PERSPECTIVE

Computer-based Information Systems

I begin my stylized historical tour in the 1940s, at the time of the Second World War, during which the first fully electronic digital computers were developed. These machines were initially applied to the "number-crunching" needs of the military and scientific communities. Indeed, much of the impetus for developing computing machines at this time came from the substantial wartime needs of the military to calculate ballistic trajectories for artillery. Before long, however, the business community recognized that it, too, could benefit significantly from the availability of powerful computing machines. The first commercial computer was delivered to the Bureau of the Census in 1951, and throughout the 1950s and thereafter, more and more businesses adopted computer-based systems for such transaction processing tasks as payroll and billing. These transaction processing systems (TPS) offered companies the benefits of greatly reducing costs and, in many cases, engaging in a volume of business activity that would not be possible without the processing power of the computer.

Given the success of transaction processing systems, which performed primarily clerical functions, the next frontier for computer-based information systems was management. As computing power increased significantly in the 1960s, and as large quantities of computer-based data were being accumulated as a by-product of processing transactions, the idea of processing these data and reporting them to management as useful information emerged. After all, it was argued, what managers do most is use information to plan and control. And plenty of data are routinely being accumulated that ought to be useful in planning and controlling. These observations led to the birth of what were commonly referred to as management information systems (MIS).

A typical management information system of the 1960s appeared to managers as a set of prespecified, standardized, often periodic, reports (the familiar printouts on ream after ream of 11 by 14 inch paper that managers would receive, say, on a weekly basis). The reports contained information acquired from data already stored as a by-product of processing transactions. Sometimes the reports contained full, detailed data. Other times managers received summary or exception reports that reduced somewhat the volume of information they received.

The implicit promise was that "if you liked transaction processing systems, you will love management information systems." But most managers did not love these systems, and many hated them. Some quipped that these were not at all "management information systems," systems providing useful information to management, but "information management systems," systems that simply managed large quantities of information. And, in the article most often cited in the information systems literature of the 1970s,[*] Russell Ackoff (1967) went a step further; he called them "management *mis*information systems."

What was the problem with these systems? As standardized, predefined reports, they frequently were not responsive to managers' needs. To see this, consider Figure 1.1, which depicts two sets of information.[†] One contains all the information relevant for solving a given managerial problem, while the other contains the information in the standardized report. Managers wanting to use the report to solve the given problem encounter two difficulties. First, much of the information they need is not in the report; they must obtain it elsewhere. Second, the information they require that is in the report constitutes only a small fraction of the information the report contains; they must therefore search the printout at length to find the needed information. Given these two limitations it might be just as easy to keep the organization-supplied report closed on your desk as a large and expensive paper-weight, delegating the information gathering for the project to a staff assistant.

---

[*]Hamilton and Ives's (1982) analysis of MIS literature in 15 journals in the 1970s found that Ackoff's (1967) article was the one most often cited.
[†]Emery (1987) describes the trade-off between displaying irrelevant information and failing to display relevant information in a reporting system. Here I have adapted his reasoning to explain why many early management information systems were unsuccessful.

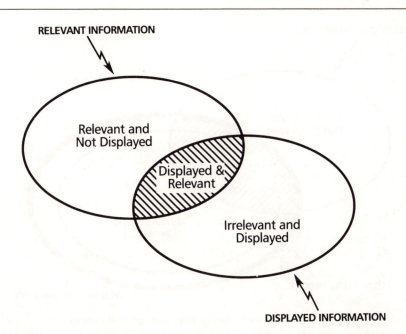

FIGURE 1.1 Using a standardized report to support a decision-making task. Note. Originally appeared as "Subsets of concern in a reporting system," James C. Emery, Lecture Notes. Reprinted with permission

Can these problems be remedied? Suppose, as in Figure 1.2, we increase the size of the report, routinely providing more standardized information to the manager. The likelihood of the necessary information being in the report increases. But the difficulty of finding the information increases as well, because the relevant data may constitute an even smaller fraction of the expanded report. What if we were to try the opposite approach, as in Figure 1.3, decreasing the size of the standardized report? Now, finding the needed information is easier, if it is in the report, but the likelihood of its being there has decreased. Either way, the standardized report does not meet the managerial needs.

Some responded to the shortcomings of these management information systems by saying, without further qualification, "MIS is a failure," or, in Dearden's (1972) words, "a mirage." Others responded less negatively, along the following lines:

> Supporting managers with computers seemed like a good idea, and, although we didn't succeed, we can certainly say we tried. The fallback position of using computers for the considerable benefits of transaction processing and the more limited ones of standardized managerial reporting isn't so bad, after all.

Still others responded by identifying the shortcomings of the early MIS and endeavoring to remedy them. A major weakness of the initial approach to MIS

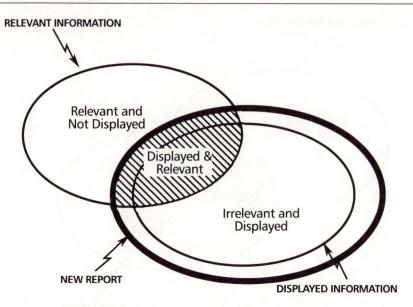

FIGURE 1.2   *Increasing the size of the report*

was that it focused on reporting information to management, rather than on supporting what management does with information, which, broadly speaking, is make decisions. More specifically, predefined, standardized reports are not responsive to the needs of managers to retrieve relevant information as they analyze problems and make decisions. The solution, therefore, may be found in designing systems that (1) give a manager ad hoc and more timely access to his or her information base and (2) provide computational capabilities specifically relevant for the manager's particular decision-making tasks.

A number of systems reflecting this philosophy were constructed in the late 1960s. For instance, Scott Morton (1971) built an interactive system that supported the production-planning decisions of the laundry equipment division of a large corporation, and Gerrity (1970, 1971) built a system that supported the investment decisions of portfolio managers in the trust division of a large bank. In 1971, Gorry and Scott Morton published their seminal paper on the subject, coining the term "Decision Support System (DSS)" to refer to this new breed of computer-based information system that focused on supporting people tackling unstructured or semistructured decision-making tasks. During the past two decades, concomitant with advances in the technology of interactive computing, the field of DSS has advanced with increasing speed.

At this point I must clarify some terminology. Until now I have used the phrase "management information system (MIS)" when describing the information reporting systems that historically followed TPS and preceded DSS. Many authors use MIS this way, restricting it to refer only to these reporting systems.

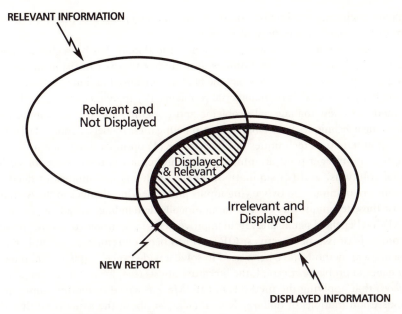

FIGURE 1.3   Decreasing the size of the report

Many others, however, use the term MIS more broadly to include the full range of managerially oriented information systems, including reporting systems as well as those systems that followed them, such as DSS and office systems.* Henceforth, I adopt the latter convention, using the term MIS to include reporting, decision support, and other more recent systems. Following Zmud (1983), I use the term ''information reporting system'' to refer to systems that produce standardized, prespecified reports.

Operations Research/Management Science

Before continuing the discussion of DSS *per se*, I must go back in history, returning to the time of the Second World War, during which the discipline now referred to both as Operations Research (OR) and as Management Science (MS) also emerged. Again, the military needs of the times spurred the scientific efforts, and again, shortly after the war, the developments were applied to industrial problems as well. During the war, Operations Research provided a scientific approach to two sets of operational problems: managing scarce resources efficiently and effectively, and planning and controlling military strategies and tactics. Since the war, the techniques of OR/MS have been applied to a wide range of business

---

*Some authors use MIS even more broadly, including TPS as well.

problems, including production and inventory management and the analysis and control of systems in a variety of domains.

Operations Research/Management Science traditionally has been characterized by the use of mathematical techniques and models to assist decision makers in solving their problems. Over the years the field has advanced rapidly: (1) developing new mathematical models of managerial problems, (2) applying existing mathematical models to new managerial problems and domains, and (3) developing new mathematical techniques for solving or manipulating these models. Among the better-known mathematical techniques of OR/MS are (1) optimization (such as linear, dynamic, and integer programming), where mathematical models are solved for optimal solutions, and (2) simulation, where mathematical models of decision problems are manipulated by varying inputs and observing changes in the outputs. Because these techniques are often computationally demanding, the advancement of OR/MS has benefited significantly from improvements in electronic computing power.

From at least two perspectives, OR/MS has been extremely successful. First, mathematical methods have been used to solve a wide range of theoretical models of managerial problems. Second, the literature attests (see, for instance, the journal *Interfaces*) that applying the methods of OR/MS has saved numerous companies millions upon millions of dollars. Nonetheless, at about the same time that the introduction of MIS was raising problems in the computer-based information systems field, OR/MS was having its own problems of acceptance by industry. Critics claimed that the field was preoccupied with mathematical techniques that were becoming increasingly remote from the real-world problems being modeled. And critics also claimed that, despite the tangible successes of OR/MS, its potential was not being realized; John Little expressed it as follows in the opening sentences of his landmark paper on models and managers:

> The big problem with management science models is that managers practically never use them. There have been a few applications, of course, but the practice is a pallid picture of the promise. (1970, p. B-466)

Why would managers resist using models? One explanation is that they are reluctant to use "black-box" optimization models that they do not understand and cannot control. Little's proposed solution was to design carefully the interface between model and manager, leading to an interactive, computer-based model—what he called a "decision calculus"—that is easy for managers to understand and to control. During the 20 years since then we have seen the development of many such models and modeling systems.

Decision Support Systems: A Confluency

Little's paper appeared in 1970; Gorry and Scott Morton's in 1971. As Figure 1.4 suggests, the histories of Computer-Based Information Systems and

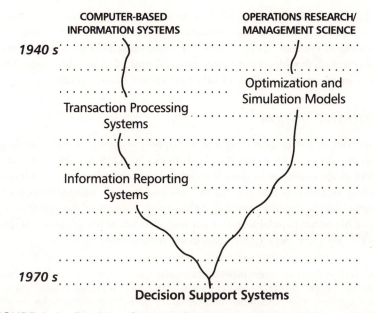

FIGURE 1.4 *Decision Support Systems: an historical perspective*

Operations Research/Management Science are first parallel and then confluent, meeting in the early 1970s. Spurred on initially by the military exigencies of the Second World War, each field's attention turned soon thereafter to problems in industry and, despite early successes, each field was seen some years later as not reaching its potential. After approximately 25 years of more-or-less independent development, the two fields reached a common conclusion: technological support for managerial decision making must not lock managers into systems they cannot control, be they prespecified reports or black-box models. Prespecified reports are not sufficiently valuable to managers who must make decisions; and black-box models may generate decisions, but they are more in the spirit of replacing decision makers than supporting them. Computer-based support for decision making, therefore, must support ad hoc retrieval of data and managerial control over model manipulation. Moreover, computational capabilities must be provided that focus on decision makers' specific problem-solving tasks, and these capabilities must be packaged in a way that makes them easy for a manager to use.

The systems we commonly refer to as Decision Support Systems flow from the confluency of Computer-Based Information Systems and Operations Research/ Management Science,* from the joining of the data-oriented and model-oriented approaches to supporting decision makers. In the mid-1970s, when Alter (1977b,

---

*In Chapter 2, I will identify several other streams of research that also feed into DSS.

1980) classified 56 DSS, he placed them in seven categories but noted that "the taxonomy can be collapsed into a simple dichotomy between data-oriented and model-oriented systems" (1980, p. 74). Today, most DSS provide at least easy access to data or flexible control over models, and most provide both. Today's DSS also incorporate a variety of other computer-based decision aids.

THE INTUITIVE NOTION

My brief tour of the origins of Decision Support Systems notwithstanding, the question remains, "What are they?" Intuitively, DSS are systems that help managers make decisions in situations where human judgment is an important contributor to the problem-solving process but human information-processing limitations impede decision making. DSS are an adjunct to the decision maker, extending his or her capabilities, but not replacing his or her judgment (Ginzberg and Stohr, 1982). Emery (1987) expressed it as follows:

> A decision support system provides computer-based assistance to a human decision maker. This offers the possibility of combining the best capabilities of both humans and computers. A human has an astonishing ability to recognize relevant patterns among many factors involved in a decision, recall from memory relevant information on the basis of obscure and incomplete associations, and exercise subtle judgments. A computer, for its part, is obviously much faster and more accurate than a human in handling massive quantities of data. The goal of a DSS is to supplement the decision powers of the human with the data manipulation capabilities of the computer. (pp. 102–103)

In a similar vein, Keen (1981) characterizes a DSS as "a staff assistant to whom the manager delegates activities involving retrieval, computation, and reporting" (p. 1). Given the limitations of humans and the strengths of computers as information processors, the notion of a DSS as a superhuman, information-processing assistant is intuitively appealing. Let us consider some examples of how computer-based systems provide information-processing assistance to human decision makers. The examples that follow are illustrative, not exhaustive.

Ad Hoc Data Retrieval

Since storing large quantities of information accurately and retrieving them rapidly is a strength of computers and a weakness of people, a basic form of computer-based decision support is providing decision makers with the ability to retrieve information selectively on an ad hoc basis. The available database might include data internal to the organization as well as data from such external sources as commercially available economic and marketing databases. The DSS might include capabilities not only for retrieving data selectively but also for aggregating the data and summarizing them statistically.

Ad hoc data retrieval gives decision makers access to information they would not have without the DSS. Would they literally not have access to the information? Perhaps. In some cases the data would be completely unavailable without the DSS. In most cases the information could be acquired without the DSS by human assistants, but either not in a timely fashion, not with sufficient accuracy, or at a cost that exceeds its value. So, practically speaking, the decision maker is able to consider information that otherwise would be unavailable. Such information might be valuable for finding problems, for discovering opportunities, for controlling actual performance against plans, and for analyzing alternative courses of action. For example, a marketing manager might, on an ad hoc basis, use a DSS to compare sales for the current period with sales for the same period last year, with projected sales for this year, with a given competitor's sales, or with sales for the industry as a whole.

Information Presentation

Presenting information in a variety of formats is another computerized information-processing facility that humans find supportive. In addition to displaying data in traditional, monochrome tables, many systems use color, computer-generated graphics, or both to present information to decision makers. Color is often used to highlight good or bad news, to contrast actual and budgeted figures, and to distinguish historical from projected data. A variety of business graphics (for instance, line graphs, bar graphs, and pie charts) are the most common graphic displays, but more sophisticated systems use such representation techniques as icons, maps, and animation. The display is frequently under control of the user, so he or she can rapidly switch from one format to another, can fine-tune a particular chart (changing coloring, shading, scale, and the like), or can combine multiple datasets into a single graphic representation.

The marketing manager, for example, might find different presentation formats appropriate for different types of sales comparisons. A pie chart might be best for comparing sales within the industry, while a line graph might be most appropriate for considering the company's own sales trend. The manager might arrive at the specific display format by trial and error, varying a number of the display parameters.

DSS enable users to examine information in formats that would otherwise not be possible. Again, should we take ''not be possible'' literally? For the most part it would be possible for a human staff assistant to produce the graphics generated by the computer by hand. But doing so would be extremely tedious and time-consuming; and some time would certainly elapse between the decision maker's requesting the visual and his or her receiving it. In reality, without the computer-based system, a decision maker's ability to study information depicted graphically would be extremely limited compared with what is now achieved with even a simple business graphics or electronic spreadsheet package.*

Manipulating Simulation (Planning) Models

Decision makers needing to predict the consequences of their actions, or of external events they cannot control, frequently employ computer-based (mathematical) planning models that simulate the key aspects of their decision problems. By manipulating the planning model, varying its inputs (either decision variables they control or exogenous variables they do not) and examining its outputs, decision makers can study the likely ramifications of their decisions. Technically known as case, parametric, or sensitivity analysis, this model-based activity is now popularly referred to as "What if?" analysis, because decision makers effectively ask the computer model "What if I do X?" or "What if Y happens?" For example, the marketing manager might ask, "What will happen to my sales and profits if I increase my price by $5 per unit?" or "What if my competitor cuts its price by $2 per unit?"

Even fairly simple simulation models can be computationally demanding, and sophisticated models can be especially so. Moreover, decision makers typically run simulation models many times, asking many "What if?" questions by systematically varying the inputs over many possible values of the decision and exogenous variables. Performing such extensive calculations by hand is, of course, theoretically possible, but is out of the question practically for most problems. With a DSS performing the laborious calculations, however, decision makers can run the models multiple times with minimal effort. And running the models more times enables users to generate more scenarios—that is, to consider more alternative actions and to evaluate more fully how each action might interact with uncontrollable events.

Executing Other Models

Simulation models constitute just one of many kinds of mathematical models decision makers employ. Decision makers often require such statistical techniques as regression analysis and time-series forecasting and such optimization methods as linear and integer programming. Executing these models is also computationally demanding, often even more so than executing simulation models, so DSS are again valuable information-processing assistants.

Other Decision Aids

DSS often include interactive decision aids that combine data retrieval, stylized display, and model-based processing to provide specialized functionality that meets

---

*The jury is still out, however, on the value of business graphics for decision making. For a quick overview of the issues see Jarvenpaa and Dickson (1986).

particular decisional needs. For instance, a decision aid that supports choosing one of many alternative solutions might help users scan relevant databases in search of viable alternatives, display the alternatives and their associated data in tabular form, produce graphical comparisons of the alternatives, allow users to identify specific alternatives they wish eliminated, select a winning alternative by applying user-defined mathematical formulae, and implement other, more sophisticated methods of choosing among the alternatives. People frequently make these types of decisions without computer-based support, but by being relieved of the information-processing burden, DSS users are able to consider more alternatives, to consider each alternative in greater detail, to see more clearly the relative merits of each alternative, and to use more sophisticated selection methods.

Outline processors exemplify a much different type of decision aid; they are a form of support for idea processing (Young, 1989), empowering decision makers to create, modify, store, retrieve, manipulate, and display textual information organized hierarchically in the form of an outline. Although the decision aid does not perform "number crunching," it does perform information processing. Of course, people manage outlines on paper all the time, but outline processors make adding items to the outline and restructuring it much easier, since the computer performs all of the information processing associated with rearranging and redisplaying the outline. Decision makers are more likely, therefore, to experiment with a variety of ways of organizing their thoughts.

Summary

We have just seen a number of ways that DSS serve as superhuman, information-processing assistants to decision makers. In each case the system performs operations that, theoretically, human decision makers could perform themselves, but that, because of their computational or data intensity, a human would not be likely to perform manually in practice. As one user of Lotus 1-2-3 observed, "Lotus can't do anything I can't do on the back of an envelope. But it would have to be *some* envelope!"

Compared with humans, DSS provide information, stylized displays, and analytical results with greater timeliness, greater accuracy, and less cost. Perhaps more importantly, these relative advantages of using a computer-based system to process information empower decision makers to engage in more intensive and extensive decision-making behavior. They can retrieve more data, display more graphs, run more simulations, and so forth. And this behavior *can* translate into better decision making. For example, DSS enable decision makers to discover problems earlier, to generate more alternative solutions to problems, to study more carefully the consequences of each proposed solution, to present and defend proposed decisions more convincingly, to control actual performance against decided-upon plans more effectively, and to understand their businesses and industries better. So DSS can improve both how efficiently and how effectively decisions are made.*

The various examples of DSS as information-processing assistants also illustrate how the DSS approach takes advantage of the relative strengths of humans and machines. Freed by the computer from responsibility for the tedious information-processing tasks associated with making decisions, the human can concentrate on judgmental activities. Easy access to otherwise unavailable information, displays, and analyses can enrich the decision maker's judgmental processes. For instance, graphical displays may enhance a person's ability to recognize patterns in data. Retrieving historical data may support a person's ability to learn from experience and to reason by analogy. The results of simulation and other model-based analyses can enlighten a decision maker's subjective assessment of alternative courses of action.

In addition to viewing DSS as information-processing assistants, the intuitive notion generally regards DSS as interactive systems that are easy to use, controlled by the user, flexible, specific to particular decision-making environments, and responsive to changes in the decision-making environment. Moreover, the intuitive notion is that DSS do ''not attempt to automate the decision process, predefine objectives, or impose solutions'' (Keen and Scott Morton, 1978, p. 2). As we probe the subject more deeply, we shall see how well these intuitive notions do or do not stand up.

THE PROBLEM WITH DEFINING DSS

On one of the first occasions that I spoke publicly about my work on Decision Support Systems, I began my talk by inviting the audience to pose questions as they arose during the presentation. Not 30 seconds later, while I was still in the middle of the title slide, a hand went up in the back of the room and a doctoral student asked, ''According to your definition, is SPSS [a popular statistical package] a DSS?'' On that day I learned that if, as Brooks (1975) claims, software engineering is a tar pit, then formally defining the phrase ''Decision Support System'' is surely one as well. The seemingly simple question ''What is a DSS?'' can entrap, and the more one struggles with the issues it raises, the more difficult extricating oneself can become. Perhaps the safest route for me to follow here, therefore, would be to move directly from the intuitive notion of DSS to the process

---

*Keen and Scott Morton (1978) distinguish efficiency from effectiveness, stating that the distinction is central to their view of DSS, and asserting that DSS ''improve the effectiveness of decision making rather than its efficiency'' (p. 1). Bennett (1983b) endorses and expands on this position, while Moore and Chang (1983) explicitly oppose it. Alter (1980) suggests that gains in personal efficiency do belong within the domain of DSS. I concur with Alter and conclude, as did Moore and Chang, that the distinction as presented in the DSS literature is ''confusing.'' The efficiency/effectiveness distinction appears to be most important for its motivational value, reminding us not that improving efficiency is unimportant, but that improving effectiveness *is* important.

view of decision making, circumventing a definition entirely. But understanding the subject fully requires confronting why so much confusion surrounds its name.

Although there is no single, agreed-upon definition of DSS (Sprague, 1980; Alter, 1981; Ginzberg and Stohr, 1982; Watson and Hill, 1983; Stabell, 1983; Rockart and DeLong, 1988, among others), historically, Decision Support Systems have been defined along the following lines:

- A *Decision Support System (DSS)* is a computer-based information system that supports people engaged in decision-making activities.

In this context, ''support'' is intended to mean that

(1) the system assists human decision makers to exercise judgment—that is, the system is an aid for the person or persons making the decision; and
(2) the system does not make the decision—that is, the system helps decision makers exercise judgment but does not replace the human decision makers.

Point (1) has been used to distinguish DSS from information reporting systems, which have frequently been criticized for not being sufficiently responsive to people's decision-making needs. Point (2) has been used to distinguish DSS from ''black-box'' optimization models, which have frequently been criticized for not involving decision makers sufficiently in the problem-solving process. Both points follow from the notion that the tasks supported by a DSS lack structure. The lack of structure explains (1) why the decision maker requires assistance and (2) why the computer-based system cannot replace the human decision maker.

I shall refer to this as the ''historical'' or ''traditional'' definition of DSS. Clearly a product of the historical context that produced the first DSS about 20 years ago, it might have remained a satisfactory DSS definition to this day. Unfortunately, by adding a variety of qualifications and refinements (for instance, who the decision maker is and how he or she is supported), we have acquired an oversupply of alternative definitions. Some definitions are explicit, others implied by the assumptions made by various DSS researchers. Some definitions differ one from another only with respect to small nuances. Others conflict directly. Still other definitions are oblique, defining DSS in completely different ways.

Sources of Disagreement

Three factors appear to explain the variance in DSS definitions: (1) early research activities, (2) ongoing developments, and (3) marketplace dynamics. Much of the early DSS research can be characterized as prescription based upon limited description. After studying a small number of systems (sometimes only one), researchers drew conclusions about what DSS should do, how they should be designed, how they should appear to the user, how they should be configured internally, who should use them, and how they should be used.* These early conclusions became, in many cases, *de facto* definitions of DSS. But different researchers, working with different systems, generated different implicit definitions.

DSS definitions also vary because as technology advances, new forms of computer-based decision support are continually being invented. One might expect that technological advances would lead to a broadening of the definition of DSS, but the effect seems to be the opposite. The current practice is to brand many of these developments new types of systems (Executive Support Systems, Group Decision Support Systems, Expert Support Systems, Idea Processing Systems, and so forth). Finding ourselves in the midst of a proliferation of system types, the issue becomes defining which of these are subclasses of DSS, which intersect the set of DSS, and which are distinct from DSS. Researchers of the newer system types often define DSS narrowly, and differently from each other, to distinguish the systems they are studying from "traditional" DSS. For instance, in comparing DSS with Expert Systems, Turban and Watkins (1986) associate DSS with problems that are ad hoc and unique as opposed to repetitive; but in distinguishing DSS from Executive Support Systems, Rockart and DeLong (1988) associate DSS with decisions that *are* repetitive.

A third source of definitional variance is that, given a highly competitive marketplace for computer software, vendors are motivated to manipulate the DSS rubric. When DSS was a new and fashionable "buzzword," vendors wanted to define it as broadly as possible so it would include their products. But since so many products have squeezed beneath the DSS umbrella, vendors now differentiate themselves by reverting to a more limited definition of DSS, claiming that what they offer is something else (whatever the latest fad may be).

The conflicts over definitions are probably best illustrated by considering some frequently asked questions such as the following, several of which have repeatedly been the themes of sessions at major conferences:

- Are ESS (Executive Support Systems, Rockart and DeLong, 1988) distinct from DSS or are they a subset of DSS? For that matter, are ESS and EIS (Executive Information Systems, Rockart and Treacy, 1982) the same or are they in some way different one from another?
- Are electronic spreadsheets, such as Lotus 1-2-3, DSS? What about planning languages, such as IFPS? Statistical packages, like SPSS and SAS? Linear programming packages?
- What is the relationship between Expert Systems and Decision Support Systems? Is an Expert Support System (Luconi, Malone, and Scott Morton, 1986) a DSS?

---

*Notable exceptions are Alter (1977b, 1980) and Keen (1980), who studied 56 and 30 systems, respectively.

The answers to these questions depend upon one's definition of DSS. Depending upon whom you ask, which journals you read, which conferences you attend, and which advertisements you consider, you will obtain different answers to each of these questions.

The conflicts center primarily around whether one adopts a broad or narrow definition of DSS. The broad definitions move in the direction of counting as a DSS any computer-based information system intended to improve decision making, but they differ among themselves in exactly where they define the boundary. The narrow definitions use one or more criteria to limit what qualifies as a DSS, often distinguishing DSS from such other systems as Executive Support Systems, Expert Support Systems, and so forth.

At the 1981 NYU Symposium on Decision Support Systems, Ginzberg and Stohr (1982) surveyed six definitions of DSS (reprinted as Table 1.1), observing a shift over time in the nature of DSS definitions, leading to a narrowing of the systems defined as DSS. While arguing that such a narrowing is a proper function of a definition, they lament the failure of recent definitions to provide a consistent focus. For instance, some define DSS in terms of how they are used, whereas others do so with respect to how they are developed.

TABLE 1.1   Ginzberg and Stohr's analysis of the concepts underlying DSS definitions

Source	DSS defined in terms of:
Gorry and Scott Morton (1971)	problem type, system function (support)
Little (1970)	system function, interface characteristics
Alter (1980)	usage pattern, system objectives
Moore and Chang (1983)	usage pattern, system capabilities
Bonczek *et al.* (1980)	system components
Keen (1980)	development process

Note. Reprinted with permission from "Decision support systems: issues and perspectives," Michael J. Ginzberg and Edward A. Stohr, in *Decision Support Systems*, North-Holland Publishing Company, 1982, pp. 9–31. Copyright (1982) Elsevier Science Publishers BV. All rights reserved.

It appears that the field cannot even agree on how it disagrees. Two years later, at the 1983 Harvard Colloquium on Information Systems, Scott Morton (1984) asserted that "[a]s many authors have pointed out, a general broadening (and consequent debasing) of the term *DSS* has caused it to lose much of its specific meaning" (p. 16). Ginzberg and Stohr claim definitions are becoming narrow; Scott Morton says they are becoming too broad. Both viewpoints have merit: while some definitions have become very narrow, others have become very broad. The broad definitions conflict with the narrow ones, and the narrow ones also conflict one with another.

Substantive Conflicts

Definitions of DSS conflict substantively on a number of points—not all independent—concerning what is and what is not a DSS. These substantive differences tend to arise either from alternative interpretations of the traditional definition, from alternative approaches to updating the traditional definition to accommodate technological advances, or from a setting aside of the traditional definition versus a strict adherence to it. For now, my purpose is to identify the conflicts; I treat most of the issues they raise in more detail later on.

Data Retrieval and Modeling Capabilities

Most DSS definitions view DSS as supporting decision makers by providing data- and model-oriented capabilities (see, for instance, Keen and Scott Morton, 1978; Sprague, 1980; Moore and Chang, 1983; Watson and Hill, 1983). At issue is whether a given system *must* provide both capabilities to qualify as a DSS. A number of authors (Rockart and DeLong, 1988; Mittman and Moore, 1984; Reimann and Waren, 1985, among others), see model-oriented capabilities as essential to the concept of DSS. In particular, many DSS observers see "What if?" simulation analysis as central to the DSS approach. These model-oriented views conflict with Keen and Scott Morton (1978), who recognized that some DSS may not contain analytical capabilities, with Alter (1977b, 1980), who identified both data-oriented and model-oriented systems as DSS in his study of 56 systems in the mid-1970s, and with Emery (1987), who more recently noted that although "a data-oriented DSS provides a relatively low degree of aid to the human decision maker" compared to a more sophisticated model-oriented system, "the information obtained from such a DSS may have great value" (p. 105).

Managerial Level

Anthony (1965) distinguished three levels of planning and control activity in organizations: operational control, management control, and strategic planning. Some researchers (for example, Gorry and Scott Morton, 1971; Sprague, 1980; Watson and Hill, 1983) argue that all three levels are appropriate targets for DSS, but two more limited views of DSS applicability have also been expressed. Some assert that DSS support only the top two levels—that is, non-operational decision making. This position maintains that the term DSS applies to supporting tasks lacking in structure, where human judgment is indispensible, and that these tasks tend to occur at the top two levels. Others claim that DSS applies mainly to operational and management control, because strategic planning is so lacking in structure that it cannot be supported by the traditional methods of DSS.

System Specificity

Generalized systems such as electronic spreadsheet packages and financial planning languages can be problematic for DSS definers. These systems are content-free, in the sense that they provide generalized modeling (and some data management) capabilities, but do not provide specific models or data structures. Instead, these systems empower people to create their own models and data. Most DSS observers agree that when professional developers use an electronic spreadsheet package or planning language to create a specific DSS, the spreadsheet package or planning language is not a DSS but a "DSS Generator" (Sprague, 1980), a software system for developing DSS. But what about when decision makers use the content-free package directly to build their own models and then manipulate these models to make decisions? Many argue that the electronic spreadsheet package or planning language is still a DSS Generator, not a DSS, but others contend that the system is now functioning as a DSS. In other words, some people assert categorically that empty electronic spreadsheet packages and financial planning languages are never DSS, whereas others claim these empty systems may or may not be DSS depending upon how they are being used.

Support

Those who abide by a strict interpretation of the historical definition consider such systems as linear programming packages, information reporting systems, and statistical analysis packages not to be DSS, either because these systems are not sufficiently supportive of the decision maker or because they tend to replace rather than support him or her. Indeed, the original notion of DSS was, in part, a response to the optimization models and information reporting systems of the 1960s. Similarly, statistical packages such as SPSS and SAS, by being neither problem-specific nor oriented toward specific decisional activities, are seen as insufficiently supportive of managerial decision-making needs to qualify as DSS. All of these systems, however, can be and are being used to assist decision makers. Many DSS researchers, therefore, count some or all of these systems as DSS.

Problem Frequency

While Rockart and DeLong (1988) associate DSS with repetitive decisions, Turban and Watkins (1986) associate them with problems that are ad hoc and unique. Donovan and Madnick (1977) adopt a broader view, identifying two classes of DSS, "institutional DSS, which deal with decisions of a recurring nature, and ad hoc DSS, which deal with specific problems that are usually not anticipated or recurring" (p. 79).

The conclusion that DSS support repetitive tasks follows from the premise that DSS need to be specific to the problems they support. If an organization is investing the time and money required to build a system tailored to a particular problem, it is argued, then that task should be one that is performed repeatedly. The conclusion that DSS support ad hoc tasks follows from the premise that DSS support tasks lacking in structure and at the top managerial levels. These tasks, it is argued, tend to be one-time decisions. Most people agree that repetitive and nonrecurring tasks each require different kinds of systems; the question is whether both should be called DSS (as Donovan and Madnick do), or whether the definition should be limited to one or the other. If so, which one would it be?

Interactive Use

Most systems that support decision makers are interactive; the system runs on a timesharing system or dedicated personal computer with which the user communicates directly. But is interactivity a prerequisite for classifying a system as a DSS? Either implicitly or explicitly, most DSS definitions assume so (Keen and Scott Morton, 1978; Sprague, 1980; Keen, 1981; Watson and Hill, 1983; Reimann and Waren, 1985; Young, 1989, among others): "It isn't a DSS if you can't see your reflection in the screen." The requirement stems from the argument that interactivity is necessary to support a manager's real-time problem-solving processes. In fact, many DSS observers go a step further, claiming that the quality of the interactive interface is essential and that DSS are interactive systems *that managers can use easily*.

Not all researchers agree that interactivity is a requirement for DSS. Moore and Chang (1983), for example, note that although a batch system would be less responsive to a user's needs, interactivity should not be an intrinsic part of the categorization of a DSS. Similarly, Alter (1981), in his critical analysis of DSS definitions and connotations, counts batch as well as interactive systems as DSS.*

A Solution

Perhaps the best solution, were it feasible, would be to abandon the appellation "Decision Support System" entirely, because it means so many different things to so many different people. But the term has proliferated too widely for that. The second best solution, in the spirit of the first, is to move toward a broad, inclusive, unifying definition. The multiple, conflicting, narrow definitions we have now make the term meaningless as a basis for communication among researchers and between researchers and practitioners. Researchers constantly draw conclusions about "DSS" that depend on how they have defined them. These conclusions about how to develop DSS, when to use them, what their effects will be, and so forth are valueless to other researchers or to practitioners unless the scope of systems to which the findings apply is clearly defined. Moreover, we

---

*Alter (1977a, 1981) argues that what matters is not whether the computer system is interactive but whether the system is used to support "interactive problem solving," which may or may not be the most appropriate usage pattern in a given situation.

cannot build a cumulative knowledge base if each study uses its own definition of the object being examined. When our findings conflict, for instance, we do not know if the differences are semantic or substantive.

Considering how much effort academicians have expended trying to distinguish "true" from "would-be" DSS, it seems likely that the commonalities across the systems variously assessed as DSS and non-DSS are much greater than the differences. If so, the best strategy is to begin by recombining all of these systems into a single class—call it DSS—and then to describe them systematically, studying how they are similar and, in particular, how they are different. This strategy does not confuse a broad definition with a melting pot. Adopting a broad definition, one that brings together the diversity of systems we find today, both enables and necessitates a careful differentiation of these systems based on their features. To this task the majority of this book is devoted. If systems differ significantly and systematically—as the arguments favoring narrow definitions suggest they will— then this will become evident from the analysis. And the distinct subclasses of systems identified in this manner will be distinguished methodically.

Systematic description and differentiation, within a broad rubric, is preferable to the current practice of comparing each new variant with one or another of the narrow definitions. After 20 years of talking about DSS, and often splitting hairs over what does and what does not qualify as one, the time has come for the field to describe systematically how the characteristics of computer-based systems that may affect decision makers can vary, and to differentiate systems on the basis of these characteristics rather than hype and hair splitting. Consequently, I employ an extremely broad definition, one more encompassing than the broadest of definitions today:

● A *Decision Support System (DSS)* is a computer-based information system that affects or is intended to affect how people make decisions.

In this book the phrase "Decision Support System" and its acronym "DSS" are shorthand for any computer-based information system that may have a bearing on how people make decisions. I include systems that are deliberately excluded from many or most definitions, for instance, data- as well as model-oriented systems, batch as well as interactive systems, content-free as well as decision-specific systems. In particular, I include information reporting systems and mathematical programming packages, as well as Executive Support Systems, Expert Support Systems, Group Decision Support Systems, and Idea Processing Systems.

My definition differs markedly from other definitions, because its purpose differs markedly from their purposes. Most of the definitions in the literature can be seen as prescriptive, defining either what a DSS *should* be to be consistent with the historical concept, or what a DSS *should* be to be as successful as possible in supporting decision makers. Such definitions are constrained, respectively, by either history or current knowledge. In contrast, my definition departs from the historical concept and is not tied to current knowledge. It is intended to lead to description, not to embody prescription. Saying nothing about what computer-based systems that support decision makers *should* be, the definition frees us to study what they are and can be.

Scott Morton (1984) argues that broadening the definition of DSS debases the concept. But the concept has already been debased by so many different narrow definitions. In the historical context of the early 1970s, distinguishing DSS from the information reporting systems and optimization models of the day was important to break with current practice, to "get the DSS bandwagon rolling." But in our current context it is more important to examine all available computer-based systems, most of which support decision making in some way, and to learn how they are similar and how they are different. Ginzberg and Stohr (1982) observed not only that DSS definitions are becoming more narrow, but also that the questions raised by the definitions "collectively ignore the central issue in DSS, that is, support of decision making" (p. 12). The broad approach taken here allows us to focus on precisely that.

THE PROCESS VIEW OF DECISION MAKING: DSS AS INTERVENTIONS

Understanding how computer-based systems affect decision makers requires knowing something about how people make decisions. When studying human decision making, we can use two approaches (Zeleny, 1982; Kleindorfer, Kunreuther, and Schoemaker, 1991): the outcome-oriented approach or the decision-process approach. The outcome orientation is concerned with the question "What is the decision?" The process view asks "How is the decision reached?"

We employ elements of both approaches in analyzing and designing DSS. Building optimization or multi-attribute utility models into a DSS is an example of using traditional outcome-oriented techniques. The model is a "black-box" that transforms inputs into outputs. Were we studying how to replace the human decision maker, such outcome-oriented models might suffice. We *might* not need to pay attention to the *process* of decision making. But our objective is to understand how DSS affect decision makers' behavior, and this requires understanding how DSS affect the processes through which decision makers arrive at decisions. Consequently, while we may draw upon both approaches, the process-oriented view must dominate.

The process view of decision making forces us to recognize that DSS are not just information-processing assistants but interventions into the processes through which decisions are made. When we augment a person's decisional apparatus with a computer-based system, we are also changing the way that apparatus operates. In the most simple case the only change may be that activities previously performed manually are now mechanized. At the other extreme the entire process may be supplanted by a new one.

A number of outcome-oriented empirical studies—see reviews by Sharda, Barr, and McDonnell (1988) and Benbasat and Nault (1990)—attest to DSS affecting decision-making behavior. The recent process-oriented studies of Jarvenpaa (1989) and Todd and Benbasat (1988), which examine how DSS affect decision makers' approaches to solving multi-attribute problems, present more convincing evidence that DSS intervene into the way decisions are made. Jarvenpaa found that how attributes and alternatives were presented affected decision makers' choice of information search strategies; Todd and Benbasat found that the existence and characteristics of decision aids affected decision makers' choice of solution strategies.

Although the designer's intention may be to improve decision making, building a DSS presents dangers as well as opportunities. The hope is that DSS interventions will leverage decision-making processes, causing or enabling decision makers to adopt superior processes. Less sanguine is the prospect that DSS interventions may cause decision makers to become further entrenched in current, ineffective processes (Stabell, 1983) or, worse yet, to adopt inferior ones.

Basing their argument on recent findings in psychology, as well as several empirical DSS studies, Kottemann and Remus (1987) suggest that DSS can have dysfunctional consequences for decision-making performance. For instance, Fripp (1985) experimented with three DSS for financial decision making, finding that users of two of the DSS achieved asset positions worse than the non-DSS users. Elam and Mead (1990) tested the effects of two DSS intended to increase the creativity of decision makers. Relative to unaided decision makers at the same task, one system increased creativity but the other inhibited it. And in a pilot study, Kottemann and Remus found, on average, subjects without computer-based aids outperformed those using a DSS for a production scheduling task.

Similar concerns have been raised in the context of group decision support. In an experimental setting, Watson, DeSanctis, and Poole (1988) found, in addition to intended consequences of GDSS use, such unintended consequences as GDSS users' perceiving that the problem-solving process was less understandable and the issues discussed more trivial. In a field study of an executive-level group decision room, Gibson and Ludl (1988) discovered a number of negative consequences that conflicted directly with the system's objectives of "truth and trust."

These findings remind us that human and system-based decision-making processes have both strengths and weaknesses. As Figure 1.5 suggests, DSS can improve human decision-making processes by amplifying their strengths and attenuating their weaknesses, whereas DSS can degrade decision-making processes by attenuating their strengths and amplifying their weaknesses.

Consider, for example, someone trying to rent a new apartment. One weakness of this person's unaided decision-making process might be that, due to limited information-processing capabilities, he or she considers only a small number of alternative units and only a small number of attributes for each unit. Another

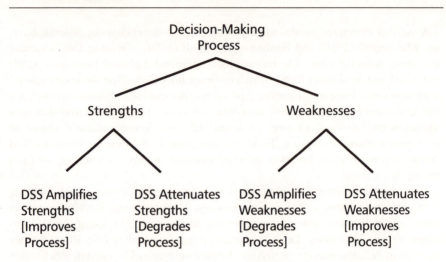

FIGURE 1.5   Effects of DSS on decision-making processes

weakness might be that he or she uses a sequential process, considering alternatives one at a time until a satisfactory apartment is found, because doing so requires less cognitive effort than evaluating the full set of alternatives to find the best apartment on the market. Among the strengths of the process might be the person's diligence and accuracy in acquiring information about available units, as well as his or her intuition when acquiring and processing the information. For instance, if a unit ''looks too good to be true'' based on the usual attributes, the person might search for additional attributes that explain the anomaly.

Suppose the prospective renter acquires a computer-based system that supports apartment selection. With such a system the person might consider more alternative units and more attributes for each, attenuating this shortcoming of the current process. The system might also enable him or her to acquire information even more accurately and in a more timely fashion, amplifying these strengths of the current process. Each of these effects constitutes an improvement to the process. On the other hand, the functionality of the decision aid might reinforce the sequential elimination process, amplifying this weakness. And by relying on the decision aid and the information it provides, the role of the renter's intuition might be attenuated. These last two effects constitute degradations in the process.

More generally, what are the strengths and weaknesses of human decision-making processes, and how can computer-based systems amplify or attenuate them? Let us concentrate first on individual decision making. With respect to the strengths of humans as decision makers, we often point to our intuition, our ability to learn from experience, and our creativity. A DSS might amplify these strengths by relieving decision makers of the tedium of mundane information processing, enabling them to concentrate on more creative and judgmental activities. Or a DSS might more directly support these characteristics; for instance, the use of computer-based systems to support creativity is now a subject of great interest. On the other hand, relying too heavily on a computer-based system, especially one with restrictive capabilities, might stifle creativity, learning, and intuition, attenuating these human strengths. Indeed, Elam and Mead's experiment showed that one DSS enhanced creativity while the other inhibited it.

Turning now to the weakness of humans as decision makers, a large body of literature in psychology, especially in behavioral decision theory, has found that due to limited information-processing capabilities, humans frequently rely on simplifying heuristics rather than normatively optimal procedures when making decisions, often leading systematically to biases in the ways they acquire and process information. By expanding a decision maker's information-processing capabilities a DSS might reduce the need for simplifying heuristics and alleviate the effects of such "systematic cognitive biases." On the other hand, the features of particular decision aids might have the opposite effect, inducing or exacerbating such biases.

Consider, for example, the various biases associated with acquiring information.* If a DSS presents decision makers with information, in a unified and readily accessible form, for which they would otherwise have to search sequentially, many of the biases that lead to decision makers' not acquiring or not weighting appropriately all relevant information might be alleviated. But the DSS might promote other biases that follow from order effects in the presentation of the information, from the mixing of quantitative and qualitative data, or from decision makers' relying too greatly on the DSS's database to the exclusion of other relevant information.

The same type of analysis can be applied to group decision making. We usually view the synergy that can follow from bringing a collection of individuals together to perform a task jointly as the strength of group processes. The weaknesses of groups are the "process losses" of group interactions, including dominance by individual group members, social pressures to conform, extreme influence of high-status members, and inhibitions against expression (Huber, 1984; Applegate, Konsynski, and Nunamaker, 1986; DeSanctis and Gallupe, 1987). Group Decision Support Systems endeavor to improve group processes by providing tools, such as "Electronic Brainstorming" (Applegate *et al.*, 1986), that enhance the prospects for group synergy, and by including features in those tools, such as anonymity, that can reduce the process losses. But these same tools and features might have the opposite effects. Brainstorming tools that support simultaneous idea generation (all group members keying at once) might create an overload of amorphous information that impedes group synergy. Anonymity, while

---

*See Tversky and Kahneman (1974), Slovic, Fischhoff, and Lichtenstein (1977), Hogarth (1980), Sage (1981), Hogarth and Makridakis (1981), and Kahneman, Slovic, and Tversky (1982) for reviews of these and other systematic cognitive biases.

ameliorating some process losses, can contribute to others, such as reducing some group members' incentives to participate actively.

Although the DSS literature has long recognized the importance of the process view, researchers have paid surprisingly little attention to exploring the effects computer-based systems have on decision-making processes. In their review of the empirical DSS literature, Benbasat and Nault (1990) found few process-oriented studies, noting that "[i]t is ironic that even though the fundamental studies in this field have placed emphasis on understanding the influence of computerized support on changes in decision processes . . . , few MSS studies that examine these relationships have emerged" (p. 222). We are just now beginning to see increasing interest in this important subject. In addition to some process-oriented empirical studies, such as those by Jarvenpaa (1989) and Todd and Benbasat (1988), methodologies for studying how computer-based support affects individual (Todd and Benbasat, 1987) and group (Zigurs, 1989; Poole and DeSanctis, 1989) decision-making processes have recently appeared.

DECISION-MAKING PROCESSES

Although process-oriented studies in the field of DSS are limited, a large literature in such disciplines as cognitive psychology and behavioral decision theory studies human decision-making processes. Understanding what is already known of these processes is a vital first step toward studying DSS from a process orientation. The process-oriented studies by Jarvenpaa (1989) and Todd and Benbasat (1988), for instance, build upon work by Payne (1982) and others on contingent decision making.

Two characteristics of human decision-making processes are central to understanding DSS:

- Decision making is not a point-event. Simon (1960, 1977) observes that we often mistakenly think of decision-making activity as occurring only at the moment of choice. In fact, decision making is a complex sequence of differentiated activities occurring over time.
- Decision making is not monolithic. Numerous distinct paths can be followed to arrive at a decision. Often choosing the path (determining the structure of the process) is more important and more difficult than traversing it (executing the process).

These two observations are the pillars on which the following basic discussion of decision-making processes rests. For more extensive treatments of human decision-making processes, see Newell and Simon (1972), Janis and Mann (1977), Hogarth (1980), Huber (1980), Sage (1981), and Kleindorfer, Kunreuther, and Schoemaker (1991), among many others.

What are Decision-making Processes?

Decision-making processes are often defined intuitively, and circularly, as the processes through which decisions are made. For many purposes the intuitive definition is satisfactory. But for our present purposes we should also note that decision-making processes are interconnected sequences of information-processing and other problem-solving activities. For an individual decision maker the process may simply be the sequence of activities he or she performs en route to arriving at a decision. In more complex contexts, where some activities are performed in parallel, the decision-making process is a collection of such sequences, which intersect one with another.

Researchers have proposed numerous models that decompose managerial decision-making processes into "phases" or "stages." The one most often cited in the DSS literature is Simon's (1960, 1977, pp. 40–41) model, which identifies four phases:

- Intelligence ("finding occasions for making a decision"),
- Design ("finding possible courses of action"),
- Choice ("choosing among courses of action"), and
- Review ("evaluating past choices").

Simon notes that

> [g]enerally speaking, intelligence activity precedes design, and design activity precedes choice. The cycle of phases is, however, far more complex than this sequence suggests. Each phase in making a particular decision is itself a complex decision-making process . . . There are wheels within wheels within wheels. (1977, p. 43)

Simon's phase model pervades the DSS literature. The model is valuable because it offers a simple vocabulary for talking about decision-making processes, one we can use to describe what takes place during decision making by identifying the major groups of decision-making activities and the connections among them.

Like any model, Simon's phase model of the decision-making process is an abstraction and simplification. When analyzing a given process more detail is required. The model is nonetheless useful, because it provides a common means of describing all decision-making processes while serving as a starting point for describing any particular process. I therefore elaborate briefly on each of the model's phases.

Intelligence

During the first phase, Intelligence, the need for decision-making activity is identified and the decision-making process is initiated. Mintzberg, Raisinghani, and Theoret (1976) divide this phase—they call it "identification"—into two parts:

"recognition," wherein the decision-making process is triggered by recognizing a need for decisional activity, and "diagnosis," during which the decision situation is clarified and defined.

How situations for making decisions are recognized depends on whether they are "opportunities," decisions initiated on a purely voluntary basis, "crises," decisions invoked by intense pressures requiring immediate action, or "problems," situations lying somewhere between opportunities and crises (Mintzberg *et al.*, 1976). Crises, such as a warehouse being destroyed by fire, are generally brought to the decision maker's attention. Opportunities, such as a desirable warehouse being on the market, and problems, such as a growing shortage of warehouse space, may be brought to the decision maker's attention or may be discovered when he or she searches for them. See Pounds (1969) for an insightful discussion of "The process of problem finding."

Design

In the Design stage, decision makers prepare alternative courses of action in response to the situation diagnosed in the Intelligence phase. Decision makers might respond by searching for ready-made solutions, by modifying ready-made solutions, or by developing custom-made solutions (Mintzberg *et al.*, 1976). If the situation is a shortage of warehouse space, for example, the decision makers might search for suitable warehouses to purchase, search for available warehouses that can be modified as needed, or design plans for constructing new warehouses. Searching for solutions is often followed by screening, where large numbers of alternatives found by the search are first pared down to a more manageable set for further analysis.

Choice

The decision is finally reached during the Choice stage. When the Design phase generates only a single option, choice consists of either accepting or rejecting that option; when a set of potential actions is passed forward from Design, the decision maker must choose among them. Researchers have studied the Choice phase heavily, identifying prescriptively and descriptively many choice processes. I will frequently use this phase as a source of examples; in the following paragraphs I present some of the basic concepts I will refer to later.

Decision makers often confront multiple, conflicting objectives. A marketing manager, for example, may want to increase both short-run profit and long-run market share, two frequently incompatible goals. And this is a simple case; having more than two conflicting objectives is not uncommon. Multiplicity of criteria is a major factor contributing to the difficulty of the Choice phase, as decision makers must choose among or trade off the various objectives.

A common, widely studied choice situation in which objectives may conflict is the "multi-attribute decision problem," characterized by a set of alternative choices, each described in terms of the same set of attributes or aspects. Consider some examples: prospective renters may evaluate the apartments available with respect to size, rent, location, age, view, and so forth. Car buyers typically look at many features, including a vehicle's price, make, year, style, color, trunk space, mpg rating, safety, and extras. High-school seniors consider tuition, location, reputation, and size, among other factors, in selecting a college. Table 1.2, which illustrates the structure of multi-attribute problems, shows an instance of the apartment selection decision.

TABLE 1.2   The apartment selection problem

Alternatives	Attributes				
	Rent ($/month)	Size (sq. ft)	Location	Age	View
123 Main St, #201	850	1000	good	7	good
1045 Broad St, #1212	900	1200	good	10	good
987 Ocean Drive, #4	800	900	poor	5	poor
987 Ocean Drive, #6	750	1000	fair	5	fair
124 Washington Blvd, #12	800	1000	fair	15	good
126 Washington Blvd, #5	850	1100	fair	12	fair
1515 Elm Road, #123	700	900	fair	20	fair
4242 Smith St, #1	700	900	poor	10	fair

Attributes often conflict. As the table shows, alternatives scoring highly with respect to one criterion may score poorly with respect to another. For instance, the larger apartment, the car more loaded with extras, the college with the better reputation all probably cost more than many other alternatives scoring lower on these attributes. The challenge for the decision maker is to resolve the conflicts among the criteria (attributes) and to select a winner.

Multi-attribute decision problems have been studied extensively, and many solution strategies have been examined. Sage (1981), expanding on Schoemaker (1980), classifies rules for choosing among alternatives as "holistic," "heuristic," or "wholistic."* Table 1.3 shows some of the decision rules within each category.

Holistic evaluation methods, sometimes called "scoring rules," evaluate each alternative independently, selecting the alternative rated most highly. Most of these rules assign each alternative a single score that is a function of its attribute values, and the alternative with the highest score is the winner. The holistic methods differ one from another in terms of the scoring functions they use. Probably the best-known of the holistic methods is the one based on the axioms

---

*See also MacCrimmon (1973) and Montgomery and Svenson (1976) for surveys and classifications of decision rules.

TABLE 1.3 Some decision rules for multi-
attribute problems

Holistic Evaluation	Multi-Attribute Utility Theory Additive Linear Models
Heuristic Elimination	Lexicographic Rules Elimination by Aspects Conjunctive Elimination Disjunctive Elimination Dominance Additive Difference
Wholistic Judgment	Standard Operating Procedures Intuitive Affect Reasoning by Analogy

Note. This classification is based, in part, on those by Sage (1981)
and Schoemaker (1980).

of "multi-attribute utility theory (MAUT)" (see Keeney and Raiffa, 1976, for an overview). Another important approach is the "additive linear model," which can be seen as a special case of multi-attribute utility theory, where each alternative's score is a weighted sum of its attribute values. In the apartment selection problem, for example, a decision maker might define the overall score for an apartment as follows:

$$(0.5 \times \text{rent}) + (0.1 \times \text{location}) + (0.2 \times \text{size}) + (0.1 \times \text{age}) + (0.1 \times \text{view}),$$

where the values for rent, location, size, age, and view in Table 1.2 have each been converted to numerical ratings on a common scale.

In contrast to holistic methods, heuristic elimination processes never evaluate an alternative entirely by itself; the decision maker determines the preferred choice through a sequential process of comparing alternatives either one with another or against some acceptable standard. Alternatives that fail in a comparison are eliminated, and the process proceeds until only the winner remains. Although they are all sequential elimination processes, the techniques in the heuristic elimination category vary significantly.

The "lexicographic decision rule" considers one attribute at a time, beginning with the most important. If one alternative is superior to the others in terms of that attribute, the alternative is selected and the process is complete. If several alternatives are tied, however, all other alternatives are eliminated and the next most important attribute breaks the tie. The process continues until a winner is selected.* A variant on this rule, the "minimum difference lexicographic rule,"

---

*Most of the heuristics may terminate or be terminated with a small group of winners rather than a unique selection.

requires that only differences greater than some specified minimum can determine a decision. That is, even in the absence of a tie, if no alternative exceeds the others by as much as the required minimum, the next attribute must be considered. The "lexicographic semiorder rule" is another variant, where the requirement of a minimum difference applies only to the most important attribute.

Like the lexicographic rules, the widely used "elimination by aspects" method (Tversky, 1972) considers one attribute at a time. But elimination by aspects (EBA) does not compare alternatives one with another; it compares them against acceptable standards. The decision maker specifies a criterion (an attribute and acceptable standard), and all alternatives not satisfying the criterion are eliminated. The process sequentially eliminates alternatives as the decision maker specifies one criterion (attribute and acceptable standard) after another until one alternative remains. In the apartment selection problem, for example, a decision maker might

- first eliminate all apartments renting for more than $825 (reducing the number of alternatives in Table 1.2 to five),
- then rule out units smaller than 1000 square feet (further reducing the set to two), and
- finally require at least a "good" view (leaving 124 Washington Boulevard, #12, as the preferred unit).

Note that the winning alternative satisfies the full sequence of criteria (the "conjunction" of these criteria).

Like EBA, "conjunctive elimination" compares alternatives against acceptable standards. But unlike EBA, the conjunctive rule considers all attributes at once. Alternatives not satisfying all of the criteria—that is, not meeting all of the standards for attributes—are eliminated. The sequence of actions can take two very different forms. In one approach the decision maker compares all alternatives with the standards, eliminating those that fail the test. By making the criteria more and more demanding the decision maker sequentially eliminates alternatives and ultimately selects a winner. In the other approach the standards are fixed and the decision maker proceeds to evaluate the alternatives one at a time until an acceptable alternative is found; this first acceptable alternative is selected.

"Disjunctive elimination" is similar to conjunction, except that alternatives need only to satisfy *any one* of the criteria to remain eligible. Alternatives are eliminated, therefore, only if they fail with respect to every criterion. Either of the two sequential approaches used for conjunction can be used here. The way many coaches select football players illustrates the disjunctive rule: a player must excel at either passing, running, receiving, kicking, blocking, or tackling, but not all of them.

Other heuristics are based on pairwise comparisons of alternatives. In the "dominance decision rule" an alternative is selected over another if it is better with respect to at least one attribute and no worse with respect to the remaining attributes. The "additive difference rule" subtracts one alternative's attribute values from the other's, transforms these differences with (increasing) functions reflecting each attribute's importance, and sums the transformed values. Whether this net difference is positive or negative determines which alternative is selected.

Both the dominance and additive difference rules can be extended to choices among many alternatives by conducting a sequence of pairwise comparisons. The loser in each comparison is eliminated, while the winner is compared with the next alternative. The process continues until all alternatives have been considered and a single alternative remains.

When studying the various holistic evaluation and heuristic elimination methods, an important question is whether high values on one attribute can compensate for low values on another. Holistic evaluation methods are usually "compensatory"; since each alternative receives a score that is a function of its full set of attribute values, a high score on one attribute can offset a low score on another. In contrast, most elimination techniques are "non-compensatory"; if an alternative is eliminated because one of its attribute values is unacceptable, high scores on the other attributes cannot help. In this respect, however, the additive difference model is unlike most other elimination techniques. Since it adds together the (transformed) differences for all attributes, high scores on one attribute can compensate for low scores on another.

Solution strategies belonging to Sage's third category, wholistic judgment, differ markedly from both holistic and heuristic rules; they are based on previous experience, without either detailed scoring of alternatives or formal comparisons of attributes. Examples of this category include using intuition, standard operating procedures, and reasoning by analogy.

Multiplicity of objectives is but one obstacle that stands between a decision maker and a decision. Another barrier to reaching a decision is the probabilistic nature of the world. In discussing multiple objectives I assumed a certain world. For each alternative I assumed we know with certainty the values of its attributes—that is, the consequences of choosing this alternative. But often we do not know what the future state of the world will be, what outcomes will follow from our actions. Consider again the marketing manager concerned with both short-term profit and long-term market share. He or she must make a variety of decisions, including the pricing and promotion of products. But he or she does not know with certainty how given prices and promotions will affect sales, profit, and market share.

We can distinguish two classes of structured problems that lack certainty (Mason and Mitroff, 1973)*: decisions under risk and decisions under uncertainty. Under

---

*Mason and Mitroff (1973) also distinguish structured from unstructured problems. In an unstructured problem not even the set of possible actions, the set of possible outcomes, and the utilities of those outcomes are all known. Care must be taken, however, when using the terms "structured" and "unstructured" in the DSS context, because various authors use them differently. Gorry and Scott Morton (1971), for example, distinguish structured from unstructured tasks by whether or not the tasks can be performed in a "programmed" manner.

"risk," although decision makers do not know with certainty the outcomes that will follow from their actions, they do know the set of possible outcomes and the probabilities of each one's occurring. For instance, for each combination of price and promotion under consideration, the marketing manager may have probability distributions for sales, profit, and market share. Among other techniques, most of the multi-attribute decision rules I described for the case of certainty can be adapted, with some increase in their complexity, to making single- or multiple-objective risky decisions.

Decision making under "uncertainty" is another matter. Here, decision makers do not even know the probabilities of the outcomes that follow from alternative actions. For example, the marketing manager may not be able to project how a given promotion will affect market share. For these problems the holistic and heuristic methods described earlier are generally not appropriate.

Post-decisional Activities

Discussions of decision-making processes frequently cite only the first three of Simon's phases, the ones on which he himself concentrates. Simon does, however, identify a fourth phase, "Review," wherein past choices are assessed. Other researchers have also identified phases that follow choice. Sprague and Carlson (1982) add an "implementation" phase, and Mintzberg *et al.* (1976) identify an "authorization" routine. Indeed, a host of activities follow choice, including the following: authorization or ratification, which require the presentation and defense of decisions to higher levels of the organization; implementation, which often triggers other lower-level decision-making processes; and review and control, which also may trigger new decision-making activity if actual performance does not conform to plans. I treat these activities collectively as a fourth phase, "Post-decisional Activities."

Structuring the Process: Deciding How to Decide

Formulating the process he or she will follow is itself a formidable task for a decision maker. For the kinds of problems we usually support with computer-based systems, unique, well-defined solution strategies seldom exist. Sometimes no well-defined method exists for solving the problem, so the decision maker must devise a new approach. One-time decisions, such as siting a nuclear power plant, often fall into this category. Other times, multiple, competing solution techniques exist, requiring the decision maker to select one of these techniques or to synthesize several of them. Within each phase of the decision-making process we can find examples of competing approaches: for Intelligence activity, numerous statistical models have been developed that might be used to forecast time-series data. During the Design stage, decision makers can generate alternative actions by searching for ready-made solutions, by creating custom-made solutions, or by customizing ready-made solutions. For the Choice phase, management scientists and behavioral decision theorists have identified numerous techniques for solving multi-criteria problems. Post-decisional Activities such as ratification and control might be performed formally or informally, by individuals or by groups.

Since different strategies and techniques will likely lead to different solutions, defining the decision-making process is not just a necessary chore but a pivotal decisional activity. Since decision makers may be better at understanding their problems than at knowing how best to solve them, defining the process may also be an especially difficult activity. In terms of both importance and difficulty, therefore, we find that defining the decision-making process—deciding how to decide, as it were—is a significant part of making a decision.*

Deciding how to decide goes by many names in the literature: meta-choice (Kleindorfer *et al.*, 1991), meta-decision (Mintzberg *et al.*, 1976), pre-decision (Wedley and Field, 1984)†, secondary decision (White, 1975), and strategy selection (Beach and Mitchell, 1978). I shall usually refer to this activity as "structuring the decision-making process."

As Figure 1.6 suggests, we can distinguish structuring the decision-making process from executing the decision-making process. Structuring the process defines how the decision will be made: which models will be used, which data, which solution techniques, and so forth. Structuring the process includes specifying the information-processing and problem-solving activities to be performed, as well as their order. Executing the process entails actually performing the various information-processing and problem-solving activities.

In a multi-attribute problem such as buying a car, renting an apartment, or choosing a college, structuring the process might be accomplished by deciding to use a particular elimination rule to reduce the set of alternatives and then to employ a particular scoring method to select a winner from the reduced set. Once this meta-decision is made, the process is executed and the decision determined by performing the elimination and running the scoring model.

Human judgment is, of course, a critical part of decision making. The judgments people make as they execute their decision-making processes are typically of two kinds (Hogarth, 1980): "evaluative" judgments, which express the decision maker's values or preferences, and "predictive" judgments, which reflect the decision maker's expectations about future conditions. Preferring one job over another, finding a given level of profit unsatisfactory, and trading off short-term profit and long-run market share are all evaluative judgments. Projecting the inflation rate for the third quarter of this year, stating the likelihood that the

---

*My purpose here is not to discuss the complex question of how people decide how to decide. See Payne (1982) for a selective survey and theoretical analysis of the literature on this subject.

†Others—for example, Pitz (1977) and Payne, Braunstein, and Carroll (1978)—use "pre-decision" differently, referring to the portion of the decision-making process that precedes reaching a decision.

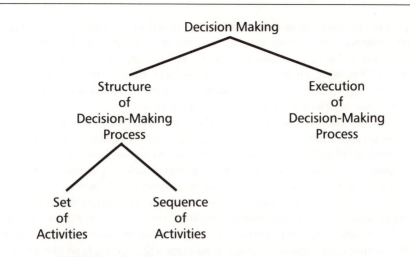

FIGURE 1.6   The process view of decision making

prime rate will exceed 10% by year-end, and claiming that next year's sales will exceed this year's are all predictive judgments.

The role of human judgment in decision making is not limited to the predictive and evaluative judgments of process execution. Deciding how to decide, structuring the decision-making process, is fundamentally a judgmental activity. The decision maker must judge which techniques, models, data, and so forth are appropriate for the task at hand. Indeed, the judgments that define the structure of the decision-making process determine which evaluative and predictive judgments the decision maker must perform when the process is executed.

The decision-making process need not be fully structured before execution begins; structuring and executing the process may be interwoven. Some decision makers may plan their processes in advance, but others may structure their processes dynamically as they proceed toward a decision. Even when decision makers plan the complete process before beginning execution, they may need to deviate from this plan as results are obtained.

People often speak of "arriving at a decision" or "reaching a decision." Traversing a path is an apt metaphor for making a decision. The path is the decision-making process, taking us from our current position, "undecided," to some other location, "decided upon X." The path is defined by three features: the places we visit, the order in which we visit them, and what we do during each visit. These correspond to the information-processing activities we perform, the sequence in which we perform them, and the judgments we make as we perform them.

How Process Complexity Can Increase

To this point I have emphasized aspects of individual decision-making behavior. Indeed, we often think of decision-making processes only in terms of individual people making personal decisions. But individual decision making is just one of several contexts for decision making, ranging from individual through group, organizational, interorganizational, and societal decision making (Kleindorfer *et al.*, 1991).* Focusing our attention beyond personal decision making, we find that as the number of stakeholders and shareholders in a decision increases, so too does the complexity of the decision-making process.

The various contexts for decision making are often "nested." For instance, since groups are collections of individuals, group decision-making processes include many elements of individual decision-making behavior. Similarly, both individuals and groups of individuals make decisions as part of broader organizational decision-making processes. In these complex, nested decision-making contexts, where many agents participate in determining the decision, the decision-making process is not a simple sequence of information-processing activities but a network of such activities, a collection of sequences that intersect at many points. Understanding the intersections, capturing the interactions among the agents, is an essential part of describing the process.

Although DSS have been used to support all five decision-making contexts— individual, group, organizational, interorganizational, and societal—most DSS research and practice concentrates on decision making that takes place within organizations. Consequently, individual, group, and organizational decision-making processes have been and continue to be the cases of greatest interest to DSS researchers. A unique aspect of decision making in organizations is that it is often hierarchical, with decisions made at one level of the organizational hierarchy constrained by those made at the next higher level and constraining those made at the next lower level (Emery, 1969). Just as contraints are passed downward, feedback (control information) is passed up the hierarchy. Understanding organizational decision-making processes therefore entails understanding the interactions among managerial levels.

Summary

Understanding the nature of decision-making processes is central to studying how computer-based systems can affect human decision-making behavior. Decision-making processes are networks of information-processing activities which, for the purpose of analysis, we often group into such phases as Intelligence, Design, Choice, and Post-decision. Moreover, defining this network of activities—that is, structuring the decision-making process—is itself a judgmental task of substantial importance. Both the structuring and executing of the decision-making process can be affected by a computer-based system. For instance, Remus and

---

*Formally defining and distinguishing the contexts is a thorny issue, especially since they are often nested (see Kleindorfer *et al.*, 1991), and not essential for my present purposes. See Hackathorn and Keen (1981) for one approach to this issue.

Kottemann (1986) propose a design for an "Artificially Intelligent Statistician" that supports process structuring by determining the appropriate data and statistical techniques to be used, and supports process execution by producing output in formats that minimize the likelihood of decision makers' misprocessing information. Analyzing how a DSS affects the structure and execution of the decision-making process complements studying how it amplifies or attenuates the process's strengths and weaknesses as a means of describing the system's effects.

WHAT THIS BOOK IS ABOUT

This book is about computer-based information systems that can affect the decision-making behavior of their users. More specifically, it is about how to describe these systems and how to differentiate them one from another. My points of departure, set forth earlier in this chapter, are the following:

- A broad definition of Decision Support Systems (DSS), which includes any computer-based information system that affects or is intended to affect how people make decisions.
- A process view of decision making, which leads to viewing Decision Support Systems as interventions into the processes through which people make decisions.
- A descriptive, rather than a prescriptive, approach. Given the broad definition of DSS, I focus on describing and differentiating these systems in terms of how they can affect the decision-making processes of their users.

The DSS research literature has been much more prescriptive than descriptive. But good prescription depends upon good and systematic description, and systematic description depends upon a common mechanism for describing and differentiating systems. The purpose of this book, therefore, is to introduce and elaborate an approach to describing and differentiating systems in terms of their likely effects on the decision-making behavior of their users.

The book is organized as follows: before focusing on the descriptive theme, I present in Chapter 2 a framework for research and practice in the field of computer-based decision support. The framework, which provides a new way of looking at and integrating the field, creates a context for appreciating the main focus of this study and introduces a number of concepts that will be important later on. In Chapter 3, I make the case for a systematic approach to describing DSS and present a three-tiered approach to doing so. The tiers build one on another, and as one moves from the first through the third tiers, the descriptions become more oriented toward the system as a whole and more directed toward how the system is likely to affect decision-making behavior. In Chapter 3, I focus primarily on the first two tiers—(1) descriptions of the system's functional capabilities, and (2) descriptions of how the system's configuration of components appears to its users. I also introduce the third tier, system attributes that describe properties of the system as a whole as it affects decision-making behavior. I devote Chapters 4 and 5 to studying two system attributes of special importance: ''system restrictiveness,'' how a DSS constrains its users' decision-making processes, and ''decisional guidance,'' how a DSS sways or enlightens decision makers' judgments. Chapter 6 concludes the book, using the descriptive approach to perform several analyses and discussing the approach's implications for research and practice.

Chapter 2
A FRAMEWORK FOR DSS RESEARCH AND PRACTICE

In terms of quantity, the Decision Support Systems literature has no shortage of frameworks, taxonomies, dichotomies, approaches, and the like. Why propose yet another framework? The problem is this: the existing frameworks lack a common focus, posing different questions and addressing different concerns from different perspectives. Many frameworks are classification schemes; others are development approaches. Some provide internal architectures; others, external views. Some are mostly descriptive; others, primarily prescriptive. Some are oriented toward research; others, toward practice. Individually, each contribution has advanced the state of DSS research, practice, or both. But collectively, the frameworks offer neither a coherent picture of DSS nor a well-defined set of issues for the field as a whole. After more than two decades of DSS research we now need a framework that is more comprehensive and unifying than the ones we have used in the past.

DSS is a complex field, comprising interacting sets of technological and behavioral issues addressable from numerous perspectives. As such the field affords great diversity of research topics. Recent analyses of the literature (Scott Morton, 1984; Elam, Huber, and Hurt, 1986; Hurt, Elam, and Huber, 1986) attest to the wide range of issues being studied. Examining this diverse body of literature, one finds, along with its strengths, a number of significant weaknesses. The literature has "gaps," important topics—such as evaluating the impact of DSS on decision-making behavior—that have been under-researched or ignored. The literature has "loose ends," promising ideas—such as Huber's (1981) discussion of DSS design in the context of organizational decision making—frequently cited but never fully developed. The literature has "rifts," latent conflicts—such as differing views of change agency (Silver, 1990)—scarcely acknowledged and not directly confronted. The literature has "fragments," isolated contributions needing to be compared to see if and how they fit together. Because our frameworks are themselves diverse, exhibiting many of these same characteristics, they do not help us solve these problems. A single, more encompassing framework is needed to ameliorate these deficiencies.

Frameworks often appear early in the development of a field of study, as a valuable starting point for initial research efforts. The field of DSS is no exception; most of its frameworks were devised in the 1970s, the early years of DSS research. These frameworks served us well, motivating and guiding early research and practice. One may contend that we have reached a point in the history of DSS where frameworks are no longer needed. I believe not. DSS is still a young field. Given the observations above, we now need an organizing mechanism to help us understand where we have been and where we should be going. In that spirit, I propose a new framework for DSS research and practice.

The framework is not a framework for developing DSS, for using DSS, for evaluating DSS, or for classifying DSS. It is a framework for understanding DSS. It invites us to step back from our positions as researchers or practitioners, to step away from whatever perspective of DSS we have adopted, and to contemplate the intricacies of the field as a whole, to recognize the elemental concepts and the connections among them. It is a way of organizing the knowledge necessary for comprehending the complex world of computer-based decision support. Some of that knowledge has already been acquired; more is still wanting.

The definition of DSS I presented in Chapter 1 includes not only systems that *are intended to* affect decision making, but also any other systems that *do* affect decision making. Including both sets of systems is important for a comprehensive program of research on the effects of computer-based systems on the decision-making processes of their users. Historically, however, DSS research has focused on guiding practice far more than on studying effects, so nearly all DSS research has focused only on those systems intended to support decision making. But studying the effects of all computer-based systems on decision making is important both as a scientific inquiry in its own right and, in the long run, as a basis for improving the state of practice. Consequently, the framework must be responsive to the dual objectives of (1) providing better computer-based decision support and (2) understanding better the effects of all computer-based systems on decision-making behavior. The framework therefore *addresses* the numerous elements involved in providing computer-based decision support but *emphasizes* factors implicated in the effects of systems regardless of designers' intentions, such as the characteristics of the affected decision-making environment, the characteristics of the system, and, especially, the effects of the system on the decision-making processes of its users. In so doing, the framework takes a vital first step toward the next frontier of DSS research: studying the effects of systems for their own sake, not just for the purpose of enlightening design.

One may think of the framework as a classification scheme for DSS concepts, but the framework's purpose is as much to identify and to connect topics as to classify them. The framework has a simple structure: three "segments," groupings of related DSS concepts, each segment connected with the other two. Some concepts fit uniquely in a single segment. Many important issues for researchers and practitioners draw upon concepts from different segments, however, thus creating the links among the segments. The segments are defined this way deliberately; they force us to identify explicitly the relationships among concepts and to decompose complex issues into their elemental parts.

I begin this chapter by describing the framework's three segments, after which I analyze the factors that distinguish each segment from the others. Then I consider the links among segments. Finally, I examine other DSS frameworks in light of the one proposed here.

THE THREE SEGMENTS

A complete understanding of DSS requires comprehending three interrelated subject areas:

- the Underlying Technology (UT),
- DSS Lifecycle Processes (LC), and
- Substantive Decision Support (DS).

These topics constitute the framework's three segments. Each segment is further divided into a set of constituent parts, as shown in Figure 2.1.

The three segments could serve as an outline for a textbook on DSS practice or a three-volume treatise on DSS research. But that would be a different book. My present purpose is to provide an overview of the three segments, to identify some of the key issues they raise for research and practice, and to refer the reader to sources that expand on many of these issues.

Underlying Technology (UT)

DSS are technological artifacts, created from and with computer-based technology. One segment of the framework, therefore, comprises the underlying technological concepts essential to the field of DSS. This Underlying Technology (UT) segment has four elements:

- basic technologies,
- development systems,
- delivery systems (platforms), and
- system architectures (internal views).

Basic Technologies

DSS draw upon a wide range of computer science and management science technologies. Historically, the most important computer technologies for decision support have been database management and dialog management, on the software side, and interactive computing, through timesharing systems or personal computers, on the hardware side. Of growing importance are telecommunications, artificial intelligence (especially expert systems), model management, and graphics. The fields of Operations Research/Management Science and Operations

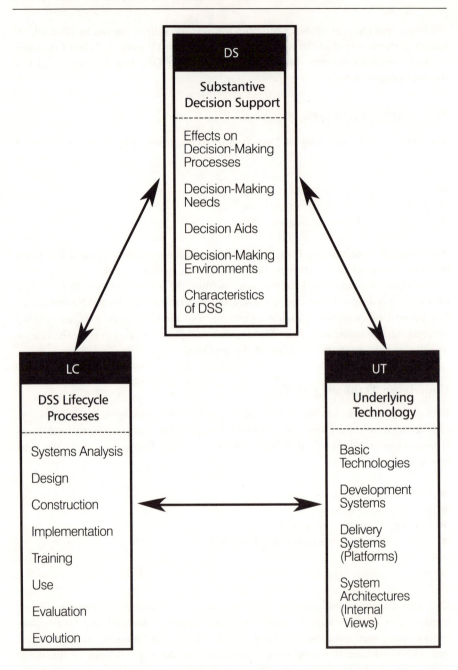

FIGURE 2.1   A framework for DSS research and practice

Management also contribute to the DSS technology base; model-based DSS frequently draw upon formulations and algorithms developed in these fields.

DSS researchers explore how the raw technologies developed by computer and management scientists can be applied to supporting human decision makers. Database management, for example, is a large and active research area within computer science. Systems intended to support decision makers have special database management needs (Clemons, 1980; Sprague and Carlson, 1982, Chapter 8), which DSS researchers study by extracting, applying, and extending the relevant fundamental database concepts. For DSS practitioners the challenge is to become conversant with the basic and extended technologies and be able to apply them as needed.

Development Systems

The software system used to create a DSS, the "DSS development system," can be an assembly language, a higher-level programming language (such as Pascal, BASIC, and APL), or a specially designed tool (such as a fourth-generation language or, in Sprague's (1980) terminology, a "DSS Generator"). The more specialized a development system is for its role in building DSS, the more likely it will embed advanced capabilities from the basic technologies such as graphics, dialog management, and model management.

More than a technological necessity, the development system plays a key role in determining a DSS's success; its capabilities constrain the DSS's features, its ease of use affects the resources expended developing the DSS as well as the quality of the DSS produced, and its flexibility influences how well the builder responds to user requests for changes. Studying the characteristics of development systems, matching them with different types of decision-making environments, and designing better and more powerful ones are important research tasks. Choosing an appropriate development system for a given project and using it well are the primary concerns for practice.

Delivery Systems (Platforms)

I shall refer to the hardware system on which the DSS executes as the delivery system (also called "the platform" in the literature). A variety of configurations are possible, including timesharing on in-house mainframes or minicomputers, timesharing purchased from a service bureau, and dedicated use on personal microcomputers. Increasingly, DSS are being operated from "executive workstations," microcomputers connected to the organization's computing network. Such workstations may be connected to other personal computers, to the organization's larger computers, or both. The software and data used by the DSS may be distributed across multiple locations in the network. See Meador, Keen, and Guyote (1986) for a discussion of the issues raised by the availability of increasingly powerful personal computers.

The choice of delivery system for a DSS constrains the choice of development system, since the development software must produce systems compatible with the delivery hardware. The features of the delivery system also constrain the capabilities of the DSS. For instance, color graphics are not feasible on a hardware system supporting only monochrome display monitors.

The choice of delivery system is often a function of which computer systems are already in place in the organization, as well as the organizational policies and procedures governing the management of information systems. Although systems intended to support decision making raise their own special issues, determining which delivery system is most desirable for a given project involves many of the same technological and behavioral factors as does addressing the more general question of centralization versus decentralization (distribution) of information systems. See King (1983) for a survey of the general case.

System Architectures (Internal Views)

Since DSS can draw upon a number of computer-based technologies, their internal structures typically integrate software components serving different functions. For instance, Sprague (1980) identifies a DSS's technological components as the database management, dialog management, and model base management subsystems, and Bonczek, Holsapple, and Whinston (1981) describe a DSS as comprising a language system, a knowledge system, and a problem-processing system. The system architecture, or "internal view," of a DSS is the way the individual software components are connected. Sprague and Carlson (1982, Chapter 10) identify four architectures for a system comprising Sprague's three components—that is, four different ways of connecting the three subsystems. Turban and Watkins (1986) consider architectures that integrate "expert system" components with Sprague's three other components. Similarly, Bonczek *et al.* define connections among their language, problem-processing, and knowledge components.

System architectures are sometimes a concern for the DSS builder, who must piece the requisite building blocks together when constructing a DSS. Other times the DSS builder is insulated from architectural issues by the development system; the builder of such a development system is the one who fits the building blocks together. No matter where responsibility rests in practice, architectures for DSS continue to be an important area for research.

Remarks

Perhaps because the field is so applied, or perhaps because the technologies are so exciting, the DSS community has always shown great interest in the underlying technology. Elam *et al.* (1985) argue that while the field of DSS has not been technology-driven, it has been technology-paced. Builders of early systems—for instance, Scott Morton (1971)—had to overcome significant technological obstacles to create their DSS. Much of the initial effort focused on hardware and software for the user interface. Not by chance, the advent of interactive computing coincided with that of DSS, and the birth of personal computing was contemporaneous with DSS's rapid growth. While behavioral issues are now receiving the increased attention they deserve, research on DSS technology continues to flourish as well. The most active topics today are model management systems (see overviews in Blanning, 1989; Blanning, Holsapple, and Whinston, 1991) and applications of expert systems (see discussions in Turban and Watkins, 1986; Luconi, Malone, and Scott Morton, 1986; Henderson, 1987).

DSS Lifecycle Processes (LC)

In addition to being conversant with the underlying technology, understanding DSS requires familiarity with the activities that are part of the DSS process, which range from project inception to system retirement. These activities constitute the framework's Lifecycle Processes (LC) segment:

- systems analysis,
- design,
- construction,
- implementation,
- training,
- use,
- evaluation, and
- evolution.

Although the term "Lifecycle" is borrowed from the Systems Development Lifecycle (SDLC),* the traditional development approach for information systems, the life of a DSS is usually much different from that described by the SDLC, which consists of a sequence of project phases passed through in order, sometimes with iterations. For DSS, development and use are often intertwined, with short feedback cycles and frequent iteration through activities as the system evolves over time. While listing distinct activities is useful for exposition, many of the activities coincide in practice. I present the activities in a logical order for discussion, not necessarily the order in which they will or should be executed in any given project.

---

*There are a number of different versions of the Systems Development Lifecycle (SDLC). For one, see Davis and Olson (1985, Chapter 18).

Systems Analysis, Design, Construction, and Evolution

We may think of systems analysis, design, construction, and evolution collectively as the process of "building" or "developing" the DSS. The DSS development literature is populated by such phrases as "adaptive design" (Keen, 1980), "middle-out design" (Ness, 1975; Hurst *et al.*, 1983), "evolutionary approach" (Grajew and Tolovi, 1978; Hurst *et al.*, 1983), "expanding subsets" (Moore and Chang, 1983), and "prototyping," all roughly synonymous expressions describing development processes with two key characteristics: the user is heavily involved in the development process and the system evolves or adapts over time.

Involving the user in the design process serves at least two purposes.* First, since each decision maker may have his or her own approach to problem solving, the decision maker's active participation in the design process improves the likelihood that the system will meet his or her needs. Second, when users participate in system design they "buy into" the project, increasing the likelihood of their accepting and using the system.

DSS designs are generally not static; DSS evolve over time in response to changes in decision makers, in organizational settings, in tasks, and, most importantly, in perceptions of tasks by decision makers (Hurst *et al.*, 1983; Keen, 1980). In fact, Keen (1980) argues that use of the DSS itself promotes learning by decision makers, which in turn leads to changes in the needs for support. DSS might be built that are self-adaptive (see Liang and Jones, 1987) or are adapted by the user, but usually the builder participates actively in the process of system evolution, modifying the DSS in response to feedback from the users.

Although the evolutionary approach dominates the prescriptive and descriptive DSS literature, this is not the only approach for building DSS (Ginzberg and Ariav, 1986). For instance, Hogue and Watson (1984) found that one-third of the 18 successful DSS they studied were developed using the traditional lifecycle rather than prototyping. See the books by Sprague and Carlson (1982) and Bennett (1983a) for discussions of how to build DSS.

Implementation and Training

The term "implementation" has many meanings in the context of DSS. Sometimes it is used broadly to refer to the full set of activities involved in building a system and putting it in place ("We are implementing a DSS"). When used narrowly it sometimes refers to the construction and installation of the system ("The implementation was on an IBM PC"). Here, I use implementation to refer to the behavioral and organizational issues—as opposed to the technological ones— involved in putting a DSS in place. Implementation includes overcoming such

---

*User involvement can also be considered part of the "implementation" process.

obstacles as user resistance, and employing such tactics as acquiring top management support, involving users in the design process, making system use mandatory, and creating a climate for change.

Researchers have found that MIS success often depends as much on the implementation process as on the technical features of the system. Moreover, Keen and Scott Morton (1978) suggest that for systems intended to support decision making, *"implementation* may be far more complex than the formal design process" (p. 189). See Alter (1980, Part 3) and Keen and Scott Morton (Chapter 7) for a discussion of DSS implementation issues; Markus (1984), Swanson (1988), and Schultz and Ginzberg (1984) provide overviews of the general case of implementation.

Training users is an especially important DSS implementation activity. Although training is important for all computer-based systems, the process may be somewhat different for systems intended to support decision making, where not only "passive" understanding, knowing how to operate the system, but "active" understanding, knowing how to apply the system to the decision-making task at hand, is necessary to take full advantage of system capabilities.* To foster active understanding, system builders may construct such computer-based training aids as tutorials, and may participate directly in the training process. While most commentators view training of DSS users as a critical activity, relatively little has been published on this subject. See Grace (1977) for an innovative approach to DSS training ("ITM," an interactive training manual) and Nelson and Cheney (1987) for a study that includes end-users' perceptions of the quantity and quality of training techniques they experienced (tutorials, courses/lectures/seminars, computer-aided instruction, interactive training manuals, resident experts, help facilities within systems, and sources external to the organization).

Use

The seemingly simple question "Who is the user?" is an important one for understanding DSS use. Many times the decision maker himself or herself is the hands-on user, interacting directly with the DSS. Often, however, the hands-on users are "intermediaries" (also known as "chauffeurs" and "integrative agents") who operate the DSS for the decision makers (Sprague, 1980; Alter, 1980; Bennett, 1974; Carlson, Grace, and Sutton, 1977). Benbasat (1984) suggests that studying the conditions under which each mode of use is most appropriate is a major DSS research issue. See Keen (1976) and Alter (1981) for discussions of this subject.

---

*Stabell (1983), following on Meador and Ness (1974), distinguishes between passive and active understanding of a system, where "passive understanding refers to the mechanics of system use," and "active understanding refers to how to use the system in the task at hand" (p. 224).

Identifying the hands-on user is one element of the broader subject of DSS usage patterns. Other important questions for comprehending DSS use pertain to if, when, and how the DSS is used. The answers to these questions have implications for other lifecycle processes. For instance, feedback from system use influences the course of system evolution. Similarly, appropriate implementation tactics must be selected to foster successful use of the system.

Evaluation

Evaluation of DSS projects serves several different purposes, operative at different points in the system's life and having different evaluative needs. Early in the project, "ex ante" evaluation is needed to justify undertaking the project and to establish expectations. In midcourse, evaluation is used to determine whether to continue with the project and, if so, what changes should be made to the DSS. Later in the project's life, "ex post" evaluation is performed to meet the organizational need to assess the project's success, to guide system evolution, and to assess the appropriateness of retiring the system.

Evaluating DSS for any of these purposes is difficult because the benefits of DSS are often intangible. Since improved decision making, the objective of most DSS projects, is not easily measured, determining the value or success of a given system may be difficult or impossible. Traditional cost/benefit analysis for information systems (Emery, 1974) may not be appropriate, and DSS evaluation therefore becomes problematic. A number of conceptual papers contemplate this problem: Keen (1975, 1981) proposes approaches to evaluating and justifying DSS, Ginzberg (1981) explores the closely related issue of measuring DSS success, and Keen and Scott Morton (1978, Chapter 8) present a "smorgasbord" of evaluation methods for DSS.

Remarks

Research in the Lifecycle Processes segment concentrates on *describing* how and how successfully the various lifecycle activities have been performed and on *prescribing* how they should be performed to be successful. The research often draws on the general MIS literature base as well as on the organizational behavior and systems theory literatures. Training, evaluation, and use are the least researched processes; the other activities—analysis, design, construction, implementation, and evolution—have been the focus of a significant share of DSS research. Most of the studies, however, have been either purely descriptive or prescriptive based on limited description. Prescriptive studies grounded in substantial description should be an important contribution to the state of DSS practice.

Substantive Decision Support (DS)

Understanding computer-based decision support requires knowing something about how people make decisions, knowing something about computer-based techniques and systems for aiding decision making, and knowing something about how the latter affect the former. Therein lies the substance of computer-based decision support. More specifically, the Substantive Decision Support (DS) segment consists of five items:

- effects on decision-making processes,
- decision-making needs,
- computer-based decision aids,
- decision-making environments, and
- characteristics of DSS.

Effects on Decision-making Processes

Perhaps the most central DSS research question is how computer-based systems can and do affect the decision-making processes of their users. In Chapter 1, I suggested two ways of approaching this issue. First, recognizing that human and computer-aided decision-making processes have both strengths and weaknesses, one can examine how a DSS amplifies or attenuates each of the strengths and weaknesses of the existing decision-making process. Second, employing the distinction between structuring and executing the process, one can study both how the structure of the process has changed and how its execution has changed after introduction of a DSS. The two approaches are complementary, and each requires an understanding of human decision-making processes, a subject that has been receiving ever-increasing research attention from behavioral decision theorists and others.

In Chapter 1, I presented a quick overview of several of the aspects of human decision-making processes most important for studying DSS: the structuring and executing of decision-making processes, the phases of decision making, the nestedness of decision-making contexts, and the nature of decision rules for multi-attribute problems. Especially important for computer-based decision support is the finding that people have limited information-processing capabilities and that these cognitive limitations can account for significant elements of human decision-making behavior (Simon, 1955; Newell and Simon, 1972; Hogarth, 1980). Its implications for DSS are threefold. First, helping decision makers overcome some of these information-processing limitations is one way that a computer-based system can improve the decision-making performance of its users. Second, the cognitive limitations of their users may reduce the potential effectiveness of some DSS. And third, by exacerbating the effects of their users' cognitive limitations, some DSS might have negative consequences for decision-making performance.

Researching how DSS can and do affect decision-making behavior serves several purposes. The findings of such research can facilitate the realization of system designers' intentions to improve decision-making behavior. Similarly, such research can also help designers avoid dysfunctional consequences for the DSS they build. Examining the likely consequences of a given DSS might even lead designers to choose not to move forward with a given project. Moreover, besides enlightening practice, studying how computer-based systems affect decision makers is a study of scientific interest in its own right.

Decision-making Needs and Decision Aids

An important element of providing support for decision making is identifying decision makers' needs and delivering computer-based capabilities that address these needs. Sometimes, decision makers recognize and express the needs themselves. For instance, a decision maker might believe that he or she is missing opportunities, failing to generate sufficient alternative strategies, or lacking necessary data. Other times, an observer—most probably the designer—might recognize weaknesses not perceived by the manager. The analyst might conclude that the decision maker is concentrating on the wrong problems, is systematically biased in making judgments, or is failing to communicate effectively with other participants in the decision-making process. Both types of needs, self-recognized and not, often follow from humans' limited information-processing capabilities; understanding these limitations can therefore be valuable in identifying needs for computer-based support.

The DSS literature contains a number of lists of managerial decision-making needs, although they do not always appear under that heading. For instance, Alter (1980) and Keen (1981) identify benefits of DSS; Zachary (1986) identifies major classes of DSS support; Meador *et al.* (1986) identify decision subprocesses; and Blanning (1979) describes the functions of DSS. Each of these lists can easily be interpreted as catalogs of the decisional needs being addressed by DSS. Table 2.1 enumerates nine common decision-making needs.

The challenge for DSS researchers is to identify commonly found decision-making needs and to devise computer-based aids that meet them. Builders must be able to apply these research findings to their own situations as well as to identify and meet situation-specific needs.

Researchers must not stop with designing decision aids; the aids must be tested to see that they both satisfy the needs and do not cause undesirable side-effects. Successful aids must also be catalogued so that DSS builders can draw upon them as appropriate in designing their systems. Humphreys and Wisudha (1987), for instance, have catalogued 58 tools for aiding decision structuring and decision making. Their catalog, structured around a framework for representing decision problems and DSS capabilities, identifies such characteristics of tools as the tool's general area of application, what the tool helps users do, how the tool helps structure

---

TABLE 2.1 Some common decision-making needs

Fuller/better exploration of alternatives
Earlier/better detection of problems and opportunities
Coping with multiple or undefined objectives
More explicit treatment of risk and uncertainty
Reducing systematic cognitive biases
Creativity
Communication, coordination, and consistency
Structuring the decision-making process
Learning

---

problems, the level of support the tool offers, and the types of users intended to use the tool. This catalog is a resource for both researchers and practitioners. Researchers can use it to identify tools that merit in-depth comparisons one with another, to select a single tool to study in greater depth, and to identify gaps in our current toolkit. Such efforts might ameliorate the widespread problem of researchers devising (and sometimes testing) their own decision aids but not studying or testing those of others. System builders can use the catalog to identify potentially useful tools for the systems they build.

Researchers can study decision makers' needs at various levels of generality. Considering more alternatives, coping with risk, and detecting problems are examples of broadly expressed needs that apply in many situations. Solving a given inventory problem with periodic review, fixed ordering costs, and backorders is a more specific decision-making need. Researching decisional needs at all levels is valuable. Studying general needs yields knowledge we can apply in many situations. Studying more specific needs is more limited in applicability, but leads to more customized decision support.

Decision-making Environments

The phrase "decision-making environment" means different things to different people. Often it connotes just the organizational setting within which decisions are made; but in this book I define decision-making environments more broadly to consist of three elements and the interactions among them:

- the people who participate in the decision-making process,
- the problem-solving tasks they confront, and
- the organizational or societal settings within which they operate.

Decision-making environments are idiosyncratic; all three components vary from one to another. Moreover, they are dynamic; decision makers, tasks, and settings all change with time. Because understanding decision-making behavior requires understanding the environment within which it occurs, knowledge of all three elements (decision makers, settings, and tasks) is important for studying DSS. In particular, understanding DSS requires comprehending the ways environments are similar and different.

The MIS and DSS literatures have studied extensively differences in *individuals* that might be relevant for understanding the design and use of information systems. In his review of this literature, Zmud (1979) groups the individual differences into three classes: cognitive style, personality (risk-taking propensity, dogmatism, extroversion/introversion, and so forth), and demographic/situational variables (age, experience, and education, among others). Cognitive style, "the process behavior individuals exhibit in the formulation or acquisition, analysis, and interpretation of information or data of presumed value to decision making" (Sage, 1981, p. 642), has received special attention in the literature on decision support. See Sage (1981) for a review of this literature, Taylor and Benbasat (1980) for a critique of it, and Huber (1983) and Robey (1983) for differing views on the importance of this research for DSS design.

Decision makers operate within a *setting* that serves as a context for their decision making. This context may be the group, organization, or society to which they belong, or, since these units are nested (Kleindorfer, Kunreuther, and Schoemaker, 1991), it may be some more complex setting. Groups, organizations, and societies each vary. Groups may have face-to-face contact or be dispersed (DeSanctis and Gallupe, 1987), may be relatively large or small (DeSanctis and Gallupe, 1987), may have scopes of activity that are mostly internal or external (McGrath, 1984), and so forth. Four conceptual models have been used to capture the varying decision-making styles of organizations: the rational, program, political/competitive, and garbage can models (Huber, 1981). Societies, may, among other things, be democratic or not. All told, decisional settings vary greatly.

Decision-making *tasks* also differ markedly. They differ in terms of how structured they are (Gorry and Scott Morton, 1971) and how they are structured (Mason and Mitroff, 1973). They vary in managerial level from operational control, through managerial control, to strategic planning (Anthony, 1965). Some decisions occur only once, whereas others are recurring (Donovan and Madnick, 1977). Decisions may be individual, group, or organizational tasks (Hackathorn and Keen, 1981). Task domains vary across such functional areas as finance, marketing, and manufacturing.

Although we often speak of decision-making tasks as though they exist by themselves, the nature of a decision-making task may depend upon the person who performs it and the setting in which it is performed. Moore and Chang (1983), for instance, argue that classifying a problem as structured or unstructured is fruitless, because the degree of structure will vary across individuals at a given point in time and across time for a given individual. Similarly, the nature of a task may vary across settings; one organization's capital budgeting process may be very different from another's.

With so many (interacting) variables, analyzing the implications of the decision-making environment for providing computer-based decision support is not an easy research task. Nonetheless, it is an important one. Understanding the key similarities and differences among environments can enlighten the design process. Research that matches environmental characteristics with features of DSS can be of even greater value to system designers.

Characteristics of DSS

While decision-making processes, needs, aids, and environments are all important parts of the substance of computer-based decision support, of special importance are the characteristics of DSS themselves. Whether we are DSS builders, DSS buyers, DSS users, or DSS watchers, we must be able to describe the features of a given DSS and differentiate it from other DSS. Builders must do so to contemplate alternative designs; buyers, to select or commission the system that best meets their needs. Users must appreciate the features of the system they are employing. Recognizing commonalities and differences across systems is a prerequisite for much DSS research.

Describing a DSS requires more than simply listing its functional capabilities. Describing a DSS requires conveying how those capabilities can meet decisional needs. Describing a DSS requires analyzing how its capabilities are packaged, how they appear to the user. Describing a DSS requires considering how the individual capabilities fit together to form a whole, contemplating the likely effects the system in its entirety will have on its users' decision-making behavior.

I devote the balance of this book to a three-tiered approach to describing and differentiating DSS. In the following paragraphs I outline the three analytic tiers, which describe a DSS in terms of

1. its functional capabilities,
2. its configuration as viewed by its users, and
3. its attributes as a "whole" system.

Beyond just enumerating a DSS's functional capabilities—"it retrieves data," "it solves linear programs," or "it draws graphs"—the first descriptive tier also relates these capabilities to the decision-making needs of the system's users. For instance, one DSS might graph historical sales data for the purpose of detecting problems, whereas another DSS might graph projected sales data to explore alternative courses of action. The first tier provides a necessary starting point for describing a DSS; the other tiers build upon it.

The second descriptive tier, referred to as the "user view," captures how a system's functional capabilities are packaged, that is, how the system's components appear to its users. This tier is necessary because the same capabilities can be configured to appear to users in different ways. One DSS might provide a set of discrete operations that can be invoked in any order, while another DSS might lock users into a predefined sequence of steps. Similarly, one DSS might provide a general-purpose linear programming capability, while another might provide a set of predefined linear programs. To be able to describe and differentiate DSS in terms of their user views, it is useful to employ a standard vocabulary, a "generic user view." Carlson's ROMC approach (Sprague and Carlson, 1982; Carlson, 1979, 1983a) can be used in this way. I present an alternative approach in Chapter 3.

The uppermost tier consists of system attributes that describe the decisional properties of the DSS as a whole. The "system restrictiveness" attribute addresses the flexibility a DSS affords its users in defining and performing their decision-making processes. "Decisional guidance" concerns how a system sways or enlightens its users as they exercise whatever judgmental flexibility they are granted. "Precustomization" describes how tailored a system is for its environment, and "customizability" captures the ability of users to tailor the system to their needs. Together, the attributes provide much information concerning the likely effects of the DSS on the decision-making behavior of its users.

Each successive tier builds on the ones before it. As we move up the tiers the descriptions pay increasing attention to those features determining the effects the DSS will have on its users' decision-making processes. Nonetheless, all three levels raise for the researcher questions of the connection between DSS features and decision-making behavior; and each level provides the practitioner with a distinct set of design issues.

Remarks

The intrasegment links are especially important for understanding the Substantive Decision Support segment. For instance, the characteristics of decision-making environments serve as a means for classifying decision-making needs and their associated decision aids. Likewise, studying decision-making needs provides a context for analyzing a system's capabilities (the first-tier descriptive analysis). But most important are the connections among decision-making environments, DSS, and decision-making processes. The key research question here is how different types of environments can interact with different characteristics of DSS to contribute to particular effects on decision-making processes. In addition to enhancing our general understanding, such research is necessary to satisfy the long-run goal of building a prescriptive mapping from characteristics of decision-making environments to characteristics of DSS, a mapping upon which DSS practitioners could draw when constructing DSS.

The Substantive Decision Support segment draws upon research in many disciplines. Organizational Behavior, Cognitive Psychology, Behavioral Decision Theory (BDT), and Cognitive Science; Operations Research/Management Science (OR/MS), especially, Multi-Criteria Decision Making (MCDM); and functional areas such as Marketing and Finance all make important contributions to this segment. Indeed, any discipline that offers theories of human or organizational decision making has the potential to contribute to the substance of DSS by providing an understanding of how decisions are made, could be made, should be made, or could be supported. The essence of providing computer-based decision support is the merger of these various decision-related disciplines with the capabilities of computer-based technology. Pursuing this merger is a challenge to be embraced by researchers and practitioners alike.

Summary

The framework disentangles the complex world of DSS, identifying elemental concepts and placing them in one of three segments: Underlying Technology (UT), Lifecycle Processes (LC), or Substantive Decision Support (DS). Our understanding of each segment benefits from knowledge acquired by a variety of reference disciplines, as shown in Table 2.2. The bodies of relevant knowledge, especially for the DS segment, are substantial. Should we fail to take advantage of these existing resources, we stand to lose much.

From a research perspective we can think of the segments as groups of closely related fundamental research issues. From a practice viewpoint one may see the segments as three aspects of the general problem of providing computer-based support. Either way, understanding DSS requires first comprehending these elemental concepts and then studying the more complex DSS issues linking them together. Before turning our attention to the vital links across segments, let us consider briefly the essential distinctions among them.

TABLE 2.2   *Reference disciplines for the segments*

UT Underlying Technology	LC DSS Lifecycle Processes	DS Substantive Decision Support
Computer Science	Organizational Behavior	Organizational Behavior
Operations Research/ Management Science	Information Systems Systems Theory	Cognitive Psychology, Behavioral Decision Theory, and Cognitive Science
		Operations Research/ Management Science (including Multi-criteria Decision Making)
		Functional Areas

DISTINGUISHING THE SEGMENTS

Until now I have discussed each of the framework's segments, UT, LC, and DS, independently of the others, concentrating on each segment's overall theme and constituent elements. Fully appreciating the segmentation, however, requires not only understanding each segment individually, but also comprehending the underlying notions that distinguish the segments from each other. Three such distinctions are important:

- an emphasis on *procedural* issues in contrast with *substantive* issues,
- a *technological* orientation in contrast with a *behavioral* orientation and
- a focus on the *ends* of providing computer-based decision support as opposed to the *means*.

Procedure/Substance*

Suppose we are trying to bake a cake. We need to know both *how* to bake the cake and *what* to use in baking it. The recipe, therefore, has two parts: the directions, which describe the procedures we will follow, and the ingredients, the substances we will employ. When we engage in a DSS project we confront the same two issues. We require "procedural" knowledge of the processes that will take place and we require "substantive" knowledge that we can employ as we perform those processes. The LC segment of the framework addresses the procedural issues, describing the various processes that take place during a system's life: systems analysis, design, construction, implementation, training, use, evaluation, and evolution. The UT and DS segments, however, contain the substantive knowledge upon which we rely, an understanding of the technological and decisional issues, respectively. For instance, adaptive design (LC) is a procedure for building DSS, whereas knowledge of decision processes (DS) and internal system architectures (UT) is part of the substance needed to build DSS.

Technology/Behavior

The segments can be distinguished in another manner: technologically oriented issues as contrasted with behaviorally oriented ones. The UT segment, of course, corresponds to the former, encompassing all the computer-based technological issues relevant to DSS. The other two segments are more behaviorally oriented. The LC segment addresses the behavior of DSS practitioners (builders,

---

*The pairing of the terms "procedure" and "substance" is borrowed from March and Simon (1958), who distinguished "procedural programs" from "substantive programs" in problem-solving processes. My use of these terms here, however, is somewhat different from their use, distinguishing not the "how" and the "what" of decision making, but the "how" and the "what" of building DSS and providing computer-based decision support.

implementors, trainers, and so forth) and DSS users (decision makers and intermediaries) during the various activities of the system's life. The DS segment is concerned with decision-making behavior and, in particular, ways of supporting and improving that behavior.

Means/Ends

A third and final distinction among the segments separates the means of providing computer-based decision support from the ends. Since improving decision making is the objective of DSS, the DS segment, which focuses on decision-making behavior and how it can be improved, corresponds to the ends of any DSS effort. In contrast, the LC and UT segments correspond to the means for achieving the ends. LC furnishes the procedural means and UT the technological means for providing computer-based decision support.

In Figure 2.1 the Substantive Decision Support segment is emphasized to signal its dominant role in the framework. The ends of DSS—that is, the substance of supporting decision makers—must be our primary focus if we are to advance significantly the state-of-the-art and the state-of-practice. But in the field of DSS, where the means include a rapidly advancing, flashy, high-powered technology, one can easily become preoccupied with these means, failing to devote sufficient attention to the ends. While all three segments are important, we must be vigilant in asserting the primacy of the DS segment. As Ginzberg and Stohr (1982) observe, "Supporting and improving decision making *is* [their emphasis] the issue in DSS." To focus on anything else misses the point.

The Substantive Decision Support segment has not received its share of attention from DSS researchers to date, with lifecycle processes such as adaptive design dominating the early DSS literature. Consequently, we do not currently understand the substance of computer-based decision support well enough to provide meaningful guidance to practitioners. How can I make this claim? We do build successful systems and we do teach courses for practitioners. We must know something of the substance of decision support. By and large, we know how to recognize support when we see it, to mimic it, and to ad-lib adaptively. We do not, however, possess a systematic understanding of the DS segment, a prerequisite for moving the field significantly forward. We need now to pursue such an understanding.

Not everyone shares the view that the Substantive Decision Support segment must dominate. For instance, Keen (1980) has argued that an adaptive design process, hence the Lifecycle Processes segment, is the key element of DSS. Presumably, this view requires adaptability in the development process to substitute for substantive knowledge of decision support. Although the nature of managerial decision-making demands adaptive designs, I believe that understanding the substance of those designs is even more important.

Ironically, while the substance of decision support is the dominant issue, the underlying technology is the *sine qua non* of DSS. Even without understanding the DS and LC segments, a practitioner familiar with the technology can produce a system that provides some measure of support to decision makers. But no matter how well one comprehends the substance of decision support and the lifecycle processes for providing it, without some understanding of the underlying technology no DSS can be produced. Given the enabling role that technological knowledge plays, we must take care to ensure that research and development are driven not by technological capabilities but by decision-making needs.

There are grounds for concern as well as for optimism. Historically, both research and practice have neglected the DS segment. With the underlying technology continuing to advance in exciting ways, such neglect could easily continue. But we are beginning to see increased research (and calls for research) on the effects of DSS on decision-making behavior. And we are starting to see a variety of theory-based, commercially available products—Arborist, Expert Choice, Lightyear, and Supertree, to name a few—sharing shelf space with the many packages that do not draw on what we know of human decision making. These are promising signs.

Summary

The framework's segmentation scheme is based on three dichotomies: procedure versus substance, technology versus behavior, and ends versus means. One might expect these distinctions to yield a three-dimensional framework with eight ($2 \times 2 \times 2$) segments. Such an approach, however, would provide too fine a grid and, perhaps, empty cells. Instead, as the discussions of the distinguishing concepts demonstrated, each concept corresponds uniquely to one of the three segments in the sense that it differentiates that segment from the other two. As shown in Table 2.3, the procedure/substance dichotomy separates LC from the others, technology/behavior distinguishes UT, and ends/means distinguishes DS. Figure 2.2 illustrates the relationships between the concepts and the segments, and Figure 2.3 illustrates how each concept separates a different segment from the other two.

LINKING THE SEGMENTS

Partitioning elemental DSS concepts into distinct segments serves two purposes. First, as we have seen, grouping closely related concepts organizes the subject and enables us to identify, explore, and understand the fundamental issues confronting researchers and practitioners. Second, distinguishing concepts one from another allows us to focus on the relationships between them. The contents of the individual segments and the links among them are equally important for understanding DSS. Together, they provide an integrated structure for the study and practice of computer-based decision support.

TABLE 2.3   *Segments differentiated by concepts*

Concept	Distinguished segment	Other segments
Procedure/Substance	LC	DS UT
Technology/Behavior	UT	DS LC
Ends/Means	DS	LC UT

Not all DSS issues are elemental concepts fitting neatly into a single segment; many complex issues cut across multiple segments. One can think of the segments as decomposing these complex issues into their constituent elements. Reciprocally, one can think of the complex issues as connecting the segments. Both perspectives yield valuable insights. Here I concentrate on the links.

Links between segments are typically based on one or more of the conceptual distinctions identified in the preceding section. Indeed, intersegment links highlight the complementary nature of the two contrasting sides of each distinction: procedure requires substance, a behavioral orientation complements a technological one, and means serve ends.

One can study the complex issues and the connections they make among the segments at two levels of detail. One can take a macro view, examining "the big picture" to sense how the three segments fit together to form a coherent view of DSS. One can also examine the individual "micro links" that connect specific concepts in one segment with specific concepts in another. I will consider each case in turn.

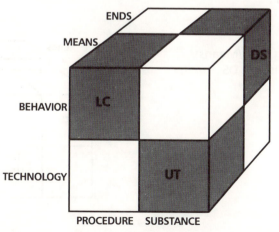

FIGURE 2.2   *Segments differentiated by concepts*

(a) Bisecting Procedure/Substance:
Distinguishing LC

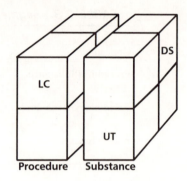

(b) Bisecting Technology/Behavior:
Distinguishing UT

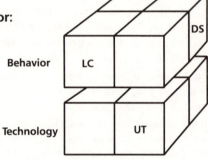

(c) Bisecting Ends/Means:
Distinguishing DS

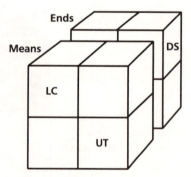

FIGURE 2.3   *Distinguishing segments*

A Macro View

Figure 2.4 depicts a macro view of a DSS project, portraying the collection of processes that occur during a DSS's life together with their inputs and outputs. The figure shows most of the major elements of the framework, identified by segment, and the relationships among them.*

The lifecycle processes (LC) are placed into two groups. Systems analysis, design, construction, and implementation constitute one group, and DSS implementation, training, use, evaluation, and evolution form the second group. The division, which separates those activities preceding initial delivery of the system from those following it, is somewhat rough, since the life of a DSS consists of overlapping and iterative activities. Moreover, implementation is placed in both groups, because implementation, as defined here, begins at the outset of the project and extends into the period of system use.

The developmental processes of analysis, design, and construction collectively take information technology (UT segment) and the characteristics of the given decision-making environment (DS segment) as inputs and produce a DSS as an output. That is, a given DSS development project applies information technology to create a DSS for the decision-making environment being supported. The DSS has an internal architecture (UT segment), which structures the technological subsystems, and external characteristics, which can be represented using the three-tiered approach to describing DSS (DS segment).

Once constructed, the DSS is placed into the decision-making environment. As it is used, the DSS interacts with its environment (the decision makers, tasks, and setting), intervening in the process through which decisions are made. As further consequences of system use, the environment may change as individual or organizational learning takes place, and the DSS may change (evolve) in response to perceived needs for modifications.

Notice the interplay between procedure and substance. The boxes represent procedures; the inputs and outputs are the substance. Clearly, procedural and substantive knowledge must fit together. As the cake-baking analogy highlights, each is only useful when joined with the other. Knowing procedurally how to build something requires knowing substantively what to use to construct it and what to produce. But despite the relatively large share of research attention DSS development processes have received, these procedures reference very little of the substance of DSS, very little of what we know about decision-making processes, needs, aids, environments, and support systems. Merely understanding lifecycle processes by themselves is not sufficient to produce an effective DSS; we must understand the substance of DSS and our procedures must be augmented to use that substantive knowledge. Development approaches for DSS must explicitly

---

*For simplicity, I have not shown all the components of all the segments. The missing elements can easily be added.

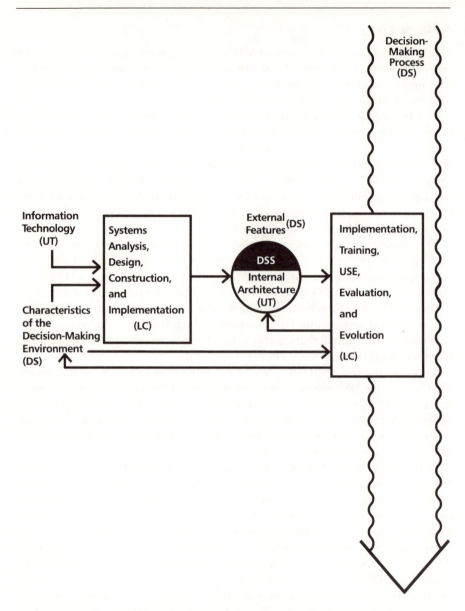

FIGURE 2.4   The big picture

reference the contents of the DS and UT segments. Conversely, we must develop procedures that take advantage of any substantive knowledge we acquire of decision making or technology. In short, we need to build stronger links between the lifecycle processes and the other two segments.

Micro Links

We see in Figure 2.4 that segments are interconnected in many ways. In addition to the interaction between procedure and substance, for instance, behavioral and technological issues are blended in the inputs to and outputs from the developmental processes. The macro view shows us the types of links that connect segments, the ways in which segments and their major components are related. Understanding the interconnections—especially in a way that enhances practice— requires studying these links at the micro-level, comprehending how an individual concept within one segment draws upon or impacts an element of another segment. Consider some examples of the links:

DS and UT

Some decision-aiding techniques require specific basic technologies. Some forms of group decision support, for example, depend upon sophisticated telecommunications facilities, shared databases, and large display screens. Support for geographically or spatially oriented decision making often requires special color/graphics capabilities. When frequent access to large, up-to-date databases must be provided, a mainframe is usually a key component of the delivery system. Understanding a given decision aid fully, therefore, entails examining the basic technologies upon which it depends.

Similarly, certain basic technologies may facilitate developing particular decision-aiding techniques. The availability of increasingly sophisticated display capabilities (color, graphics, animation), for instance, raises the question of how this technology can best be used to support decision makers. Inventing decision aids drawing on these capabilities is not sufficient; the aids must be studied to assess their impacts on decision-making behavior. Indeed, much research has centered on the best way to display information for decision makers (for surveys, see Ives, 1982; DeSanctis, 1984; and Jarvenpaa and Dickson, 1988). Along the same lines, many researchers are now asking how artificial intelligence and expert systems technologies can be fruitfully embedded in DSS. The issue is not just how to embed the technologies, but what effect they will have on decision-making behavior.

The internal architectures and external features of a DSS have an important connection one with another: the internal subsystems must be configured so as to produce a DSS with the desired external features (functional capabilities, user view, and attributes). While internal architectures and external features are each significant topics by themselves, to produce an effective DSS the DSS builder must also understand how they are related.

DS and LC

The characteristics of the decision-making environments being supported and the types of decision aids being employed influence how some lifecycle processes are carried out. The following are representative examples: the organizational setting plays a major role in determining which implementation tactics are used; the relative efficacy of voluntary and mandatory use, the importance of top management support, and the best means of fostering change all depend on the setting. Features of the decision aid contribute to determining the appropriate type of training. Some aids require extensive training by humans; others require little training or embed appropriate computer-based training facilities. Characteristics of the environment and of the DSS both affect patterns of use— for instance, whether or not a chauffeur is used. To understand fully a given decision aid or decision-making environment, therefore, we must understand its implications for the lifecycle processes.

Influence also occurs in the opposite direction, from the LC to the DS segment. Since design and analysis methodologies shape the systems they produce, different approaches to the analysis and design processes may systematically lead to differences in the computer-based support provided. Some analysis and design methodologies may tend to produce DSS with particular special features, while others may be more "robust," producing a broader spectrum of DSS. Some of these more robust methodologies may even provide a means for choosing among alternative DSS features. Understanding a given DSS design methodology must include considering how it shapes the systems it produces.

LC and UT

For a given DSS the nature of its lifecycle processes may impose requirements on the underlying technologies employed in its construction. In particular, certain development approaches may require specific technologies. Effective use of adaptive design and the middle-out approach demands development systems sufficiently flexible to facilitate rapid initial implementation and subsequent modification. For these reasons, Keen and Gambino (1983) have advocated the use of APL as a DSS development language. For similar reasons, Sprague (1980) advocates the use of DSS Generators. To understand fully a development approach requires appreciating its technological requirements.

Conversely, the underlying technology influences DSS development processes. Increasingly sophisticated and powerful development systems, for example, can improve significantly the processes of system construction and evolution. Moreover, how one approaches the technology may affect how one views the lifecycle. To wit, Sprague and Carlson (1982) use the three technological levels of Sprague's (1980) framework to interpret Keen's (1980) adaptive design process.

Remarks

We have just seen many examples of the links that connect elements of one segment with elements of another. Many more links can be considered. Most of the examples were somewhat abstract in that they did not reference specific decision aids, specific design methodologies, specific development systems, and so forth. For the most part I described the kinds of connections that can occur between elements of different segments, but did not define specific links such as "Decision Aid X requires Development System Y" or "Design Methodology A systematically produces DSS with Attribute B." These more specific cases, however, are the ones that constitute the majority of micro links between segments. For each decision aid we invent, for each design methodology we propose, for each development system we construct, we must study how it affects and how it is affected by the other segments of the framework. All told, the number of micro links among segments is vast.

The examples suggest that links are often the connections between means and ends. Particular ends—that is, certain types of substantive support—may depend upon particular means, either procedural (lifecycle processes) or substantive (underlying technologies). Conversely, particular means (processes or technologies) may lead systematically to particular ends (forms of support). Moreover, particular procedural means (processes) may be compatible or incompatible with particular substantive means (technologies).

Summary

The links between segments are an integral part of the framework. Together with the segments' contents, they create a structure that organizes the field of DSS. Although researching within a given segment is both important and a natural place to begin, we must extend our understanding of each elemental concept to include its interactions with those in other segments. The more that researchers explore the links between the segments, the richer will be our understanding of DSS.

A final thought on intersegment links: the essence of providing computer-based decision support is the combining of support for decision making with the capabilities of computer-based technology. It follows that at least three constraints limit the success of computer-based decision support. First, research in decision-making theory is still limited in its understanding of how to improve human decision-making processes. Second, current information systems capabilities limit what is technologically feasible. Third, we lack a satisfactory merger of the current states of decision-making theory and information systems technology. All three constraints are binding. Advances either in prescriptive decision research or in computer technology would enhance our capacity to support human decision makers. Even without such advances, however, an integration of current decision-making theory with currently available technology should lead to significant improvements in DSS.

EXAMINING OTHER FRAMEWORKS

How does the framework described above relate to other frameworks in the DSS literature? In this section I study this question by analyzing existing frameworks in terms of the new one. Fitting well-known elements of the DSS literature into and across the segments of the new framework serves two purposes. First, the new framework's structure becomes more concrete when its segments are associated with familiar components from the literature. Reciprocally, the roles played by each existing framework, as well as the interactions among the frameworks, become clearer when we analyze each one with respect to the new framework's segmentation scheme. The analysis also provides an opportunity to survey each framework's key concepts and contributions.

The 15 frameworks, taxonomies, and approaches I survey have most in common that they are fundamental contributions to the DSS literature, providing general insights into fairly broad topics rather than detailed discussions of narrowly defined issues. Moreover, the pieces are either among the most frequently cited in the DSS literature or present concepts of special importance later in the book. All are from the "early" DSS literature, ranging from 1971 to 1985 and concentrated about the late 1970s and early 1980s. Since my main purpose in this section is to study these contributions as they relate to the new framework, detailed debates over the substance of these works, as well as consideration of other research contributions, are either deferred to subsequent chapters or omitted.

TABLE 2.4   *Fitting the DSS literature into the framework's segments*

UT Underlying Technology	LC DSS Lifecycle Processes	DS Substantive Decision Support
Ginzberg and Stohr (1982)	Ginzberg and Stohr (1982)	Ginzberg and Stohr (1982)
		Gorry and Scott Morton (1971)
		Hackathorn and Keen (1981)
Donovan and Madnick (1977)		Donovan and Madnick (1977)
		Lerch and Mantei (1984)
	Alter (1980)	Alter (1980)
	Gerrity (1971)	
	Stabell (1983)	
	Hurst *et al.* (1983)	
	Keen (1980)	
	Moore and Chang (1983)	
Sprague and Carlson (1982)	Sprague and Carlson (1982)	Sprague and Carlson (1982)
Bonczek *et al.* (1981)		
Ariav and Ginzberg (1985)	Ariav and Ginzberg (1985)	Ariav and Ginzberg (1985)
	Keen and Scott Morton (1978)	

Tables 2.4 and 2.5 depict how the 15 pieces relate to the framework's three segments. Table 2.4 positions each piece in the appropriate segment(s), whereas Table 2.5 lists the pieces, their fundamental concepts, and the associated framework segments. Several of the books and articles deal with multiple segments because (1) they employ dimensions oblique to those of the new framework, (2) they explicitly address links among segments, or (3) they do not attempt to distinguish fundamental concepts.

Ginzberg and Stohr (1982)

Of the existing approaches to organizing the DSS field, the outline Ginzberg and Stohr used for their survey of DSS research is the one most resembling the new

TABLE 2.5   Frameworks, taxonomies, approaches . . .

Source	Key Concepts	Segment
Ginzberg and Stohr (1982)	Anatomy, Ontogeny, and Physiology	UT, LC, and DS
Gorry and Scott Morton (1971)	Task Structure	DS
	Managerial Level	DS
Hackathorn and Keen (1981)	Task Interdependencies	DS
Donovan and Madnick (1977)	"Ad Hoc" versus "Institutional"	UT and DS
Lerch and Mantei (1984)	Phase of Process	DS
	Task Structure	DS
Alter (1980)	Taxonomy	DS
	Implementation	LC
Gerrity (1970, 1971)	Decision-centered Design Methodology	LC
Stabell (1975, 1983)	Decision-oriented Design Methodology	LC
Hurst *et al.* (1983)	Evolutionary Approach and Middle-out Design	LC
Keen (1980)	Adaptive Design	LC
Moore and Chang (1983)	Meta-design Methodology	LC
Sprague and Carlson (1982)	DSS Generators	UT
	Three Technological Subsystems	UT
	ROMC	DS
	Managerial Objectives	DS
	Building Process	LC
Bonczek, Holsapple, and Whinston (1981)	Language System, Knowledge System, and Problem-Processing System	UT
Ariav and Ginzberg (1985)	Systemic View	UT, LC, and DS
Keen and Scott Morton (1978)	Motivational Material	—
	Design, Implementation, and Evaluation	LC

framework. Theirs is also a three-part organization, identifying DSS anatomy, physiology, and ontogeny. Figure 2.5 maps Ginzberg and Stohr's organization onto the new framework. Ontogeny, "the processes by which DSS are designed and implemented" (p. 12), corresponds very closely to the Lifecycle Processes segment; anatomy, "the underlying technological components from which DSS are built" (p. 12), to the Underlying Technology segment. Some anatomical components—for instance, Alter's (1977b, 1980) taxonomy*—are more closely related to decision making than to technology, however, and they are found in the Substantive Decision Support segment. The bulk of physiology, "the ways in which DSS are used" (p. 12), is divided among Substantive Decision Support and Lifecycle Processes.

Gorry and Scott Morton (1971)

Nearly 20 years have passed since Gorry and Scott Morton's influential framework first appeared. Observing it from today's perspective leads to a pair of conclusions. First, the article has played a seminal role, coining the term "Decision Support System," being one of the most-often cited MIS papers of its decade, and affecting significantly both research and practice. Second, the article's importance stems not so much from its ongoing value as a framework for research or practice as from the historical role it has played in focusing attention and resources on computer-based systems for supporting decision makers.

Although popularly cited as a framework for Decision Support Systems this article is best characterized by its title, "A Framework for Management Information Systems," positioning DSS within the broader MIS context as systems that do not replace human decision makers but do provide meaningful assistance to the decision-making process. The essay is a well-crafted argument; its two dimensions appear carefully chosen to support the article's two primary assertions.

The first component of Gorry and Scott Morton's argument advocates what was in 1971 a new breed of computer-based system. Using two of Simon's (1960) concepts as a foundation, the framework's "task structure" dimension distinguishes DSS from other systems by creating a niche for them: supporting tasks not sufficiently structured to be automated fully, but with enough structure to be assisted by computer-based aids. Indeed, the concept of "supporting, not replacing, the decision maker" has become the cornerstone of DSS research and practice.

Gorry and Scott Morton use the second dimension of their framework primarily to oppose the "total systems" concept popular in the 1960s. By differentiating systems on the basis of Anthony's (1965) three levels of managerial activity

---

*This rearrangement seems very much in the spirit of Ginzberg and Stohr's (1982) article, where they advocate strongly—and lament the lack of—a focus on support for decision making in DSS research.

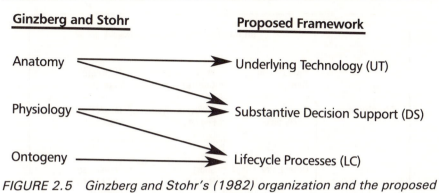

Ginzberg and Stohr   **Proposed Framework**

Anatomy ──────────────────► Underlying Technology (UT)

Physiology ───────────────► Substantive Decision Support (DS)

Ontogeny ─────────────────► Lifecycle Processes (LC)

FIGURE 2.5   *Ginzberg and Stohr's (1982) organization and the proposed framework*

(operational control, management control, and strategic planning) and arguing that different levels of decision making require different types of information, they conclude that the total systems approach is often inappropriate.

Although Gorry and Scott Morton depict their framework as a rectangle thoroughly filled with tasks (see Figure 2.6), their two dimensions are not theoretically orthogonal. Both dimensions depend on Simon's distinction between programmed and non-programmed tasks. As one moves along the "task structure" dimension, from structured through semistructured* to unstructured tasks, the portion of the task that is programmed decreases. But Anthony observes that as one moves across managerial levels, from operational control through managerial control to strategic planning activities, the activities are increasingly non-programmed. We should expect, therefore, that tasks would cluster about the diagonal of the Gorry and Scott Morton framework.

For nearly two decades Gorry and Scott Morton's framework has been the dominant one in the field of DSS. Its two dimensions have played well their roles in starting the DSS bandwagon rolling. In terms of the current needs of DSS research and practice these two dimensions—task structure and managerial level—are characteristics for differentiating decision-making environments. As such, both are contained within the Substantive Decision Support segment of the new framework.

Hackathorn and Keen (1981)

Hackathorn and Keen propose adding a third dimension, "task interdependency," to Gorry and Scott Morton's framework. Drawing on Thompson's (1967) analysis

---

*In the course of defining this dimension, Gorry and Scott Morton introduce the now-popular term "semistructured." The word is rarely used as formally defined—tasks where a non-empty, proper subset of Simon's three phases are "programmed"—but is used casually to connote the tasks most likely to be supported by DSS, those lying in that "squishy" region between the extremes of highly structured (candidates for automation) and unstructured (not easily supported).

Information Systems: A Framework

	Operational Control	Management Control	Strategic Planning
Structured	Accounts Receivable	Budget Analysis— Engineered Costs	Tanker Fleet Mix
	Order Entry	Short-Term Forecasting	Warehouse and Factory Location
	Inventory Control		
Semi-Structured	Production Scheduling	Variance Analysis— Overall Budget	Mergers and Acquisitions
	Cash Management	Budget Preparation	New Product Planning
Unstructured	PERT/COST Systems	Sales and Production	R&D Planning

FIGURE 2.6   *Gorry and Scott Morton's framework. Note. Reprinted from "A framework for management information systems," G. Anthony Gorry and Michael S. Scott Morton, Sloan Management Review, **13**(1) (Fall 1971), pp. 55–70, by permission of the publisher. Copyright (1971) by the Sloan Management Review Association. All rights reserved*

of the types of task interdependencies in organizations, Hackathorn and Keen suggest separating decision support into three distinct, but interrelated components: Personal Support (for decision makers whose tasks are relatively independent of others), Group Support (for individuals engaged in separate but highly interrelated tasks), and Organizational Support (for tasks involving a sequence of operations and actors). Task interdependency is a characteristic that differentiates decision-making environments and, like Gorry and Scott Morton's original dimensions, belongs to the Substantive Decision Support segment.

Hackathorn and Keen's article serves multiple purposes: to assert the importance of considering interactions among individuals when providing computer-based

TABLE 2.6   *Donovan and Madnick's comparisons of institutional and ad hoc DSS*

	Institutional DSS	Ad Hoc DSS
Number of decision occurrences for a decision type	many	few
Number of decision types	few	many
Number of people making decisions of same type	many	few
Range of decisions supported	narrow	wide
Range of users supported	narrow	wide
Range of issues addressed	narrow	wide
Specific data needed known in advance	usually	rarely
Specific analysis needed known in advance	usually	rarely
Problems are recurring	usually	rarely
Importance of operational efficiency	high	low
Duration of specific type of problem being addressed	long.	short
Need for rapid development	low	high

Note. Reprinted with permission from "Institutional and ad hoc DSS and their effective use," John J. Donovan and Stuart E. Madnick, *Data Base*, **8**(3), Winter 1977, pp. 79–88. Copyright (1977) John J. Donovan and Stuart E. Madnick. All rights reserved.

support; to suggest that mismatches may occur between support needs and support provided, especially if the DSS field concentrates only on personal support; and to emphasize the organizational implications of using personal computing for decision support.* Hackathorn and Keen's messages have been heard and heeded; although the definitions vary somewhat from theirs, a large share of DSS research today focuses on group support, and organizational decision support is receiving increasing attention.

Donovan and Madnick (1977)

While Hackathorn and Keen increase the dimensionality of the Gorry and Scott Morton framework, Donovan and Madnick introduce a concept that aligns with an existing dimension, managerial level. They distinguish two classes of DSS, contrasted in Table 2.6: "institutional DSS, which deal with decisions of a recurring nature, and ad hoc DSS, which deal with specific problems that are usually not anticipated or recurring" (p. 79). Portfolio management systems exemplify institutional DSS; systems supporting new product and merger decisions illustrate ad hoc systems. Institutional DSS tend to be found at the operational and management control levels, and ad hoc DSS occur at the management control and strategic planning levels.

---

*Hackathorn and Keen's observations concerning the organizational implications of using personal computers as delivery systems for decision support suggests that the task interdependency dimension has important links with the Underlying Technology segment.

After contrasting the two types of DSS, Donovan and Madnick focus on a technological approach to providing ad hoc decision support and its application to energy-related decision making in New England. Elsewhere, Donovan (1976) discusses this technology, the Generalized Management Information System (GMIS), and its use in greater detail.

The first section of the Donovan and Madnick article belongs in the Substantive Decision Support segment, whereas the second part contributes to the Underlying Technology segment. As a whole, the article bridges these two segments nicely by discussing a need for support together with an underlying technology for meeting it.

Lerch and Mantei (1984)

Lerch and Mantei propose a two-dimensional DSS framework, noting that their scheme classifies *types* of decision support rather than Decision Support *Systems*. The distinction is important not only because it reminds us that a DSS may incorporate many different forms of support, but because it motivates us to look beyond the labels we use for classifying systems and to examine the substantive support a system provides.

Lerch and Mantei's first dimension, phase of the decision-making process (Intelligence, Design, and Choice), consists of the first three stages of Simon's phase model. The second dimension, degree of decision structure (structured under certainty, structured under risk, structured under uncertainty, and unstructured), is based on Mason and Mitroff's (1973) framework. Taken together, the two dimensions classify decision-making activities—as opposed to complete decision-making tasks—in terms of (1) the decision-making phase to which they belong and (2) how structured they are. Since the two dimensions can also classify the computer-based techniques used to meet the needs of these decision-making activities, the framework fosters a matching between decision-making activities and support techniques. The framework clearly belongs to the Substantive Decision Support segment, although the article suggests a number of links with the other two segments.

Comparing Lerch and Mantei's structuredness dimension with that of Gorry and Scott Morton helps identify a key difference between the two frameworks. Gorry and Scott Morton classify whole tasks, while Lerch and Mantei classify individual activities. Gorry and Scott Morton, therefore, determine task structuredness by first assessing whether or not each phase is structured (programmed) and then arriving at an overall assessment for the entire task. Lerch and Mantei, however, concentrate on individual activities, considering how structured they are and to which phase they belong.

Lerch and Mantei's classification scheme serves two purposes: to facilitate communication (among researchers and practitioners), and to provide design aid and guidance. Indeed, they establish these objectives as criteria for evaluating

DSS frameworks and use them to review and reject other candidate dimensions. I will return to these criteria at the end of this chapter.

Alter (1980)

Based on 56 DSS case studies performed in the mid-1970s, *DSS: Current Practices and Continuing Challenges* is best known for its unidimensional taxonomy (Alter, 1977b), reprinted here as Table 2.7. Systems are classified by the generic operations or functions they perform, and the taxonomy "is based on what can be called the 'degree of action implication of system outputs,' i.e., the degree to which the system's output can directly determine the decision" (1980, p. 73). Alter observes that the taxonomy can be collapsed into a dichotomy between "data-oriented" and "model-oriented" systems. As I noted in Chapter 1, this distinction reflects the dual origins (MIS and OR/MS) of the field of DSS; it is one of the key concepts necessary for understanding computer-based decision support.

Given rapid advances in computer-based technology, coupled with dramatic shifts in the use of that technology by decision makers, a decade-old taxonomy based on descriptive studies must play a different role today than at the time it was created. Then, it provided a snapshot of the various kinds of support systems being used and the differences among them. Today, we would view what Alter described as distinct types of systems as distinct operations likely to be found within a single system. And, of course, we would need to add newer functions to the list. Furthermore, since Alter found that the types of systems differed with respect to many characteristics (type of task, hands-on user, decision maker, key role, key usage problem, system initiator, key design and implementation problem, key

TABLE 2.7 Alter's taxonomy

Data-oriented
A. *File drawer systems* allow immediate access to data items.
B. *Data analysis systems* allow the manipulation of data by means of operators tailored to the task and setting or operators of a general nature.
C. *Analysis information systems* provide access to a series of databases and small models.

Model-oriented
D. *Accounting models* calculate the consequences of planned actions on the basis of accounting definitions.
E. *Representational models* estimate the consequences of actions on the basis of models that are partially nondefinitional.
F. *Optimization model* provide guidelines for action by generating the optimal solution consistent with a series of constraints.
G. *Suggestion models* perform mechanical work leading to a specific suggested decision for a fairly structured task.

change issues, and key technical problem), today's hybrid systems raise numerous research questions with respect to these issues.

Following the taxonomy chapter, Alter identifies five ways DSS can increase the effectiveness of individuals: improving personal efficiency, expediting problem solving, facilitating interpersonal communication, promoting learning or training, and increasing organizational control. Both the taxonomy and the list of increases in effectiveness fit neatly into the Substantive Decision Support segment.

Less often cited than the taxonomy, but perhaps of greater long-run importance is Part 3 of Alter's volume, "Toward successful implementation," containing significant discussions of implementation patterns, situations, risk factors, and strategies. These contributions belong to the Lifecycle Processes segment.

Gerrity (1970, 1971)

In one of the early DSS research efforts, Gerrity developed the Portfolio Management System (PMS) by using a "decision-centered design methodology" subsequently endorsed by Keen and Scott Morton (1978) and extended by Stabell (1975, 1983). Central to Gerrity's approach, whose purpose is to direct changes in decision-making behavior, are normative, descriptive, and functional models of the decision-making process. The normative model, created first, defines how decisions should be made, whereas the descriptive model characterizes how decisions are currently made. The gap between these two models defines the design problem confronted by the practitioner, whose functional model of the computer-based support system represents a compromise between the descriptive and normative models. The functional specification represents "a reasonable balance between long-run decision process goals and short-run limitations in resources and capacity for change" (p. 64). Building a DSS conforming to the functional model is intended to move the decision maker from his or her current decision-making process, captured by the descriptive model, in the direction of the normative model.

As a methodology for DSS design and implementation, Gerrity's approach belongs to the Lifecycle Processes. The decision system models that pervade his methodology link the LC segment with the DS segment.

Stabell (1975, 1983)

Stabell's "decision-oriented approach" to building DSS (1983) posits that "increasing decision-making effectiveness through changes in how decisions are made should be a principal objective of DSS development" (p. 225). Sharing Gerrity's view of DSS as a vehicle for directed change, Stabell (1975) critiques and extends Gerrity's methodology, finding it inadequate to cause the desired changes in decision-making behavior.

Both Stabell and Gerrity's methodologies fit squarely in the Lifecycle Process segment, but Stabell augments Gerrity's decision-modeling framework in ways that build stronger connections to the DS segment. For example, Stabell (1975) suggests using Simon's (1972) concept of "bounded rationality" and Cyert and March's (1963) observations concerning "local rationality," "uncertainty avoidance," "local search," and "simple learning" in organizations as bases for diagnosing gaps between actual and desired decision-making behavior. These analyses lead him to propose a set of DSS features that ought to be widely applicable in directing change, or, as he calls it, "decision channeling."

Hurst, Ness, Gambino, and Johnson (1983)

"Growing DSS: a flexible, evolutionary approach," uses an agricultural metaphor to discuss the nurturing and cultivation of DSS. As the verbs "grow," "nurture," and "cultivate" suggest, this article provides insights into procedures for systems development and belongs to the Lifecycle Processes segment. While concentrating on the evolutionary nature of DSS, it touches on all the other processes (analysis, design, construction, implementation, training, use, and evaluation) as well.

The article's major theme is captured by the following observation: "The only constant is change, and you can't even count on that" (p. 123). Responding to the variety of changes that occur in decision support environments over time requires a flexible, evolutionary approach to DSS development. The authors therefore advocate the "middle-out" design approach, a technique that "begins close to the level of the problem at hand, and . . . involves a cyclical process of generalizing (bottom-up) and specifying (top-down) at each stage of the problem-solving process" (p. 124). Middle-out design relies heavily on rapid development of prototype systems, often using a "breadboarding" technique of synthesizing systems from existing components.

Although the article belongs to the Lifecycle Processes segment, it has a number of connections with the Underlying Technology segment. For instance, using an evolutionary development approach influences one's choice of development and delivery systems.

Keen (1980)

Adaptive design—a development process whereby the system, user, and builder adapt in response to each other over time—is the basis for Keen's definition of DSS. In this article Keen defines a system as a DSS if and only if it emerges through an adaptive process of design and use where all six bidirectional influences among system, user, and builder are operative. Although I have opted to define DSS more broadly, Keen nonetheless offers persuasive arguments that adaptive design is often the most appropriate approach to building computer-based systems that are intended to support decision makers. For instance, the unstructured nature of many decision-making tasks may prevent users and builders from creating adequate functional specifications in advance of DSS construction, but these users and builders can react to an initial version of the system, indicating ways it should be adapted. Likewise, if decision makers learn from using a system—a concept central to Keen's viewpoint—their support needs are likely to change, necessitating adaptation of the system.

Adaptive design clearly belongs to the Lifecycle Processes segment, touching in some way all eight of its constituent elements—design, analysis, construction, implementation, training, use, evaluation, and, in particular, evolution. The adaptive development process is consonant with Hurst *et al.*'s evolutionary view of DSS design and employs their middle-out approach. The relationship between adaptive design and the decision-centered/decision-oriented approaches of Gerrity and Stabell, however, is open to interpretation. Keen asserts that the two views are compatible, claiming that adaptive design can be used to achieve the improvements in effectiveness advocated by Gerrity and Stabell. Stabell, however, is critical of designers' relying too greatly on adaptability in place of specifying explicitly how system features support decision making in a given situation.

Moore and Chang (1983)

Moore and Chang's "meta-design methodology" for DSS is not "a step-by-step procedure or even an exhaustive list of topics that are important in designing DSS" (p. 174), but a basis from which DSS practitioners can develop their own design frameworks. By addressing design *methodologies*, albeit at the "meta-design" level, the article contributes primarily to the Lifecycle Processes segment.

Moore and Chang present four key ideas: system/problem migration, subset evolution, "soft" versus "hard" DSS capabilities, and a "weak–strong" design continuum. Their "migration effect"—the tendency for DSS and decision-making problems to migrate over time toward support for more structured tasks—motivates the other three ideas, each of which has a connection with the DS or UT segments.

The concepts of subset evolution and "soft" versus "hard" capabilities are both components of an adaptive development process for DSS. Subset evolution is an approach to designing the external features of a DSS such that the user sees a set of extensible capabilities that expand over time. In choosing between "soft" and "hard" capabilities, Moore and Chang advocate beginning with "soft, initial, generalized system capabilities" that eventually are " 'wired down' into hard, streamlined, powerful operators" (p. 174). The concepts have implications for both the DS and UT segments, since they affect the substantive support the decision maker receives and also place demands on the development system the builder employs.

Moore and Chang's final concept defines a design continuum ranging from "weak" designs that follow "the user's current preferences and existing capabilities" through "strong" designs that deliberately attempt "to shape or refine the user's decision-making process'' (p. 174). The intended strength of a DSS design, a function of the system's objectives, has important implications for the design of a system's attributes.

Sprague and Carlson (1982)

Building Effective Decision Support Systems blends and extends two widely cited elements of the DSS literature: Sprague's (1980) "Framework for the development of DSS" and Carlson's (1979, 1983a) "ROMC approach." The book concentrates primarily on the technology for constructing DSS and secondarily on the process of building DSS, giving some attention to substantive decision support, as well.

Sprague's framework for DSS development, reprinted as Figure 2.7, identifies three levels of technology, associated with five roles for people. Builders use DSS Generators (packages of related hardware and software capabilities) to construct Specific DSS (the systems actually employed by the user) quickly and easily. Technical supporters build the DSS Generators from a variety of DSS Tools (system building blocks such as database systems and dialog managers).

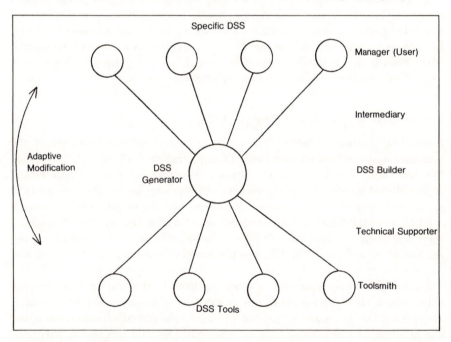

FIGURE 2.7   *Sprague's framework for the development of DSS. Note. Reprinted by special permission from the MIS Quarterly, 4(4), (Dec. 80). Copyright 1980 by the Society for Information Management and the Management Information Systems Research Center at the University of Minnesota. All rights reserved*

The DSS Generator, as a special type of DSS development system, is part of the UT segment. The UT segment also includes the three main technological subsystems of a DSS (Dialog Management, Model Management, and Database Management), which Sprague treats extensively because they are essential for understanding the framework's middle and lower levels. For analyzing the upper level, the level of the managerial decision maker, Sprague identifies six performance criteria; these criteria, which relate to such topics as task structure, task interdependency, and decision-making phase, contribute to the DS segment. The relationships among the three levels are also important parts of the framework, since the interactions among levels define Sprague's approach to adaptive system development (the LC segment).

Carlson's ROMC is usually billed as an approach to DSS analysis and design, which would make it part of the LC segment, but ROMC fits better in the DS segment because it is mostly a generic user view of DSS components. The "approach" consists of using the ROMC generic user view (DSS comprise Representations, Operations, Memory aids, and Control mechanisms), subject to the guidelines that representations are designed first and that the system includes operations focusing on each of Simon's phases. The ROMC chapter is contained within the part of Sprague and Carlson's book devoted to the process of building DSS, the remainder of which belongs to the LC segment. A strength of this portion of the book is that it builds a bridge between LC and UT by applying Keen's concept of adaptive design to the use of DSS Generators.

Bonczek, Holsapple, and Whinston (1981)

Foundations of Decision Support Systems concentrates on two elements of the computer-based technology underlying DSS, placing the book in the UT segment. Bonczek *et al.* describe network database management systems and formal logic/artificial intelligence in the context of proposing an architecture for DSS comprising three elements: a Language System (LS), the linguistic facilities made available to the DSS user; a Knowledge System (KS), the DSS's body of knowledge about a problem domain; and a Problem-Processing System (PPS), the interfacing mechanism between an LS and KS that produces information supporting a decision process.

Some readers may also wish to place the book in the DS segment, because it presents a classification scheme for DSS that is based on a partial generic user view. The key concept behind the two-dimensional classification is the degree of non-procedurality of user requests. The first dimension partitions languages for directing computation into three cases of increasing non-procedurality: the user states the model explicitly, the user invokes a model by name, and the user simply states the problem. Similarly, the second dimension partitions the language for directing data retrieval into three cases: the user states the retrieval procedure explicitly, the user invokes a report, and the user simply

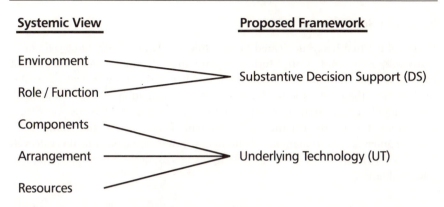

Systemic View   **Proposed Framework**

Environment

Role / Function   Substantive Decision Support (DS)

Components

Arrangement   Underlying Technology (UT)

Resources

FIGURE 2.8   Ariav and Ginzberg's (1985) systemic view and the proposed framework

states the problem. The cartesian product of the two dimensions yields a nine-cell scheme.

Ariav and Ginzberg (1985)

"DSS design—a systemic view of decision support" is consistent with many of the positions I presented here but, being itself a broad-based approach to DSS, it is not easily analyzed with respect to the new framework. Observing that most existing DSS studies concentrate on only one of three critical sets of issues—sets that align with the DS, LC, and UT segments—Ariav and Ginzberg present an integrated view of DSS by applying the "systems approach" (Churchman, 1968) to DSS analysis, thus characterizing a DSS by its environment, its role or function, the components it comprises, the arrangement of its components, and the resources it consumes.

Figure 2.8 depicts the mapping from the systemic view onto the new framework. The first two aspects, environment and role/function, pertain to Substantive Decision Support, while the next two aspects, components and arrangements, relate to the internal components and architecture of a DSS and are contained in the UT segment. The final aspect, resources, includes hardware and software and therefore also belongs, at least in part, to the UT segment.

None of the five aspects map into the Lifecycle Processes segment. Perhaps this is because the article as a whole is an approach to DSS design—although not a detailed design methodology—so the systemic view in its entirety can be seen as belonging to the LC segment. That the five aspects of DSS featured by the systemic view are divided among the other two segments indicates the strong links that must exist among segments. Moreover, the systemic view itself emphasizes the crucial relationships among the aspects.

Keen and Scott Morton (1978)

In one of the first books dedicated to the subject of DSS,* *DSS: An Organizational Perspective*, Keen and Scott Morton expend much of their effort making the case for DSS and placing DSS in perspective. Most of this motivational material—for instance, their discussions of management, information, systems, and MIS; their models of decision making; and their examples of DSS—is more of a foundation for the subject than a component of any one of the framework's three segments. The remainder of the book, however, belongs to the Lifecycle Processes segment, concentrating on design, analysis, evolution, implementation, and evaluation.

Summary

My review of other frameworks, as summarized in Table 2.4, might suggest that the Substantive Decision Support segment has received an appropriate share of DSS researchers' attention, contrary to my earlier assertions. One must keep in mind, however, that the review included only frameworks, taxonomies, and other broad-based approaches to DSS and did not attempt to list all, or even most, DSS research. Moreover, most of the contributions to the DS segment cited here are classification schemes requiring detailed follow-up research to furnish any true substance. These initial contributions are shells waiting to be filled.

Unfortunately, the follow-up research has been slow in coming. Although many of these classification schemes have been cited in other general commentaries on DSS, we are only now beginning to see studies that utilize the classifications in any meaningful way. Recognizing the vast potential for this segment, we see that our understanding of the Lifecycle Processes and Underlying Technology segments is much more complete than that of Substantive Decision Support, the relative lengths of the lists notwithstanding.

CONCLUSION

Lerch and Mantei (1984) propose two criteria for evaluating DSS frameworks: (1) how well the framework facilitates communication among researchers and practitioners, and (2) how well the framework provides aid and guidance for DSS design. They offer these criteria in the context of frameworks that are classification schemes for decision-making activities, but the criteria are valuable for evaluating DSS frameworks in general. If pushing forward the state-of-the-art as well as the

---

*Keen and Scott Morton's (1978) book is often cited as the first devoted to DSS, but it was preceded by Scott Morton's (1971) *Management Decision Systems* and was contemporaneous with McCosh and Scott Morton's (1978) *Management Decision Support Systems*.

state-of-practice is an objective of a DSS framework, then satisfying these two criteria is a prerequisite.

The new framework meets both evaluative criteria. One can look at the framework's three segments as a means of structuring the DSS knowledge base and elucidating its contents, thereby increasing its value for both those who contribute to and those who draw upon that knowledge. When researchers or practitioners add to the knowledge base, the framework's structure classifies the new contributions, relating them to what is already there. When researchers or practitioners need to draw from the knowledge base, the framework makes it easier to find what is needed and to see how that knowledge fits into the larger scheme of computer-based decision support.

The segments, their major components, the intrasegment connections between these components, and the intersegment links tying the framework together remedy problems with the current state of our DSS knowledge base. Fitting the DSS literature to the framework highlights the gaps (under-researched areas), fragments (isolated contributions), loose ends (partially connected contributions), and rifts (conflicting contributions) in our knowledge. In short, the framework facilitates communication among researchers, among practitioners, and between researchers and practitioners.

The framework's structure also enlightens DSS design. The fundamental concepts that distinguish the three segments separate complex design issues into more basic ones. The framework separates the *ends* of the design process—the "system design" itself—from the procedural and technological *means* of developing the design and constructing the system. It separates the *technological* issues that influence a DSS design from the *behavioral* ones. And it separates the *procedures* for designing a system from *substantive* concerns about the design's content.

Designing DSS successfully entails understanding how the segments differ and then combining them effectively, merging carefully the two sides of each dichotomy. Designers must unite computer-based technology with an understanding of human decision making and its needs for support. For instance, they must appreciate how the underlying technology constrains what decision aids and system characteristics are feasible and, conversely, how particular decision aids and system characteristics place demands upon the underlying technology. Likewise, designers must understand how the means serve the ends: for instance, how particular development processes lead systematically to particular forms of support and, conversely, how particular forms of support demand particular development approaches. Finally, designers must blend the procedural and substantive aspects of design. For instance, when employing an adaptive design strategy they must know how to define the initial system characteristics and how to change these characteristics over time.

All of these connections among segments require much more research for us to provide sufficient aid and guidance to DSS designers. The framework provides a structure for such research. Before we can seriously consider the crucial bonds with the Substantive Decision Support segment, however, we must first understand the contents of this segment better. In particular, before we can enhance our design procedures to refer to design characteristics of DSS, we must develop a means of describing and differentiating DSS in terms of their characteristics. The chapters that follow address this challenge.

Chapter 3
DESCRIBING DSS: A THREE-TIERED APPROACH

Beginning with this chapter, I concentrate on the Substantive Decision Support segment of the framework, presenting an approach to describing computer-based systems that can affect the decision-making behavior of their users. Being able to describe Decision Support Systems (DSS) systematically is a fundamental requirement for both research and practice. Just as physicists employ mathematical equations and chemists enlist molecular models to describe the systems they study, members of the DSS community require a mechanism for describing the computer-based systems with which they are concerned. Among the many activities that would benefit from a mechanism for describing DSS, two stand out:

- *Designing DSS*. Creating a DSS requires analyzing the decision-making environment to be supported and producing a computer-based system that matches its needs. Without a systematic way of characterizing how the features of DSS vary, one lacks a systematic means for considering alternative designs when defining a system's features.
- *Studying DSS Effects*. Describing the association between DSS characteristics and DSS effects requires a systematic means of describing the characteristics of DSS. Understanding why different DSS affect decision making differently requires being able to distinguish DSS in terms of these characteristics.

Given its importance and fundamental nature, surprisingly little attention has been given to systematically describing and differentiating DSS. Although many have given names to one subclass of DSS or another, Alter's (1977b, 1980) taxonomy is still the only major attempt to characterize and distinguish systematically the spectrum of systems that support decision making. Recognizing the significant changes in computer-based technology and decision-support capabilities that have occurred during the 15 years since Alter studied the systems from which he derived his taxonomy, a new examination of this subject is now called for. In this chapter, after examining in more detail why such a descriptive mechanism is needed, I introduce and elaborate a three-tiered approach to describing DSS.

WHY AN APPROACH TO DESCRIBING DSS IS NEEDED

Figure 2.4 presented a macro view of how the pieces of the DSS picture fit together. Figure 3.1 simplifies that snapshot, eliminating the underlying technology and

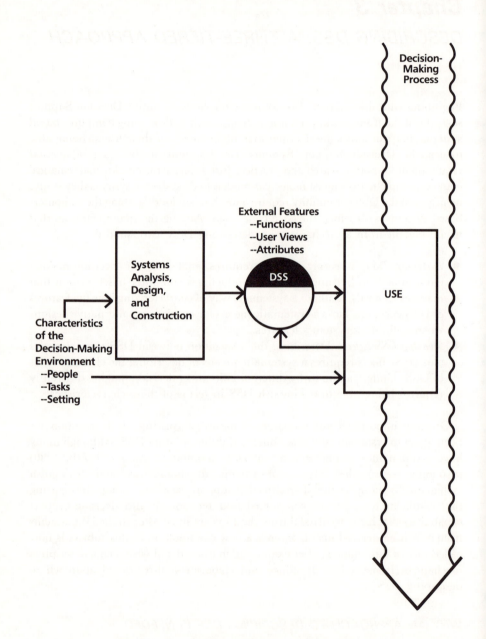

FIGURE 3.1   A context for describing DSS

focusing on the Substantive Decision Support segment of the framework. The diagram illustrates why both designing systems and studying their effects depend critically on systematic description of DSS.

Designing DSS

It is useful to think of systems analysis and design as a matching process, a function that accepts decision-making environments as inputs and produces corresponding computer-based information systems as outputs (see the left portion of Figure 3.1). The goal of this process is to create or to select that one computer-based system from the universe of possible systems that best meets the needs of the environment. DSS analysis and design could be both more efficient and more effective if we understood better the inputs to these processes (environments), the outputs from them (systems), and how the inputs relate to the outputs. More specifically, we need

- to identify and describe the key characteristics of decision makers, tasks, and organizational settings;
- to describe how DSS differ one from another and how those differences affect the way decisions are likely to be made; and
- to prescribe a mapping that translates characteristics of environments into characteristics of systems that successfully support them.

Each of these tasks poses a considerable challenge for researchers. The ultimate goal—not yet on the horizon and perhaps not fully attainable—is the last item, a prescriptive mapping from environments to systems. Before we can even consider such *prescription*, however, we must first have more meaningful *description*. The immediate focus of research attention, therefore, should be the first two items, developing appropriate means for characterizing environments and systems.

To date, a relatively small share of DSS research has addressed these issues. The most widely cited portion of DSS research has addressed the "procedural" issues of building systems rather than the "substantive" questions concerning their content. For instance, the terms "Adaptive Design" (Keen, 1980), "Middle-Out Design" (Ness, 1975; Hurst *et al.*, 1983), "Evolutionary Development" (Grajew and Tolovi, 1978; Hurst *et al.*, 1983), and others like them dominate the DSS literature. Although involving users in an evolutionary development process is no doubt important, the time has now come to ask the question: What do we do *substantively* as we design in an adaptive, middle-out, and evolutionary manner?

Within the relatively small segment of the DSS literature that is substantive and descriptive, decision-making environments have received far greater attention than have DSS themselves. In fact, a number of promising characteristics—for instance, task structure (Mason and Mitroff, 1973; Lerch and Mantei, 1984), task interdependency (Hackathorn and Keen, 1981), and organizational style

(Huber, 1981)—have been proposed for categorizing environments. To a large extent, however, these characteristics have remained loose ends in the literature. They have been introduced, and in some cases widely cited, but never developed. There is little to indicate how these environmental differences might translate into differences in systems. We are left to conclude that the mapping would be an identity: type "X" systems would be built for type "X" environments.

Perhaps the reason these environmental characteristics, the inputs to the design process, could not be pushed further is that so little attention has been paid to the outputs, the DSS themselves. Other than Alter's (1977b, 1980) taxonomy, we have done relatively little to describe systematically how DSS differ one from another. And we have certainly not considered how they differ with respect to what ought to be the central substantive issue in DSS design: how system features affect decision-making behavior.

While we do not find systematic approaches to DSS description, we do find growing interest in naming particular classes of DSS. Recent conference proceedings and some journals are replete with such labels as GDSS (Group DSS), ODSS (Organizational DSS), NSS (Negotiation Support Systems), ESS (Executive Support Systems), EIS (Executive Information Systems), IPS (Idea Processing Systems), and so forth. Some of these labels given to systems belong, in fact, to people, tasks, and settings—that is, to decision-making environments. They describe systems only through the identity mapping (the systems are type "X" systems because they serve type "X" environments). Others of these labels do properly identify classes of systems, but the rush to label rather than describe is nonetheless problematic. Some years from now, if not already, we will have a plethora of such labeled classes—some distinct, some overlapping—without a systematic way of describing how the systems are similar and how they are different. Unless we adopt a descriptive mechanism, we will have impressive labels, but we will not have an enlightened approach to DSS design.

Studying the Effects of DSS

A fundamental research issue, which has considerable significance for practice as well, is how, if at all, DSS affect decision-making behavior. Do DSS succeed at improving decision making? If so, how? Which process strengths do they amplify, which weaknesses do they attenuate? What other effects do DSS produce? When and how do DSS degrade decision making? Which process strengths do they attenuate, which weaknesses do they amplify?

The DSS literature does not have very much to say about these questions. Several reviewers (Scott Morton, 1984; Elam, Huber, and Hurt, 1986; Hurt, Elam, and Huber, 1986; Kottemann and Remus, 1987) note how little attention has been devoted to such topics as DSS impacts, evaluation, and effectiveness. And collectively, the few evaluative studies do not present a coherent picture. Sharda, Barr, and McDonnell (1988), in their review of research on DSS effectiveness, observe that the empirical findings have been inconsistent and conclude that "the studies appear to have been conducted independently, without any progressive improvements in experimental design, DSS employed, or variables examined" (p. 156). Similarly, Benbasat and Nault (1990) conclude from their review of the empirical research literature that "the research evaluating the effects of MSS use has mostly been ad hoc in its selection of variables and devoid of theoretical linkages" (p. 224). Moreover, Benbasat and Nault's search found mostly outcome-oriented studies; they discovered few studies adopting the process view. A coherent approach to studying DSS effects, one that pays special attention to how DSS affect the processes through which decisions are made, is now needed.

Figure 3.1 provides a starting point for considering the effects of DSS. How a DSS affects decision-making behavior, if at all, depends upon if and how it is used, which, in turn, depends on the interaction of the system with its environment (the people, task, and setting).* The computer-based system alone does not determine the consequences of its use. As Poole and DeSanctis—drawing on Markus and Robey (1988) and Poole, Holmes, and DeSanctis (1988)—note, "people display a vast variety of reactions to technologies and only rarely is there a simple one-to-one determinism by which technology imposes definite, unequivocal effects on users" (1989, p. 155). Nonetheless, evidence (for instance, Markus, 1984) does suggest that a system's characteristics play a role in determining its effects. To study systematically what this role is—that is, how the characteristics of DSS interact with the environment to affect decision making—we need a means for describing DSS characteristics and for distinguishing DSS based on their characteristics.

Summary

Both designing DSS and studying their effects require a means of describing systems: DSS design entails describing prospective system features, and studying DSS effects entails describing how system features can affect decision-making behavior. Moreover, both activities require descriptive mechanisms that clearly differentiate one system from another: DSS design involves comparing and choosing among alternative designs, and studying DSS effects involves analyzing how differences across systems can contribute to different decision-making behavior. Furthermore, both activities, not just the second, require descriptions that help explain how the system affects decision-making processes, because a central consideration in designing system features is whether they will foster the desired effects without engendering unintended consequences.

Although I focused here on two activities, designing DSS and studying their effects, these are not the only ones requiring a means of systematically describing

---

*Recall that Figure 3.1 is a simplification. The effects will likely depend on other factors as well, such as the implementation tactics employed and the training provided.

systems. Consider a few other examples: DSS buyers need a basis for selecting or commissioning the system that best meets their needs. DSS trainers need a way to present system features to novice DSS users. And DSS researchers addressing a variety of issues—for instance, ''Do different analysis methodologies systematically produce DSS with different characteristics?''—need to analyze commonalities and differences across systems. Indeed, most DSS research and practice activities could benefit from a way of describing and differentiating systems.

A THREE-TIERED APPROACH TO DESCRIBING DSS

The discussions of why DSS description is needed, and the purposes it would serve, suggest a number of desirable properties for a descriptive mechanism:

- The mechanism should meet the needs of the full range of DSS research and practice, including, but not limited to, designing systems and studying their effects.
- The mechanism should differentiate as well as describe DSS.
- The mechanism should describe DSS in a way conducive to understanding how they affect decision-making processes.

Since any simple descriptive schema for DSS will not possess all of these properties, I propose a sequence of three levels of description, with each tier building on the descriptions generated by the previous levels of analysis. The three analytic tiers, shown schematically in Figure 3.2, describe a DSS in terms of

1. its functional capabilities,
2. its configuration as viewed by its users, and
3. its attributes as a ''whole'' system.

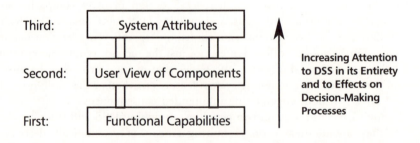

FIGURE 3.2   *A three-tiered approach to describing DSS*

These tiers correspond to three questions commonly asked by DSS users:

1. "What can it do?"
2. "What does it look like?"
3. "How will it affect my decision making?"

Moving upward from the first through the third tier, two shifts of perspective become apparent. First, the descriptions pay increasing attention to decision-making processes and to the perspective of DSS as process interventions. Second, the descriptions take more and more of a holistic outlook rather than focusing on individual system components in isolation one from another. Consequently, the uppermost tier, the system attributes level, plays an innovative, culminating role in satisfying the need for systematic description.

THE FIRST TIER: FUNCTIONAL CAPABILITIES

The most basic, and most commonplace, way of describing a DSS is in terms of what it does. This first descriptive level reflects the intuitive notion of DSS as information-processing assistant, identifying the information-processing capabilities that a given DSS offers its users. "Solves linear programs," "solves the product-mix linear program," "allows ad hoc queries of historical sales data," "graphs inventory levels over time," "forecasts income and expense," and "performs multi-attribute utility calculations" are all functional descriptions of DSS capabilities.

Although some DSS perform a single function, most DSS include more than one information-processing capability. A functional description of these systems might be as simple as the "laundry list" of functions (information-processing capabilities) commonly recited by software vendors and DSS developers promoting their products. Such lists might also be used for simplistic comparisons of DSS—for example, "System Y contains capabilities A, B, and C, whereas System Z includes capabilities A, C, D, and E." But such simple descriptions are not very valuable because they offer little or no information concerning the specific contributions the system's capabilities make to supporting the decision maker. The system comparisons are similarly uninformative; because they do not provide insights into how the individual functions are similar or different, we do not have a meaningful comparison of the systems. For the first tier to yield useful descriptions, we need to describe each functional capability more fully. A meaningful way to classify functions would be especially helpful.

What more do we want to know about a functional capability than the information-processing activity it performs? We want to know something about the role it plays in supporting the decision maker. One way to capture the decisional role of a system function is to identify the decision-making need it is intended to meet. After all, functional capabilities are generally included in systems to be responsive to their users' decision-making requirements. What better way to classify support functions, then, than by associating them with the managerial needs they address?

Fuller exploration of alternatives, earlier detection of problems, and coping with multiple or undefined objectives are but a few of the needs commonly felt by decision makers (refer back to Table 2.1 for a list of common decisional needs). Each represents an obstacle to reaching a decision, an element of problem-solving activity that, when present, makes decision making difficult. And the difficulties that humans and organizations encounter in making decisions create the potential for computer-based support systems to be of value. To describe the functional capabilities of a DSS, therefore, is to convey if and how the functionality can help decision makers satisfy these and other decisional requirements.

Identifying the needs associated with particular DSS functions should be a natural process for both researchers and practitioners. Nonetheless, one can easily become preoccupied with analyzing capabilities in terms of their information-processing functions rather than their decisional roles. "Graphs data," "queries databases," and "solves optimization models" are all perfectly good descriptions of what a system does, but they do not convey why the system does what it does. They do not convey why decision makers care whether these functions are included in or excluded from the system. And they do not capture the effect these functions can have on the way in which decisions are reached.

Augmenting simple descriptions of functions with analyses of the decisional needs they meet would be most valuable. For instance, if a functional capability "graphs data," does it graph historical data for the purpose of detecting problems, or does it graph projected data for the purpose of exploring alternative courses of action? This is the kind of question a functional description must answer if it is to help explain the role of the DSS in supporting problem solving.

Decision-making needs can be expressed in more or less general terms. Each of the needs mentioned previously (exploring alternatives, detecting problems earlier, and coping with multiple or undefined objectives) were expressed very generally and are found, therefore, in a wide range of environments. But "solving my spare parts inventory problem," "determining the profitability of my foreign loans," and "setting the price for my new skin-care product," are much more specific descriptions of decision makers' needs. These more specific needs correspond very closely to statements of the decision problems themselves, whereas the less specific needs reflect the general requirements of human and organizational problem solving.

Why speak in general terms at all when we can describe more specific decision-making needs? First, the functionality of some DSS can be described only in general terms. Many systems today are intended to be broadly applicable, requiring additional customization before being applied to a given decision-making environment. Electronic spreadsheet packages are good examples; as "content-free" entities, waiting for a user to imbue them with problem-specific content, the decisional needs they meet can be described only in the more general terms.

Second, general decision-making needs classify more specific ones. Decisional needs can be organized in a hierarchy, with needs at one level refined into more specific ones at the next level, as in Figure 3.3. Special leaf nodes representing information-processing functions can be attached to those nodes whose needs they are intended to satisfy. These leaves might be placed at any level of the tree, depending on the degree of specificity of the needs they meet. Figure 3.3 shows a small portion of a sample needs–functions tree, where circular nodes correspond to decision-making needs and rectangular (leaf) nodes represent information-processing capabilities. The general need, "coping with the lack of a single objective," is divided into two more specific needs, each of which is addressed by different computer-based capabilities. "Coping with multiple objectives" is supported by a variety of computer-based choice models (a "multi-attribute utility decision aid," an "elimination by aspects decision aid," and so forth) and "defining an objective" is supported by "idea-processing software." The general need is itself associated with "computer-based planning models,"

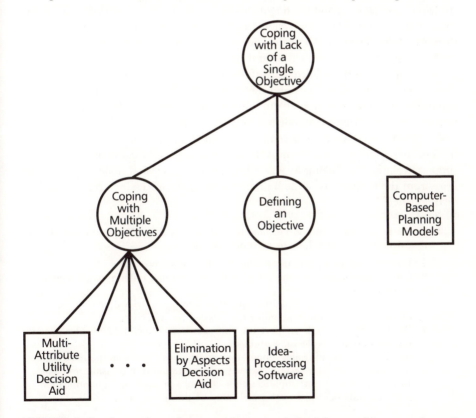

FIGURE 3.3   A portion of a sample tree of decision-making needs and information-processing functions

since these computer-based systems can be applied to meeting all of the more specific needs.

We see that decision-making needs can be used as a multi-level classification scheme for DSS functionality. Trees such as the one in Figure 3.3 might be drawn for several distinct purposes. First, a tree whose leaves are exactly the functional capabilities of a given system would represent the first-level description of that system, the tree's structure indicating how the system's functional capabilities are intended to satisfy decisional needs. Second, by coding leaf nodes with different shapes or colors, a tree could represent a comparison of the first-level descriptions of two or more systems. The tree's structure would immediately highlight differences in how the systems meet decisional needs. Third, independent of any particular systems, a tree could be a graphic catalog, representing the state-of-knowledge concerning how to meet decisional needs with functional capabilities. The leaves would describe all known means of meeting the various needs included in the tree.

This last use of tree diagrams suggests two paths of inquiry that DSS researchers studying functional capabilities might choose to follow. They might take functional capabilities currently found in systems and consider which decision-making needs those capabilities meet and how they do so, or they might select a decision-making need—at any level of specificity—and propose functional capabilities to satisfy it. Either approach should prove fruitful in developing the "state-of-knowledge" tree of decision-making needs and information-processing functions. The more expansive the tree, the greater our understanding of the role of information-processing technology in supporting decision making.

Zachary (1986) has made a significant contribution to our understanding of the first tier by devising a cognitively based, functional taxonomy of decision-support techniques. Taking as a starting point the decision-making needs that arise from the limitations of the human information-processing architecture, he distinguishes

> six classes of decision support techniques that identify the six major kinds of support that decision aids give human decision makers:
>
> 1. Process models support the prediction of complex processes.
> 2. Choice models support the integration of individual criteria across aspects or alternative choices.
> 3. Information control techniques support the storage, retrieval, and organization of data, information, and knowledge needed for a decision.
> 4. Representational aids support the expression and manipulation of a specific representation of a decision problem.
> 5. Analysis and reasoning aids support the performance of problem-specific reasoning processes based on a certain (expert) representation of a decision problem.
> 6. Judgment refinement/amplification techniques support the quantification of heuristic judgment processes which may be prone to bias. (pp. 30–31)

These six classes are each decomposed into more specific decision-aiding methods using a (mostly) hierarchical organization. Zachary also proposes a design methodology for employing this taxonomy to design computer-based decision aids that meet the needs of a given decision-making environment.

The first-tier description of DSS, the one most commonly found in practice today, is the *sine qua non* of descriptions, for without an understanding of a system's functional capabilities we can say very little about that system. In particular, the information provided by the first-tier analysis serves as the basis for descriptions at the upper two levels.

THE SECOND TIER: THE USER VIEW

Beyond knowing what it can do, understanding a DSS means being able to describe how it is organized. One can examine a system's configuration from two perspectives: the internal view and the external view. The internal view describes the architecture of a system's underlying technological building blocks (in terms of Sprague's (1980) framework, the database, dialog, and model base management components). The external view describes how a system's functional capabilities are packaged. The external view is the user's view, capturing how the operators, data, models, representations, and so forth appear to the user. The user view* is the one that matters for studying how a system affects decision makers' behavior; it constitutes the second tier of analysis.

A given set of functional capabilities can be packaged for users in more than one way. Consider the following questions we can ask about a system's (external) configuration: Do users see discrete operations that can be invoked in any order, or do they encounter a predetermined sequence of steps? Do users see a modeling capability independent of individual models, or do they access a set of fully packaged models? Do users employ database and graphics capabilities that exist independently of specific datasets, or do they see a package of particular databases and retrieval capabilities? Can users modify the system's operators, data, models, and representations? In short, what does the system look like to the user? These questions and others like them are answered by the second analytic level.

The second tier builds on the information provided by the first-tier analysis. Since the same information-processing functions can be packaged in various ways, however, the user view represents a significant level of analysis in its own right. How a system's components appear to its users can play a determining role in how they use it and, therefore, how it affects their decision-making behavior.

Asking how a DSS appears to its users brings to mind the topic of user interfaces. After all, what the user "sees" is the interface. But human–machine interfaces are a different subject. Studies of user interfaces concentrate on the nature of the interaction between human and machine, including such issues

---

*User views of DSS should not be confused with user views in the database management literature, a different concept.

as dialog styles,* input devices, and menu formats. The second-tier analysis describes not how the user interacts with the system's components, but what those components are and how they are configured. The two topics are related, however, since the interface connects the user with the system's external components.

Generic User Views

We could describe in an ad hoc manner the external configuration of each DSS we encounter. Establishing a vocabulary that can be applied to describing the user view of *any* DSS is more desirable, especially for the purpose of comparing one system with another. We may think of such a schema as a "generic user view." A generic user view must serve two analytical purposes: to develop ex ante (pre-construction) as well as ex post (post-construction) descriptions of DSS.

From the ex ante perspective, the generic view must provide a design vocabulary, a way of describing the alternative designs a DSS builder is contemplating. Adopting such a vocabulary can help designers be more systematic in addressing how their systems will appear to users. The generic view they adopt, however, can influence, and may even constrain, the external design.

From the ex post perspective, the generic user view must provide a language for describing and comparing DSS that have already been constructed. It can provide a basis for communication about user views among researchers, among practitioners, and between researchers and practitioners. Devising a generic view that is broadly applicable but still captures the essential aspects of each system, however, is not an easy task.

The remainder of this chapter concentrates mostly on exploring generic user views. I begin by surveying existing approaches, and then I present the generic user view that is employed throughout the study.

Existing Approaches to the User View

In this section I study four approaches that contribute to an understanding of user views:

- Sequence of Steps,
- ROMC,
- Verbs/Commands, and
- Degree of Non-Procedurality.

We can think of the first two items as candidates for adoption as a generic user view. The other two are not intended to be complete generic views, but offer important insights concerning how users see DSS.

---

*See Sprague and Carlson (1982, Chapter 7) or Carlson (1983b) for an overview of dialog styles for DSS.

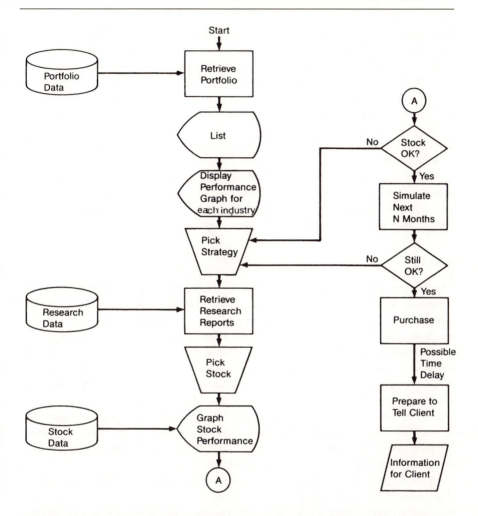

FIGURE 3.4   *Flowchart for a Sequence-of-Steps user view. Note. Reprinted with permission from "An approach for designing Decision Support Systems," Eric D. Carlson, Data Base, 10(3) (Winter 1979), pp. 1–15. Copyright (1979) Eric D. Carlson. All rights reserved*

Sequence of Steps

Many systems appear to users as predefined sequences of steps. At each step, users provide the DSS with any inputs it requires, and the system responds with a set of results. Users control the sequence of activities only to the extent they can choose to bypass a step or to branch to some other point in an otherwise predefined sequence of activities. Systems that can be described by this generic user view are typically depicted by traditional flowcharts, such as the one reprinted in Figure 3.4. These systems commonly use a question–answer dialog style.

Sprague and Carlson (1982) argue convincingly that the Sequence of Steps view is undesirable for DSS because it is highly process dependent.* That is, DSS describable by this user view impose a great deal of structure on decision makers' problem-solving processes. Users see such systems as one long sequence of activities rather than as a set of individual functions. This limitation of the Sequence of Steps view makes it problematic for both ex ante and ex post analysis. From the ex ante perspective, employing this view leads to constructing exclusively process-dependent systems. From an ex post perspective, this view cannot describe process-independent systems, a significant share of the DSS population. Although one can argue the merits of process-dependent versus process-independent systems, we are best off with a generic user view that can handle both.

ROMC

The generic user view most widely cited in the literature is the ROMC approach (Sprague and Carlson, 1982; Carlson, 1979, 1983a), which identifies four DSS components: Representations, Operations, Memory aids, and Control mechanisms. Representations, such as tables, lists, graphs, and maps, are conceptualizations of the information used in decision making. Operations are invoked by users to process information; they may be simple manipulations or more complicated decision aids such as simulation and forecasting models. Memory aids, such as databases, workspaces, libraries, and profiles, meet users' needs to store and retrieve information as they use the representations and operations. Control mechanisms—for example, menus, help facilities, natural language error messages, and procedure construction languages—assist decision makers in using the other DSS components.

In the ROMC approach, representations are the dominant system components. They are designed first and are the entitities on which the operations operate. Operations supporting the Intelligence, Design, and Choice phases of decision making can be attached to each representation. The approach fosters DSS that include a range of operations covering all three phases.

The greatest virtue of the ROMC approach is that it identifies and distinguishes different types of entities (components) encountered by DSS users. To a large degree, however, Sprague and Carlson's argument that ROMC is superior to the Sequence of Steps approach reduces to an argument that *any* generic user view identifying distinct entities and, in particular, distinct capabilities users can invoke individually, is better than one depicting systems as predefined sequences of activities. The ROMC approach, with its emphasis on visual representations,

---

*The issue of process-dependent versus process-independent DSS is closely related to the system restrictiveness attribute, the subject of Chapter 4.

seems to be particularly well-suited for the illustrative system chosen by the authors, the Geodata Analysis and Display System (GADS), which supports geographic and spatially oriented decisions such as defining school districts, assigning policemen to beats, and assigning salesmen to territories. For other classes of decisions, however, visual representations may not be so important. Moreover, the reverse of the criticism leveled against the Sequence of Steps approach can be applied to ROMC. While ROMC handles process-independent DSS well, this user view copes awkwardly with systems that are intended to be process dependent.

Verbs/Commands

Keen and Gambino (1983) propose an approach to DSS design that emphasizes translating into DSS commands the "verbs" or "action words" that decision makers use when solving problems. For example, they implemented a decision maker's demand to "give me descriptive statistics" as a "DESCRIBE" command that performs this action. Keen and Gambino do not present a generic user view, but by concentrating on commands (ROMC's operations) as the most important system component, they raise a significant challenge to ROMC, wherein representations dominate.

Degree of Non-procedurality

Bonczek, Holsapple, and Whinston's (1981) two-dimensional classification scheme for DSS captures the degree to which a system's users access its functionality non-procedurally. The scheme's first dimension is the degree to which users must specify procedures for directing computation, ranging from stating the model explicitly, through invoking models by name, to simply stating the problem. The second dimension is the degree to which users must specify procedures for retrieving data, ranging from stating the retrieval procedure explicitly, through invoking predefined reports, to simply stating the problem. Since a system's degree of non-procedurality provides significant information about how its capabilities appear to its users, being able to identify systems' procedural and non-procedural elements is a desirable property for a comprehensive generic user view.

Remarks

Of the approaches presented here, only ROMC is truly viable as a generic user view for DSS. Although the Sequence of Steps approach is often appropriate for other computer-based information systems, it is too simplistic and limited to be adequate for systems intended to support decision makers. And the other two approaches are not themselves generic user views: Keen and Gambino's concentration on commands offers us a useful contrast with ROMC's emphasis

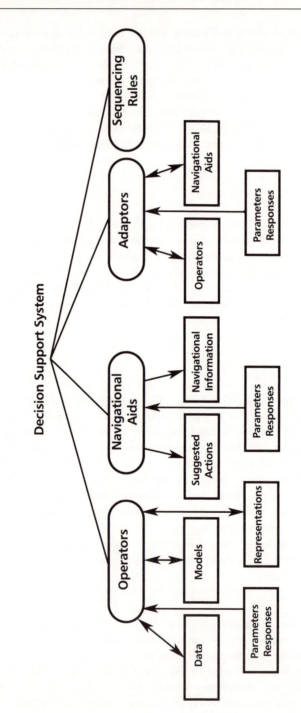

FIGURE 3.5   A new generic user view of DSS

on visual representations, while Bonczek *et al.*'s dimensions for assessing non-procedurality can be valuable additions to a generic user view.

Although ROMC is the most useful of the existing approaches, as a generic user view, it, too, provides an inadequate basis for describing the effects a DSS can have on decision-making processes. One difficulty ROMC poses is its emphasis on representations rather than operations. While representations are important, it is the operations that define what the system can do and what the user can do with the system. Another problem is that ROMC accommodates very well those systems that give users free reign in choosing operations, but it cannot be used effectively to describe systems that deliberately limit user discretion in defining decision-making processes. Finally, in stressing a process-independent approach to DSS, ROMC does not emphasize those DSS components that are most important for understanding how a system affects its users' decision-making processes. In contrast, the generic user view proposed in the next section highlights those components that determine how DSS affect their users' decision-making behavior.

A New Generic User View

The generic user view proposed here consists of four types of principal components:

- operators,
- navigational aids,
- adaptors, and
- sequencing rules.

Operators perform the system's information-processing activities, navigational aids help users choose operators, adaptors allow users to create or modify operators and navigational aids, and sequencing rules control when each of the other components can be be invoked by the user. Figure 3.5 shows this generic user view of DSS, including the principal components with their inputs and outputs.

Operators

The workhorses of a DSS are its operators, which users invoke to access the system's functional capabilities. The commands typically found in DSS—for example, "LIST," "QUERY," "CALCULATE," "REGRESS," and "OPTIMIZE"—are all operators. Given the notion of a DSS as an information-processing assistant, a system's operators are formally defined as the components that perform information-processing activities for users, or provide information to users, in support of their decision-making processes. As such, the operators are the dominant components of the generic view. To perform their functions, operators require informational *inputs* such as data, models, parameter values, control options, and visual images. While performing their functions, operators produce informational *outputs* in the form of data, models, and visual representations.

Inputs   The inputs required by an operator can be specified in two ways: users may explicitly identify the inputs, or the inputs may be embedded within the operator itself. Generalized support capabilities are usually of the former variety. For instance, a regression package may require the user to indicate the data to be analyzed, and a linear programming package may require the user to provide the model to be solved. More specialized operators, however, are more likely to be of the latter type. For example, an operator supporting a given product-mix decision may contain a fully specified linear programming model, with the user supplying at most a few parameter values.

Figure 3.5 can be interpreted as follows: the data, models, parameters, options, and representations shown feeding into the operators are those explicitly provided by the user. Sometimes users enter (key in) these data or models at the time they use an operator (for instance, by filling in a data table), but often, the data or models have already been stored and labeled, and users identify these existing datasets and models by name. We can think of these named datasets and models as separate entities in the DSS, distinct from the four principal components. In contrast, inputs embedded within operators are part of those operators' definitions; not only are they not separate entities, but they do not appear at all in the diagram.

The distinction between user-specified and embedded inputs is an important one. When inputs are embedded in operators, users do not see the operators as distinct from their inputs. Users may forget or ignore these inputs, leading them to misinterpret the outputs. Moreover, since users cannot specify the inputs, they have less control over the information-processing these operators perform. The operators are also less powerful, in the sense that they cannot be applied to more than one set of inputs. The operators may, however, be easier to use, because the system's non-procedurality is increased as users are spared the task of specifying inputs. Given the many consequences, how each of an operator's inputs is to be specified is an important design decision.

Let us concentrate on each type of input in turn. *Data* constitute one type of input. The data that operators use vary widely in form and content both within and among systems. For instance, data may be highly aggregated or may be disaggregated to a variety of levels of detail. Data may be for a single time period or may range over many periods. Common DSS data describe such items of interest as sales, personnel, economics, and costs, among many others.

Data inputs illustrate the contrast between user-specified and embedded data. Suppose a DSS designer is providing operators for listing and graphing data. If he or she chooses not to embed the data in the operators, then creating two operators, "LIST" and "GRAPH," may suffice. Users invoke these operators and specify the data to be displayed. They might type "LIST SALES" or "GRAPH COSTS" where "SALES" and "COSTS" refer to predefined datasets. Or, depending on the interface, users might just type "LIST" or "GRAPH," and then be prompted for the name of the dataset.

In contrast, if the designer chooses to embed the data in the operators, the operators "know" what data they will employ. One approach to embedding data is to create a separate operator for each dataset. For instance, the user might invoke the operators "LISTSALES" or "GRAPHCOSTS" to produce the displays.* At first glance, the difference between the two approaches may appear minimal, but it is very significant. Suppose the DSS also includes the dataset "SALARIES." With user-specified inputs, the user could type "LIST SALARIES" or "GRAPH SALARIES" to display this dataset. With embedded data, however, the system does not support listing or charting "SALARIES." Moreover, with user-specified data, the same display format is generated for all datasets, since the operator does not have knowledge in advance of the inputs. In the embedded case, the displays may be tailored for the given dataset; the operators corresponding to different datasets may have different stylized displays.

Models constitute another type of input. "Model" is a tricky term in the context of DSS because people use it so many different ways. Even limiting ourselves to computer-based models for decision makers—as opposed, for instance, to behavioral models *of* decision makers—we find great diversity. I will use "model" broadly, much the way Alter (1977b, 1980) did in distinguishing data- and model-oriented systems. For present purposes a model is an abstraction of the relevant aspects of (some portion of) a decision problem represented in a form that decision makers can manipulate with a computer-based system. This definition is intended to include the full range of computer-based models used by decision makers. A DSS model might be a statistical model, an optimization model, a simulation model, a choice model, or some other form of computer-based model.

Unfortunately, the definition does not resolve all the terminologic ambiguity. People frequently fail to differentiate models from the programs and methods that manipulate them, referring to both as "the model." But the distinction matters. Taking linear programming as an example, a given model (linear program) can be solved using any one of several different techniques (the simplex algorithm, Khachiyan's algorithm, and Karmarker's algorithm). Conversely, any one of these three techniques can be used to find optimal solutions for many different models (linear programs).

Recognizing the conceptual distinction between models and their "solvers," the operators that manipulate them, is a prerequisite for describing how a given DSS appears to its users, because some systems package models and solvers such that the user sees them as combined entities while other systems package them

---

*An alternative approach is to have only the two operators, "LIST" and "GRAPH," but for each of these operators to embed several datasets, allowing the users to choose among them. Despite the difference in approach, the same conclusions apply.

such that they appear as distinct entities. When a model-based operator embeds the model it uses, the user does not see a separation between the model and the solver; the operator is a combination of the model and the solver. When a model-based operator requires users to specify the model to be used, however, the user does see the model as distinct from the solver. The operator is the solver, and the user supplies the model.

When operators and models are distinct, a given operator might be applied to many different models. But not any operator can be applied to any model; operators can be applied only to compatible models. To understand what makes operators and models compatible, it is useful to consider four levels of model abstraction (adapted from Geoffrion, 1989).*

- ''A 'specific model' is a completely definite instance of a model, including all data values (e.g., a particular Hitchcock–Koopmans transportation model)'' (Geoffrion, 1989, p. 4).
- A ''nearly specific model'' is an otherwise specific model that is missing some data or parameter values.
- ''A 'model class' is a collection of conceivable, similar, specific models; it is definite neither as to data values nor as to the identity or even number of items of various types, but is otherwise quite specific as to mathematical form (e.g., the class of all Hitchcock–Koopmans transportation models)'' (Geoffrion, 1989, p. 4).
- ''A 'modeling paradigm' is a collection of similar model classes that has established its conceptual value and influence (e.g., the class of all network flow models)'' (Geoffrion, 1989, p. 4).

Using these distinctions we see that the models embedded in operators or supplied by users are specific or nearly specific models. And operators without embedded models are solvers designed to operate either on a given class of model or on all classes within a given modeling paradigm. For instance, the simplex algorithm can operate on all linear programs (a modeling paradigm) and, in particular, on all ''product-mix'' linear programs (a class within the paradigm). Operators that manipulate decision trees might be designed to manipulate any decision tree (the paradigm) or only trees with a particular structure (a class within the paradigm). So a given operator is compatible with specific models or nearly specific models of the class or paradigm for which it is designed. When invoking a given operator, therefore, users must specify compatible model instances as inputs— that is, model instances of the appropriate classes or paradigms. And if the model is nearly specific, the users must also supply the missing data or parameters.

---

*Geoffrion (1989) distinguishes four levels of model abstraction: specific models, model classes, modeling paradigms, and modeling traditions. Only the first three are needed here for the discussion of user views. I have added nearly specific models between specific models and model classes.

This discussion notwithstanding, people often informally refer to model-based operators, whether or not they embed their models, as models. When a specific model or nearly specific model is embedded in the operator, this should not lead to much confusion. After all, the operator does contain a model instance. When the operator does not embed its models, however, some confusion can ensue. The proclivity to call such an operator a model probably follows from the operator being tied to a particular model class or modeling paradigm.

Parameter values and *control options* constitute a third type of input. Data and models make up most of the information that operators need to perform their functions, but often users must provide some additional information that sets the values of parameters or controls the execution of operators.

Consider, first, examples of parameters: an optimization model, such as a linear program, might require values for bounds and coefficients. A statistical operator—say, a stepwise regression—might require the critical *t*-value. A simulation operator might need the parameter values (mean and standard deviation) for the normal random variables it uses. A database search operator might require the values (salesperson = ''JOHN'') that define the selection conditions. This operator might also require values for search parameters such as depth-first versus breadth-first search.

Now, let us turn to control options, options users specify that control how an operator will perform. Some control options are selected before an operator commences execution; others are entered interactively as conditions warrant during operator execution. Consider some examples: an integer programming operator might include several different solvers; the user chooses the one that is used. After completing each run, a simulation operator might ask the user whether to run the model again (using a new set of pseudo-random numbers). A graphics operator might support line charts, bar charts, and stacked bar charts for plotting data; users select their preferred representations.

The line between parameters and options is fine; many control options can be thought of as parameters. Selecting depth- or breadth-first search, for instance, can be seen either as providing a parameter value to, or choosing a control option for, the search operator. Indeed, one might regard control options as a special case of parameters. Drawing a sharp line is not important; what matters is recognizing that sometimes users see themselves as providing needed values and other times they perceive themselves as controlling the information-processing activities performed by the operator.

Parameter values and control options are especially important inputs because they often reflect judgments, such as evaluations and predictions, made by the decision maker. Choice rules that employ user inputs (utilities, weights, trade-offs, acceptable ranges) to select a winner from a set of alternatives are good illustrations, as are projection models that prompt users for subjective assessments of rates of change (inflation, sales growth).

Visual representations constitute the fourth and final type of input. Although we tend to think of representations as outputs, the ROMC approach reminds us that operators sometimes operate on visual representations. Electronic spreadsheet packages with business graphics capabilities offer a familiar example; often the user specifies the data to be plotted by highlighting a section of the spreadsheet represented on the screen. Other examples of operating on visual images include zooming in on maps, transposing tables, and re-scaling graphs.

Outputs   After processing information for users, operators typically return results to them. The usual way of providing information to users is through *visual representations*, either displayed on a video screen, printed, or plotted. Common representations include lists, tables, graphs, charts, and stylized reports.

We generally think of *data* and *models* as inputs to operators, but they may also be the outputs from operators. To see this, consider the datasets and models in Figure 3.5 that are not embedded in a given operator. These datasets and models might be predefined by the designer, but often designers provide users with special operators that enable them to create and modify such datasets and models themselves. These special operators produce datasets and models as outputs. For instance, a "MAKE-TABLE" operator might enable users to key in an array of data, assign the dataset a name, and store it for use as an input to other operators.* Moreover, some operators, in addition to, or instead of, displaying their results visually, store their results as datasets that other operators can access. This is another instance of data serving as an output.

Navigational Aids

Navigational aids help users with the often difficult task of steering a course through the DSS. For decision makers using a complex system that offers many operators from which to choose, determining what to do next may be a formidable task. Decision makers may have difficulty finding an operator that suits their purposes. They may find too many operators that seem to suit their purposes, forcing them to choose among competing operators—for example, alternative choice rules or forecasting techniques—any one of which is satisfactory. They may be uncertain which models, data, or representations to specify as inputs for the operators they select. Or they may know which operators and inputs they will use, but be undecided about the order in which to use them.

Users sometimes find navigating through a complex DSS difficult because they lack sufficient understanding of the system, either "passive" understanding of the system's capabilities and how to invoke them or "active" understanding of how

---

*When users are given operators for constructing and naming their own datasets and models, the system's non-procedurality is increased because users can now invoke these data and models by name without going through the steps needed to create them.

to apply those capabilities to solving the task at hand. Other times, lack of understanding is not a problem, but given the many options they confront, decision makers nonetheless could benefit from assistance in navigating through the system. For both reasons a system's designers may wish to provide navigational aids that assist decision makers in selecting a course to follow.

Context-sensitive help messages and look-ahead menus are simple navigational aids commonly found in systems today. Help messages designed specifically for a user's current position within the system can provide information useful in choosing what to do next. Menus that look ahead to the selections that follow from each of the current choices can also help users plan ahead and structure their sessions.

Navigational aids come in a variety of forms and can be far more complex than these simple examples. As Figure 3.5 indicates, some navigational aids produce suggested courses of action, but others offer pertinent information without recommending what to do. Some navigational aids are short range, helping only with choosing the next step; others are more long range, helping define a longer sequence of activities. Some navigational aids interact heavily with users, eliciting parameter values and control options from them; others generate their information and suggestions without user involvement. All these forms of navigational aid are discussed more fully and illustrated in the context of decisional guidance in Chapter 5.

When decision makers rely on computer-based systems to support their problem solving, the operators they select and the order in which they use these operators are key determinants of their decision-making processes. By advising the selection and sequencing of operators, navigational aids play a critical role in determining decisional outcomes. Unfortunately, DSS designers can easily become preoccupied with the system's operators and overlook the need for navigational aids. Given the importance of these devices in determining a system's impact, builders should be vigilant in viewing navigational aids as an important design consideration.

Navigational aids present a combination of technological and behavioral issues for DSS researchers. The technological challenge is to invent more supportive navigational aids than are prevalent in DSS today. The behavioral challenge is to determine if and how such aids do, in fact, affect users' decision-making processes.

Adaptors

A DSS's customizability, or adaptability, is determined by its adaptors, the components users invoke to modify existing operators and navigational aids or to create new ones. Consider some examples: a user modifies an operator to measure angles in radians instead of degrees; a user modifies a statistical operator that calculates "population" standard deviations (n in the denominator) to produce "sample" standard deviations ($n-1$ in the denominator); a user creates a regression operator, in a system that has none, from the system's matrix algebra functions.

DSS vary widely in their customizability. Some DSS only let users create new operators and navigational aids; others only allow users to modify existing ones. Some DSS allow both activities; still others, neither. Moreover, the adaptors vary widely in how much power they give users to create and to modify. The "macro" facilities offered by most advanced electronic spreadsheet packages are a common example of adaptors. These facilities enable users to create their own operators (macros) from the operators (functions) included in the system.

As in the case of spreadsheet macros, adaptors frequently define the operators they create in terms of existing ones. Adaptors that are not very powerful can only create new operators that are sequences of existing operators, but more sophisticated adaptors provide some or all of the power of a programming language, including such features as complex branching and conditional execution. Some adaptors can also create new operators that contain information-processing functions not supported by existing operators. This last feature is especially important, because without it, users of DSS with limited or highly specialized sets of operators are greatly constrained when creating new operators. For example, a new operator might require such basic functions as simple arithmetic that were not part of the DSS's original operator set.

Consider an APL-based DSS, where the DSS operators are APL functions. One design approach is to treat the "function-definition" mode of the APL interpreter as an adaptor. Users can "open" existing APL functions (DSS operators) and change their definitions. Users can create new functions using the full power of the APL language. In particular, they can call any other APL functions (DSS operators) within the definitions of new ones. A less adaptable DSS might lock the existing function definitions so that users cannot modify them.

An alternative approach for the APL-based system is to deny users access to function-definition mode and, instead, to provide special APL functions as adaptors. These functions would likely give users more limited power to create or modify operators, since the designer can carefully control the adaptive capabilities provided.

Since the function of adaptors is to create and modify operators and navigational aids, these are their primary inputs and outputs (Figure 3.5). As users work with adaptors, they also input parameter values and control options. Note that adaptors are not used to create or modify independent datasets and models; doing so is the responsibility of special-purpose operators.

Adaptors can change the degree of non-procedurality of a DSS. Suppose a DSS requires its users to retrieve data procedurally. With an adaptor, users might create new operators that contain procedures for retrieving specific data items or generating certain reports. Thereafter, such operators would be invoked by name as a non-procedural means of accessing the desired information.

Sequencing Rules

Operators, navigational aids, and adaptors are invoked by the user. The user selects one of these "devices" and instructs the system to execute it. In contrast, sequencing rules govern the operation of the DSS by the user, determining which of the operators, navigational aids, and adaptors users are allowed to invoke at any point during a session. More generally, the sequencing rules determine which sequences of devices (and their inputs) are legal and which are not.

The set of all DSS can be partitioned into two classes based on the types of sequencing rules they enforce. If a system has a "trivial rule set," then the DSS does not impose any restrictions on the sequence in which users invoke its operators, adaptors, and navigational aids. Any device is allowed to be used at any time. If, however, a system uses a "non-trivial rule set," then the DSS limits the sequence of activities in one or more ways. With non-trivial rules, the path a user has already taken through the system constrains the directions in which he or she may move in the future. At different points in the decision-making process, therefore, different operators, navigational aids, or adaptors are allowed.

We can think of a system's sequencing rules collectively as a function that takes the history of system use (what the user did and, in some cases, how the DSS responded) as an input and produces constraints, in the form of a set of allowable next steps, as an output (Figure 3.6). Sometimes these constraints prescribe what must be done next. For instance, sequencing rules might require decision makers to examine certain key ratios immediately after projecting a budget. Other times, the constraints prescribe what cannot be done next. For example, sequencing rules might prohibit users from running regressions on datasets that have been determined to be autocorrelated.

DSS vary with respect to how much of the history of system use they consider when constraining their users' behavior. They also vary in the types of constraints they employ. All told, non-trivial rule sets vary in complexity along three dimensions: (1) the length of the relevant history, (2) the content of that history, and (3) the nature of the constraints imposed. Each dimension distinguishes two cases, relatively simple rules from those that are more complex.

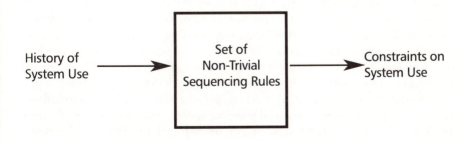

FIGURE 3.6   Non-trivial sequencing rules

The first dimension: length of relevant history   The first dimension distinguishes the following types of sequencing rules:

- rules that depend only on the device most recently invoked,
- rules that depend on the entire sequence of devices previously invoked.

Rule sets vary in terms of how far back they go when analyzing what the decision maker has done with the system. In the least complex case, the rules consider only the operator, navigational aid, or adaptor that the decision maker invoked most recently. In this case, what you do next is constrained by what you just did. Consider these illustrations: immediately after running a linear program, users might be required to study the sensitivity analysis; immediately after examining a graph, users might be required to look at the underlying data; immediately after projecting a budget, users might be required to examine key ratios.

In the more complex case, the rules consider the full history of system use. Here, what you do next is constrained by everything you have done previously. Some examples follow: once they have modified a simulation model, users might not be allowed to run "What if?" analyses until they execute tests to validate the changes; once they have projected a deficit budget, users might not be allowed to project another budget until they balance the first one. Notice how in both of these examples it is the combination of more than one action in the past that determines what a user can do in the future.

The second dimension: content of relevant history   The second dimension distinguishes the following types of sequencing rules:

- rules that depend only on which device(s) were invoked previously,
- rules that depend on which device(s) were invoked previously and the information they processed.

Rule sets vary in terms of which aspects of system use they treat as part of the history that is relevant for constraining the user. In the more simple case, sequencing rules consider only which devices the user invoked. In the more complex case, however, the relevant history consists not only of which devices were invoked, but also of the information provided as inputs and the results produced as outputs. In particular, the results an operator produces may preclude (or may require) users' taking certain actions in the future. In an integer programming environment, if an operator discovers that the constraint matrix is unimodular, users might be precluded from using branch and bound techniques to solve for optimality. In a financial planning system, when a projection operator generates a deficit budget, users might be required to eliminate the deficit immediately. In a linear programming package, when the solution is not very robust, users might be forced to examine the sensitivity analysis.

The more complex rule sets differ in two ways from the more simple ones. First, the rules consider not just the devices invoked, but also their inputs. Such rules are important because, when operators do not contain the data and models they use, the history of what users have done is best described by identifying the operators used, as well as the inputs they were given. Second, decision makers are not constrained simply because they use a device, but because of the results that device yields. The rules do not constrain users because they projected budgets, checked for unimodularity, or ran a linear program, but because the budget had a deficit, unimodularity was present, or the results were not robust.

The third dimension: nature of constraints   The third dimension distinguishes the following types of sequencing rules:

- rules that constrain only the choice of devices,
- rules that constrain the choice of devices as well as their inputs.

Whereas the first two dimensions address the complexity of the history that drives the sequencing rules, the third dimension concerns the complexity of the constraints the rules impose. In the more simple case, only the choice of devices is constrained, but in the more complex case, the devices as well as their inputs are constrained.

The more complex case of the second dimension usually demands the more complex case of the third, because rules that consider past inputs and outputs usually constrain future inputs. More specifically, when an operator's inputs produce outputs that trigger a sequencing rule, that rule usually constrains using the same inputs with other operators. Some examples clarify the point: if a Durbin–Watson statistic shows that a dataset is autocorrelated, then regression *on this dataset* is not allowed until it has been transformed; when the solution to a linear program is not very robust, sensitivity analysis *on that solution* must be performed; when an unbalanced budget is projected, *that budget* must be balanced; when an integer program has a unimodular constraint matrix, branch and bound is ruled out for solving *that program*.

The more complex constraints are also used when designers believe that a given operator is not compatible with particular datasets or models. The more complex rules can prohibit such combinations: users might not be allowed to perform regression analyses on "Dataset X" or create pie charts from "Dataset Y."

Combining the dimensions   Considered together, these three dichotomies of rule complexity define eight possible types of non-trivial rule sets, the vertices of the cube illustrated in Figure 3.7. The arrowheads in the diagram point in the direction of increased complexity.

Consider the most simple case, the lower left-hand corner of the cube, where rules depend only on which device was invoked most recently and constrain only which device will be used next. For each device in the DSS, the rules identify which devices can follow immediately after it. The rules can be represented, there-fore, as a collection of sets of legal next moves, one set for each device in the system. Suppose such a system contains only five operators—say, "QUERY," "REGRESS," "CALCULATE," "INTERNAL RATE OF RETURN (IRR)," and "NET PRESENT VALUE (NPV)"—and no adaptors or navigational aids. The sequencing rules can be represented by five sets, as shown in Figure 3.8(a). The rules and legitimate paths can also be shown diagrammatically by a simple network whose nodes are the system's devices and whose directed arcs indicate legitimate paths through the system, as in Figure 3.8(b).

For more complex rule sets, the rules and paths become difficult, if not impossible, to enumerate or show diagrammatically. Suppose we move along just one dimension, the length of relevant history dimension, to consider rules depending on the full sequence of previously invoked devices. The relevant history is now an ordered list of those devices the user invoked. This list is finite, but of unlimited maximum length because devices can be used more than once. For each possible input list, the rules generate a set of legitimate devices; but although each list is finite, the number of possible lists is not. Explicitly enumerating or charting the rules is therefore problematic. Were we now to move along the other

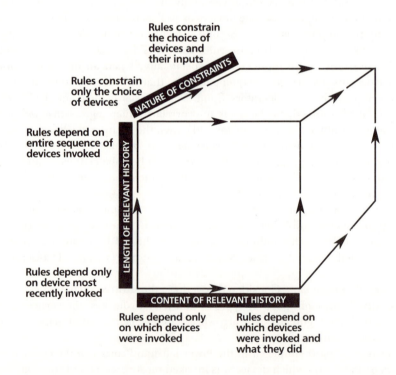

FIGURE 3.7   Increasing complexity of non-trivial rule sets

(a) Enumeration of Rules

Last Device Invoked by User	Legitimate Devices for User to Invoke Next
NPV	Query, IRR
IRR	Query, NPV
Query	NPV, IRR, Calculate, Regress
Calculate	Query
Regress	Calculate

(b) Network Diagram of Rules

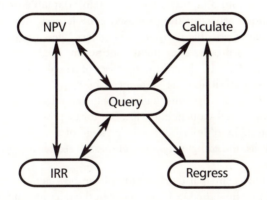

FIGURE 3.8   *The least complex case of a non-trivial rule set*

two dimensions, trying to cope with the multitude of possible inputs and outputs, the situation would become even worse.

Sequencing rules raise technological and behavioral research questions similar to those raised by navigational aids. Technologically speaking, building systems with complex, non-trivial rule sets is a non-trivial problem. Such technology only matters, however, if it succeeds in improving decision-making performance. We must therefore study under what circumstances such constraints on decision-making behavior are appropriate and effective.

Remarks

The generic user view introduced here is quite similar in spirit to ROMC. Each view sees a DSS as consisting of a set of discrete components. In particular, the operators of the proposed view are very similar to ROMC's operations. A major difference, however, is that ROMC subordinates operations to representations, whereas here, operators are dominant and representations are seen mostly as their outputs. Operators dominate because they provide the information-processing support central to the intuitive notion of DSS. Another difference is that the proposed view explicitly recognizes all of the inputs and outputs seen by users— data, models, parameters, and options, *as well as* representations.

ROMC would classify navigational aids and adaptors as control mechanisms. Indeed, Sprague and Carlson use "help commands" and "macro construction languages"—instances of navigational aids and adaptors, respectively—as examples of control mechanisms. The roles these two types of components play are so significant and different one from another, however, that they must be recognized explicitly rather than mixed with other utilities in a single category. The importance of navigational aids and adaptors stems from their roles in the decision-making process: navigational aids assist users in structuring their decision-making processes, and adaptors make a system adaptable or customizable.

The most unique aspect of the proposed generic user view is the sequencing rules, which make it possible to apply this generic view to systems all along the process-independent/process-dependent continuum. Highly process-independent DSS, such as those ROMC describes, are cases of trivial rule sets. Highly process-dependent DSS, describable as sequences of steps, are instances of tightly constrained rule sets. Systems falling between these extremes have less constraining, non-trivial sequencing rules. So, for ex post analysis, the sequencing rules make it possible to describe the wide range of systems existing today; and for ex ante analysis, the complexity and tightness of sequencing rules are important design variables.

Each of the four principal components of the new generic user view plays a role in determining how the DSS intervenes in the decision-making process. The assortment of operators included in a system has a major impact on what the user can and cannot do with that system. Navigational aids can help decision makers structure their decision-making processes, and may also lead users to adopt certain approaches to problem solving. Adaptors affect decision making more indirectly, by creating and modifying the operators and navigational aids. Given the raw capabilities of a DSS, the rule set controls what can be done when.

Summary

How a system's components are packaged—that is, how the system appears to its users—is an important aspect of describing a DSS. A generic user view, such as the one presented here, can assist both ex ante and ex post analysis by providing a vocabulary for describing the external view of any DSS. Indeed, whether or not one adopts a generic view, such questions as whether inputs are embedded in operators, whether operators can be used in any order, whether users can modify operators, and whether navigational assistance is provided are key pre-design considerations for builders and post-construction concerns for researchers and other system evaluators.

The external view is at the hub of DSS design, linked in all directions to other design considerations (Figure 3.9). It is tied to the internal view, since DSS designers must create and connect technological subsystems (internal components) in a way that produces the arrangement of external components the user sees. Likewise, it is tied to the user interface, since the interface is the technological link between users and the components with which they interact.*

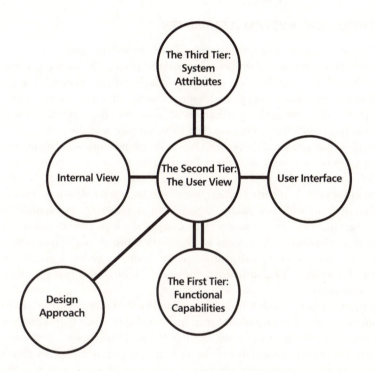

FIGURE 3.9   *The user view: the hub of DSS design considerations*

---

*At a different level of analysis, there is another relationship between interfaces and external views: the generic user view a designer adopts may influence his or her choice of dialog style. For instance, the Sequence of Steps view most often uses a question–answer style, whereas Keen and Gambino's command-oriented view entails a command-driven style.

User views also interact with design approaches. ROMC is not just a generic user view. It is an approach to DSS design that is centered about a particular generic user view. Similarly, Keen and Gambino's approach to DSS design emphasizes a particular component of the user view. When designers adopt a given design approach, that approach influences the external view of the systems they produce. Conversely, if designers first adopt a generic user view, that generic view may constrain the design process they follow.

As the middle level of the three-tiered approach to describing DSS, the user view is linked to the tiers above and below. Important in its own right, the external view is also a link between the functional capabilities (first tier) and the system attributes (third tier). Describing how the individual functional capabilities are packaged and organized is the first step toward being able to describe the collective attributes of the entire DSS.

THE THIRD TIER: SYSTEM ATTRIBUTES

The first tier describes systems in terms of their functional capabilities and how those capabilities correspond with decision makers' needs. The second tier describes how the functional capabilities are packaged—that is, how the system's components appear to its users. Each level provides some insights into how the system is likely to affect the decision-making behavior of its users. But together, these two descriptions do not suffice, because they focus on pieces of the system—the first on individual functions and the second on system components—and do not describe the properties of the system as a whole. Studying the system in its entirety is crucial to understanding how it is likely to affect decision-making behavior, because the elements of a DSS fit together synergistically to form a whole whose effects may be different from what we would expect from considering its capabilities and components individually. Consider, for example, the logical relationships among a system's elements. A system's information-processing functions might complement one another, substitute one for another, or be unrelated one to another. These are critical differences for understanding how that system is used by decision makers.

The third tier builds on information provided by the lower two descriptive levels but moves beyond the individual functional capabilities and their configuration to attributes of the system as a whole. The "system attributes" that constitute the third tier capture properties of the system that can help explain how it will interact with its environment: whether it is likely to be used, how it is likely to be used, and the likely consequences of its use. For example, attributes help us understand how well a system fits its environment. Attributes help us understand how much flexibility users have in controlling the system, whether they can choose their own paths through it, and whether they can specialize it to meet their own needs. Attributes help us understand how the system assists or influences users in choosing among functions that are substitutes, or in piecing together seemingly unrelated functions to form a coherent decision-making process. Using such attributes to study the system as a whole is essential to explaining its effects on decision-making behavior.

If studying system attributes is so important, why has this endeavour received so little effort to date? Apparently, system attributes address issues that lie at the intersection of two subjects, describing DSS and studying their effects, neither of which has received much research attention. Since describing DSS has itself received little treatment in the literature, one is not surprised that the scant attention it did receive concentrated on the more simple and more obvious first two analytic tiers. Similarly, DSS effects have received limited research attention, and the attention they received has been mostly outcome-oriented, not process-oriented. Consequently, the issue of system attributes was never raised. The field focused on what systems can do, rather than on the more important question, "What are users likely to do with the systems?"

My purpose in the remainder of this book is to remedy some of that neglect. I devote Chapters 4 and 5 to studying two system attributes of special importance: "system restrictiveness," how a DSS constrains its users' decision-making processes, and "decisional guidance," how a DSS sways or enlightens decision makers' judgments. In Chapter 6, I introduce two additional attributes: "precustomization," how a DSS is tailored for its decision-making environment, and "customizability," how users are empowered to tailor a DSS to fit their needs.

Chapter 4
SYSTEM RESTRICTIVENESS

Human judgment plays a central role in the computer-aided decision-making process. Indeed, we build Decision Support Systems to enhance human judgment. But the line between supporting judgment and replacing it is often fine; DSS can deprive users of their judgmental powers as easily as they can enhance them. How a DSS affects decision making is determined both by how the DSS supports and by how it restricts human judgment.

Using the verb "restrict" to describe a DSS may seem counterintuitive. After all, when a manager receives a DSS, his or her information-processing capabilities are augmented, not reduced. Nonetheless, DSS are at once expansive and restrictive. Since any given DSS will include some finite set of functional capabilities, when a decision maker relies on a given system to solve a problem, his or her decision-making process is constrained by that system's functionality.

Consider a DSS supporting a multi-attribute decision problem such as buying a car, renting an apartment, or choosing a college. We saw in Chapter 1 that numerous "choice rules" for solving this class of problems have been studied and many of the proposed techniques differ significantly. We could construct a different set of computer-based decision aids for each multi-attribute approach. For instance, "multi-attribute utility," a scoring rule, requires different information-processing support from "elimination by aspects," a sequential elimination process. Since a given DSS will include some subset of the full range of multi-attribute decision aids, it will restrict its users to some subset of the possible solution techniques.

My point is not that restrictions in a DSS are inherently good or inherently bad, but that they are inevitable. Understanding these restrictions is essential to understanding the DSS intervention. When analyzing DSS, however, we often neglect their restrictiveness, concentrating instead on the following kinds of questions: What features are included? What actions are permitted? What behavior is supported? We tend to ignore the reciprocal questions: What features are excluded? What actions are not allowed? What behavior is constrained? If our purpose is simply to describe the system, then answering only the first set of questions may be adequate. If we wish to understand how the system affects decision-making behavior, both sets of questions are equally important. For instance, if a DSS supports many decision-making processes but does not support the current one, then recognizing what has been excluded from the system is surely as significant as knowing what has been included.

The two sets of questions bring to mind the glass of water seen by an optimist as half full and by a pessimist as half empty. The issue here, however, is not one of perspective but of completeness. Either description of the water glass captures completely the state of its contents. But neither set of questions by itself leads to comprehending fully how the DSS is likely to affect decision-making behavior. Only by studying both what users can and cannot do with a DSS will we truly understand how the system affects their behavior.

I have been discussing intuitively a system attribute defined formally as follows:

System Restrictiveness: the degree to which, and the manner in which, a Decision Support System limits its users' decision-making processes to a subset of all possible processes.

System restrictiveness is portrayed schematically in Figure 4.1. The outer ellipse corresponds to the universe of decision-making processes for solving a given problem, while the inner ellipse represents those processes supported by a given DSS. The degree of restrictiveness is determined by the relative sizes of the outer and inner ellipses, whereas the manner of restrictiveness is determined more specifically by what is inside and what remains outside the inner ellipse. The *manner* of restrictiveness is usually of greater interest than the *degree* of restrictiveness. That is, we are more concerned with *how* the DSS is restrictive than with how *restrictive* the DSS is.

System restrictiveness is a quality, not a measurable quantity. Scoring the restrictiveness of a DSS on a scale from 1 to 10 would be neither practicable nor of much value to users and builders. Describing which decision-making processes are supported and which are not is more easily accomplished and more informative.

Not only can we not use restrictiveness as a measure, but, in general, we also cannot use it as a comparator. Figure 4.2 shows three possible relationships between the sets of processes supported by two different DSS. Notice that only in Figure 4.2(c), where DSS B is a proper subset of DSS A, can we say which

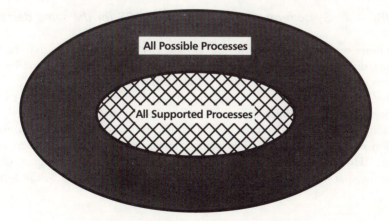

FIGURE 4.1 *System restrictiveness*

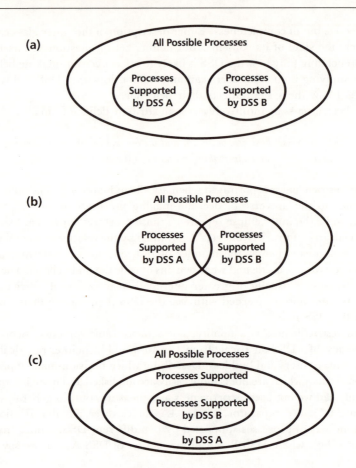

FIGURE 4.2   System restrictiveness of two DSS for the same decision

is the more restrictive system. In cases (a) and (b) we can conclude that the two systems differ in their restrictiveness—and we may be able to describe the differences—but we cannot identify the more restrictive.*

What are the determinants of a system's restrictiveness? This question can be interpreted in two very different ways. The first interpretation raises the descriptive question, ''How do the features of a DSS determine how it restricts its users' decision-making processes?'' The second interpretation is more prescriptive, asking, ''How should the design objectives for a DSS be applied purposefully to determine that system's restrictiveness?'' As shown in Figure 4.3, the former

---

*One reason we cannot always use system restrictiveness as a comparator is that restrictiveness can vary in several different ways, as described later in this chapter.

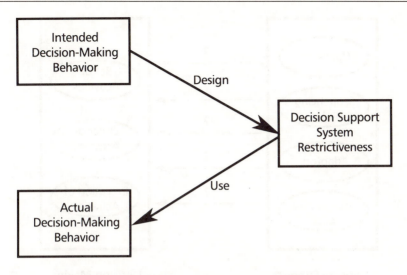

FIGURE 4.3   What determines restrictiveness?

question addresses the link from the DSS to user behavior, whereas the latter question considers the reverse connection, how intended user behavior affects DSS design. Together, the answers to these two questions provide an understanding of the restrictiveness attribute and its implications for DSS design and use.*

DESCRIBING SYSTEM RESTRICTIVENESS

For system restrictiveness to be a useful concept, we must be able to describe formally how DSS constrain their users' decision-making processes. A formal description of restrictiveness has three parts, as shown in Figure 4.4. The box on the left, representing the DSS, contains system components; these are the sources, or causes, of process restrictions. The box on the right, representing the decision-making process, identifies the aspects of decision-making that a DSS can restrict. A set of undefined arrows, representing the constraints imposed by DSS components on decision-making processes, points from the left to the right box. Describing restrictiveness means defining the arrows.

The descriptive task, then, is to identify potentially restrictive DSS components and depict if and how they constrain particular elements of decision-making behavior. The building blocks for constructing such descriptions are already

---

*System restrictiveness may remind some readers of Moore and Chang's (1983) weak–strong continuum. Indeed their continuum was an important motivation for studying restrictiveness. A key difference is that restrictiveness is an attribute of systems, whereas the weak–strong continuum is a "meta-design consideration," characterizing intentions of designers. I discuss the continuum, therefore, in the context of attitudes toward directed and nondirected change (Chapter 6).

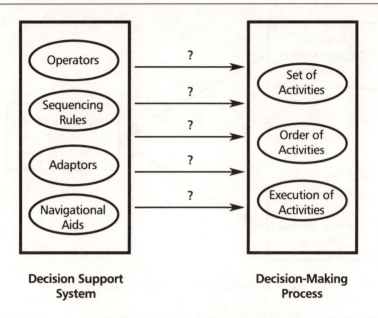

**Decision Support   Decision-Making
System   Process**

FIGURE 4.4   How do DSS restrict?

in place: DSS components were described in Chapter 3; decision-making processes, in Chapter 1. What remains is to construct a bridge between these descriptions by identifying the causal links that connect system characteristics with process restrictions.

The generic user view presented in Chapter 3 offers both a vocabulary and a structure for discussing the restrictiveness of DSS components. The analysis of restrictiveness will build upon that second-tier description, considering each of the four principal DSS components, in order of decreasing restrictive significance:

- operators,
- sequencing rules,
- adaptors, and
- navigational aids.

The best way to describe each component's restrictive effects is in terms of a single model of decision making. Chapter 1's tree-like model, shown again as Figure 4.5, differentiates nicely the ways DSS restrict decision-making processes. Each leaf of the tree corresponds to a different form of judgmental restriction:

- constraints on the structure of the decision-making process that limit the set of available information-processing activities;

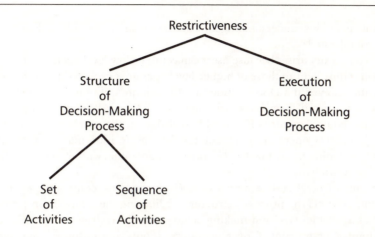

FIGURE 4.5 How decision-making processes can be restricted. Note. Reprinted by permission, "Decision Support Systems: directed and nondirected change," Mark S. Silver, Information Systems Research, 1(1) (Jan.–Mar. 1990). Copyright (1990), The Institute of Management Sciences, 290 Westminster Street, Providence RI 02903. All rights reserved

- constraints on the structure of the decision-making process that limit the ways in which information-processing activities can be combined; and
- constraints on the execution of the decision-making process that limit the judgmental inputs that drive the information-processing activities.

In the following analysis, therefore, each of the four DSS components will be associated with some subset of these three forms of restriction.

Operators

The most noticeable way DSS restrict decision-making processes is by providing constrained sets of operators. For instance, if a DSS does not provide operators supporting regression analysis, linear programming, or multi-attribute utility, then its users will not be able to employ these techniques in their problem solving. Similarly, if a DSS implements only one choice rule—perhaps, elimination by aspects or multi-attribute utility—then users will be compelled to employ that particular decision-making technique.

When a system's information-processing functions are all implemented as high-level operators such as statistical models, mathematical programming techniques, and choice rules, studying which operators are included and which are excluded may be adequate to understand how the DSS is restrictive. When a system's operators are more primitive, such as simple arithmetic functions and basic data retrieval operations, understanding how the DSS restricts decision making becomes more complicated.

The complexity arises because users can combine low-level operators to perform functions equivalent to those of higher-level operators excluded from the system. For example, even if a DSS excludes multi-attribute utility models, such models can be constructed from basic arithmetic operators. Although using the basic functions requires greater effort and knowledge on the user's part, the absence of the high-level operators does not restrict the decision-making process.* In general, including many low-level or primitive operators within a DSS makes that DSS less restrictive.

In terms of the tree-like model of decision making, constraining the set of operators restricts the process's structure by limiting the information-processing activities available. Decision-making behavior can be restricted further by giving users limited or no control over operators' inputs and outputs: data, models, parameter values, and visual representations.

Data

Since data are crucial inputs to most operators, restricting access to data severely limits decision-making behavior. Data can be restricted in several ways. Operators that have embedded in them all the data they need are the most constraining, since users have no control over which data are used. For operators that allow users to specify the input data, those data can come from two sources: (1) datasets provided as part of the DSS and (2) datasets created by the user, each of which can be restricted.

Data made available by the DSS can be limited in two ways, *globally* or *locally*. Global data restrictions determine what data the DSS provides. That is, when collections of data are restricted globally, the DSS does not provide any access to them; such data do not exist within the realm of the DSS. In contrast, a set of data is restricted locally when it is included in the system but is accessible only by certain operators.

Consider the global case first. Data deemed unreliable or inappropriate for the given task may, by design, be excluded completely from a DSS. For instance, Gorry and Scott Morton (1971) mapped Anthony's (1965) managerial levels (operational control, management control and strategic planning) onto several characteristics of information (source, scope, level of aggregation, time horizon, currency, required accuracy, and frequency of use). This mapping might be the basis for ensuring that the data available in a DSS are appropriate for the managerial level being supported.

---

*Objectively, the absence of high-level operators in this DSS does not restrict the decision-making process. Users may perceive the DSS as more restrictive, however, as discussed later in the chapter.

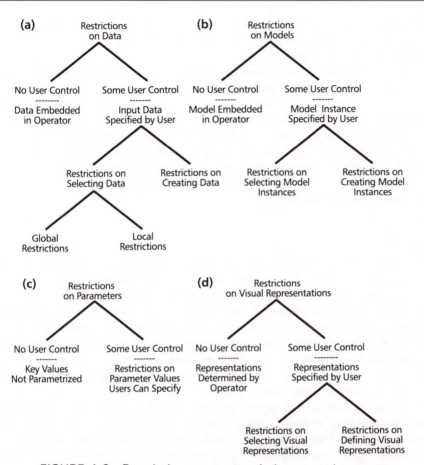

FIGURE 4.6   Restricting an operator's inputs and outputs

Turning to localized data restriction, consider operators supporting the Intelligence phase of decision making. To encourage more environmental scanning in the search for corporate problems and opportunities, these operators might be defined to work only with external data and not with internal corporate data. Similarly, to counter backward-looking analyses with more forward-looking studies, a DSS might allow certain historic data only to be used as inputs to forecasting models and not to be perused directly.

Many DSS provide operators that enable users to create their own datasets. Systems with such data-entry operators are less restrictive than systems without, since users can employ them to create datasets equivalent to those not available in the DSS. In particular, such operators can reduce system restrictiveness by empowering users to bypass global and local data restrictions. Although entering data by hand requires more effort than accessing predefined datasets, if the system allows users to do so, then the restrictions on data access have been diminished. Of course, data-entry operators themselves may have limitations on the data structures they can create.

Figure 4.6(a) shows the relationships among the types of data restriction. The extreme case, where data are embedded in the operator and the user has no control, contrasts with the various constraints that may limit users when they have some control over the specification of input data. User selection of data can be limited by global and local constraints on the availability of data; user creation of data, if supported at all, can also be constrained. Each form of restriction limits the information-processing activities that can take place within the DSS. In terms of the decision-making model, therefore, data limitations restrict the structure of decision-making processes.

Models

Many DSS operators embed specific or nearly specific models, where user control is limited to providing, at most, a few parameter values. Other operators, however, are designed to operate on any model from a given class or paradigm, with users specifying an appropriate specific model when the operator is invoked. Consider, for example, a ''simplex'' operator that can solve any linear program. An instance of the linear-programming paradigm is defined by objective function coefficients, bounds for constraints, and variable coefficients for constraints. Each time the user invokes the simplex operator, he or she can supply a different linear program, that is, a different specific linear-programming model.

How much control users have in specifying model instances varies across DSS. Systems that limit users to choosing from a set of predefined model instances are more restrictive than systems where users create their own instances, which are themselves more restrictive than systems that allow users to do both. When users choose among predefined model instances, the set of instances may be large or small. When users build their own models, they may be locked into particular model structures or they may be able to construct their own structures. For instance, with a linear-programming operator, the basic structure of the model is defined; only the coefficients and constraint values can be specified. With an electronic spreadsheet package, although the basic matrix structure is defined, users can create complex structures of their own as they define the various cells of the matrix.

Figure 4.6(b) shows the forms of model restrictiveness. The greatest restriction, of course, occurs when models are fully embedded in operators. In contrast, when models are not embedded in operators, users have some freedom in specifying model instances. How much freedom they have depends upon the power the system grants them to choose or build model instances.

Selecting among existing models and constructing new ones are both part of the meta-process of defining an appropriate decision-making approach.

Constraining the construction and use of models, therefore, restricts the structure of the decision-making process by limiting the allowable information-processing capabilities.

Parameters and Responses

Operators, especially those that embed models, often require a set of values to control their performance. These necessary values can either be hardcoded into the operator or they can be parametrized and supplied by users, as input parameters or responses, when the operator is executed. Naturally, operators whose values are hardcoded as constants are more restrictive than those whose values are supplied by users at the time of execution.

Consider statistical operators that perform hypothesis testing. The level at which the null hypothesis is rejected may be provided by the user or predefined at some fixed value, such as 0.01. Similarly, the critical *t*-value for a stepwise multiple regression procedure might be predefined or might be supplied by the user. Likewise, parameters that control database retrievals may be either preset by the system or provided by users. In each case, hardcoding the values is more restrictive than parametrizing them.

While parametrized operators are less restrictive than nonparametrized ones, they still can place restrictions on the input values supplied by users. For instance, an operator might limit the range of values allowed for a given parameter. Such restrictions might reflect limitations of the operator (it can operate only in certain ranges), reasonableness checks on the inputs, or attempts to constrain users' judgments.

Studying the parametrization of operators is a two-step process. First, we determine which values are hardcoded and which are parametrized. Then, for the parameters, we consider whether any constraints have been imposed on their values. Either form of restrictiveness, hardcoding values or constraining parameters (see Figure 4.6(c)), restricts decision-making processes by limiting users' control over the system's operators. The more an operator's values are restricted, the less influence decision makers can exert over the information processing it performs and the less opportunity they have to express their own subjective judgments. Moreover, restricting an operator's values may constrain the set of solutions it can produce.

Visual Representations

Until now, we have concentrated on the inputs to operators: data, models, and parameter values. DSS can also impose restrictions on the visual representations that operators produce as outputs. With advances in display technologies, many DSS generate a variety of forms of monochrome and color output: text, tables, graphs, charts, and even pictures. Individual operators, however, may be limited in the representations they support. Some operators may produce only text, others only graphics. Some may produce only softcopy, others only hardcopy.

When analyzing the restrictiveness of a DSS, therefore, it is important to consider constraints on representations. Are particular operators limited to a single form of output, or does the user have some control over output formats? For instance, can users choose between text and graphics, between hardcopy and softcopy? Can users choose between alternative types of graphs, such as line charts and bar charts? Can users choose to display data tables horizontally or vertically, with color or without? Can users define their own output representations, or are they limited to those predefined by the system?

Figure 4.6(d) depicts the various ways that visual representations can be restricted. Operators whose predefined displays allow no user control contrast with those that allow users some control over output formats, either allowing users to choose among several representations, to define their own, or both.

We tend to think of calculation and manipulation when we think of information processing. But drawing a graph and producing a data table are also distinctive information-processing activities. We see that restrictions on the visual representations constrain the structure of a decision-making process by limiting the information-processing activities that can be performed.

Sequencing Rules

The collection of operators provided by a DSS establishes a bound on the set of decision-making processes supported, but it does not define fully how the system restricts decision making. The way operators can be combined and ordered is also an important aspect of system restrictiveness.*

Controlling the use of a system's operators is the job of its sequencing rules. If a DSS has only trivial rules, then no constraints are imposed on combining and ordering operators. Non-trivial rules, therefore, are the ones of interest here.

Chapter 3 discussed how sequencing rules limit the use of DSS. As Figure 3.7 illustrated, three dichotomies of rule complexity lead to eight possible cases. Sequencing rules

- may depend on the device recently invoked or may depend on the entire sequence of devices previously invoked,
- may depend only on which device(s) were invoked previously or may depend on which device(s) were invoked previously and the information they processed, and

---

*Keen (1980) has observed that whole tasks—for example, portfolio management and media selection— are composed of subtasks, such as calculating a sum and searching for a value. He suggests that "user behavior and user learning can be described in terms of the *sequence of* [emphasis added] and change in subtasks" (p. 19).

● may constrain only the choice of devices or may constrain the choice of devices as well as their inputs.

When decision-making processes are complex and DSS have many operators, the sequencing rules play the decisive role in determining which sequences of activities are supported and which are not. The rules can be used to impose a single sequence of activities, or they can be used to prohibit some of the many possible decision-making processes.

In addition to imposing or prohibiting full decision-making processes, sequencing rules can control portions of processes, ensuring that specific actions are taken if certain conditions are met. For example, if a decision maker projects an unbalanced budget, a rule could force him or her to balance the budget before proceeding. Technical data analyses are likely places for such restrictions. For instance, if a Durbin–Watson statistic indicates autocorrelation, a DSS could require the data to be transformed before running a multiple regression.

Since sequencing rules control how operators can be combined, they can be used to construct highly restrictive DSS that nonetheless contain low-level primitives. Rules can be defined that prevent users from combining low-level functions in a way that emulates higher-level operators excluded from the system. Similarly, careful rule definition can restrict data significantly without barring data-entry operators from the DSS.

In terms of the model of decision making, sequencing rules clearly restrict the process's structure by limiting the order in which information-processing activities can be performed. Because sequencing rules also determine if and how low-level primitives can be combined to perform higher-level functions, they can also constrain which information-processing activities are supported.

Adaptors

Adaptors, DSS components that allow users to modify or create operators, can confound significantly the analysis of system restrictiveness. If a system's adaptors can only be used to construct new operators by combining existing ones, their effect on restrictiveness is minimal. If, however, the adaptors enable users to create new operators employing functions not otherwise available through the system, then these adaptors reduce the restrictiveness of the DSS. Similarly, adaptors allowing users to modify existing operators reduce system restrictiveness.

Adaptors affect decision-making processes indirectly, by creating or modifying the operators that directly affect decision-making behavior. So limiting a system's adaptors indirectly constrains its set of operators. In terms of the tree-like model of decision-making, therefore, adaptors restrict decision-making processes the same ways operators do: restricting adaptors limits the process's structure by constraining the information-processing activities that can be performed. Moreover, since adaptors can be used to increase the parametrization of operators or to change hardcoded values, limiting adaptors can also constrain the execution of decision-making processes.

Navigational Aids

Since navigational aids help users structure their decision-making processes, one might assume they play a role in determining system restrictiveness. Such is not the case. Navigational aids influence decision-making processes by informing and suggesting, not by imposing. They guide; they do not restrict.

Although navigational aids do not affect system restrictiveness, restrictiveness does affect navigational aids. The more a DSS restricts the structure of decision-making processes, the fewer navigational choices users have, hence, the less opportunity for the system to provide meaningful navigational aids.

Summary

In the language of the generic user view, we have found that DSS can limit decision-making processes by restricting

- the set of operators;
- the inputs to the operators (data, models, and parameters);
- the outputs from the operators (representations);
- the sequencing of operators; and
- the modification and creation of operators by adaptors.

In studying these five complementary means of restriction, we encountered instances of all three forms of process restrictions: constraints on the set of information-processing activities, constraints on the order of information-processing activities, and constraints on the execution of information-processing activities. Figures 4.7 and 4.8 build on earlier diagrams and summarize the analysis. Figure 4.7 shows how DSS components can affect the aspects of decision-making processes, replacing the undefined arrows of Figure 4.4 with arrows indicating which components can constrain which aspects of decision making. The key word here is *can*; in any given situation the descriptive task is to determine if and how each of these possible limitations is being realized.

Figure 4.8 conveys the same information, but takes the opposite perspective, depicting how each element of decision-making can be constrained by DSS components. The three kinds of process constraints—the leaves of the original tree (Figure 4.5)—are now designated by rectangular nodes. Hanging from each process constraint are new, elliptical leaves representing the DSS components that can cause the restrictions.

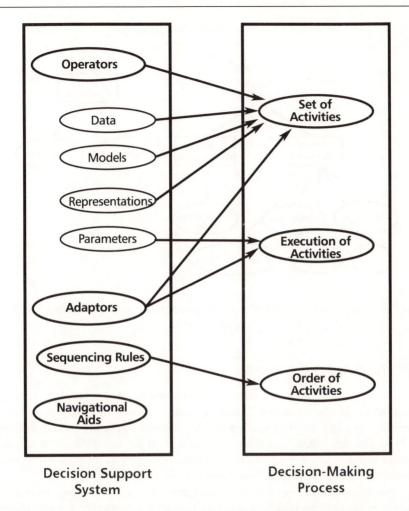

FIGURE 4.7   How DSS components restrict decision-making processes

All three forms of restriction are likely to have significant impacts on decisions. In some cases we may understand how a DSS restricts decision-making processes, although it may be unclear what the impact will be on the ultimate decision. For example, we can describe the differences in process that will take place by using a multi-attribute utility model rather than conjunctive elimination, but this is insufficient to comment substantively on the impact these process differences will have on the decision. In other cases, understanding the restrictiveness of a DSS will provide some information concerning the decisions that will be made with it. For example, when a linear program is not parametrized and the constraints are hardcoded, we know in advance how the solution space has been constrained.

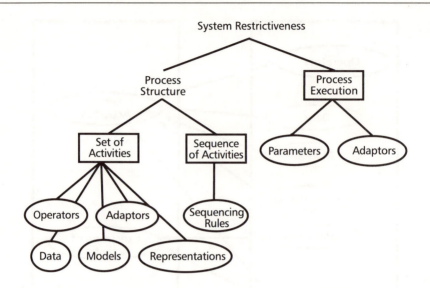

FIGURE 4.8   *How decision-making processes are restricted by DSS components*

PERCEIVED RESTRICTIVENESS

Until now I have presented system restrictiveness as an absolute concept, independent of the observer. Treating restrictiveness this way is certainly legitimate. For any decision-making problem there is some, presumably infinite, set of all possible decision-making processes. And for any DSS there is some, possibly infinite, set of processes it can support. Together, these two sets define absolutely, or objectively, the restrictiveness of a DSS.

In theory, we may consider system restrictiveness an absolute quality; in practice, restrictiveness is in the eyes of the beholder. Experimental results (Silver, 1988a) show that users' subjective assessments of system restrictiveness often differ from objective restrictiveness. These results also indicate that perceptions of restrictiveness vary from one user to another.

How users perceive restrictiveness is determined by how they perceive the sets of possible and supported decision-making processes. What matters to decision makers is not the full set of possible processes, but those processes they see as candidates for solving the problem. What matters is not the full set of processes supported by the DSS, but those processes they are able to execute with the DSS. Subjective restrictiveness is determined, therefore, by subsets of the processes that define objective restrictiveness.

Figure 4.1 shows the absolute view of restrictiveness; Figure 4.9, the perceptions of an individual user. Figure 4.1 contains only two ellipses, representing the actual

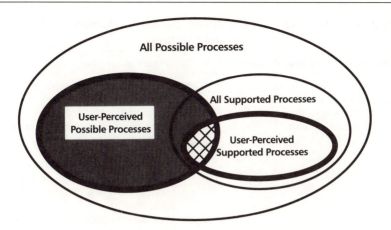

FIGURE 4.9   Perceived restrictiveness

sets of possible and supported processes. Figure 4.9 has two additional ellipses, drawn with thick borders, representing the subsets of these processes perceived by the user.

Absolute restrictiveness is determined by the original ellipses. They identify which of the possible processes the DSS supports (cross-hatched in Figure 4.1) and which it does not (shaded). Perceived restrictiveness is determined by the added ellipses. They identify which user-perceived processes are seen by the user as supported (cross-hatched in Figure 4.9) and which are not (shaded). The key to comprehending perceived restrictiveness, therefore, is understanding how and why the added ellipses are smaller than the originals.

Consider how a given decision maker perceives the outer ellipse, the universe of possible decision-making processes. He or she may not even know that some of these processes exist. He or she may be familiar with others but believe they are inappropriate for performing the task. The universe of processes is reduced to a collection of processes the decision maker sees as candidates for solving the problem. This set of user-perceived processes, not the full set of processes, is the user's frame of reference for assessing how the system restricts him or her.

For instance, the set of possible processes for solving multi-attribute problems is large. But a given decision maker may be familiar with only a few of these approaches—say, multi-attribute utility theory, elimination by aspects, and additive difference. Suppose the user will not use elimination by aspects because it is non-compensatory. His or her perceptions of restrictiveness, therefore, will be determined only by if and how the DSS supports the other two processes.

Now, consider how a user perceives Figure 4.1's inner ellipse, the set of decision-making processes supported by a given DSS. If the DSS is complex, the user may not be aware of some of the system's functional capabilities. And a combination of poor design, unclear documentation, and inadequate training may make the user

TABLE 4.1   Sources of differences between absolute and perceived restrictiveness

Differences in set of possible processes	Differences in set of supported processes
• User is not aware of some decision-making processes. • User finds some decision-making processes undesirable.	• User is not aware of some of the DSS's functional capabilities (lack of passive understanding). • User cannot operate some functional capabilities correctly or effectively (lack of passive understanding). • User cannot apply or combine operators effectively to perform the decision-making task (lack of active understanding). • User chooses not to use operators that he/she finds too cumbersome or tedious.

unable to operate properly some features of which he or she is aware. In addition to such instances as these, where a lack of passive understanding leads users to perceive restrictions in the system, insufficient active understanding can also contribute to perceived restrictiveness. That is, even if the user can control the individual operators, he or she may have limited ability to apply and combine them to solve the problem at hand. Finally, even if the user encounters none of these obstacles, he or she may ignore operators that are cumbersome or tedious to use. Each of these effects causes the user to perceive the DSS as supporting fewer decision-making processes than it actually does.

Table 4.1 recaps why users consider only a subset of the possible processes for solving a problem and why they recognize only a subset of the processes supported by a DSS. Each item in the table not only explains why subjective and objective restrictiveness differ, but also suggests that perceived restrictiveness varies across users. Differences in preferences, knowledge, and skills lead users to assess restrictiveness differently. We must remember, therefore, that Figure 4.9 shows perceived restrictiveness for a single user; showing restrictiveness for a population of users would require adding numerous ellipses.

Absolute Versus Perceived Restrictiveness

Just how dramatic are the discrepancies between absolute and perceived restrictiveness? Are perceptual differences great enough to affect comparisons of DSS?* For instance, if one DSS is objectively more restrictive than another one, will subjective comparisons produce the same conclusion? If not, will different users' subjective comparisons at least be consistent one with another?

---

*Although two arbitrarily chosen DSS cannot necessarily be compared in terms of which is more restrictive, this discussion considers two DSS that can be ordered in terms of their absolute restrictiveness.

Intuitively, one might expect objective and subjective comparisons of two DSS to agree. By definition, if DSS A is more restrictive than DSS B, then A supports a proper subset of those processes supported by B. And for each DSS, the user perceives a subset of the full set of supported processes. Consequently, it is likely, but not guaranteed, that the processes perceived as supported by DSS

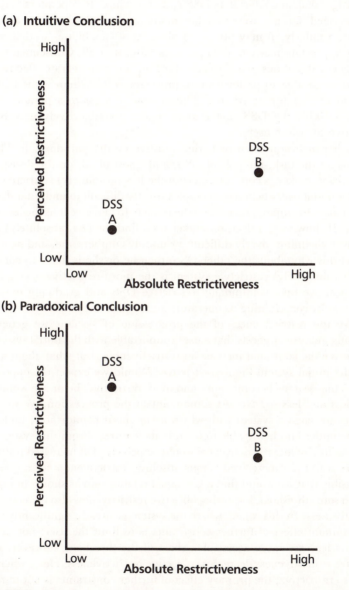

(a) Intuitive Conclusion

(b) Paradoxical Conclusion

FIGURE 4.10 Absolute versus perceived restrictiveness for two DSS

A will be a subset of those perceived as supported by B. If so, A will be seen as the more restrictive DSS. This relationship between absolute and perceived restrictiveness is shown in Figure 4.10(a).

Unfortunately, the matter is not so simple. The features that make DSS B less objectively restrictive may also make it more complex, requiring of the user more knowledge, skill, and effort than DSS A. For instance, B's operators may be highly parametrized, forcing users to define many inputs and select from among many options. Similarly, B may provide a plethora of capabilities so that some users cannot appreciate many of the operators fully, if at all. Consequently, DSS A, with fewer capabilities, may be easier for some users to operate effectively. These users may be able to perform more processes with A than with B. If so, they will find DSS A less restrictive. This reasoning leads to a paradox, shown in Figure 4.10(b): the DSS that is more restrictive objectively may be the less restrictive for some users.

Which conclusion is correct, the intuitive or the paradoxical? The answer depends on the task, the pair of DSS, and, most of all, on the decision maker. If a decision maker is comfortable with the less (absolutely) restrictive DSS and does not find it overwhelmingly complex, overly difficult to understand, or unduly cumbersome to employ, then he or she is likely to perceive it as the less restrictive system. If, however, a decision maker does find the less (absolutely) restrictive DSS overwhelming, overly difficult, or unduly cumbersome, and he or she does not feel this way about the other DSS, then he or she is likely to conclude that the less (absolutely) restrictive system is the more restrictive.

Suppose we take a minimally restrictive DSS and gradually make it more restrictive by constraining its operators and sequencing rules. How would a user perceive the restrictiveness of the progression of systems we generate? The foregoing analysis suggests that a user comfortable with the initial system is likely to perceive the continual increase in restrictiveness. But what about a user who finds the initial system highly restrictive? Would we expect the opposite trend, that, as the systems become more and more restrictive, he or she would perceive them less and less so? No. At some point in the progression, we would expect the user to reach a system with which he or she is comfortable, understanding its capabilities and being able to operate its features. From this system forward, increases in absolute restrictiveness would be perceived as increased restrictiveness.

Were we to plot perceived versus absolute restrictiveness for a given user, it is plausible that we would find a U-shaped relationship as shown in Figure 4.11. Beyond some threshold, increasing objective restrictiveness also increases subjective restrictiveness. In this range, where the system is already significantly restrictive, the dominant effect of further constraints is to limit the user, not to make the system's features more accessible. Short of the threshold, however, increasing objective restrictiveness decreases subjective restrictiveness. Here, where the DSS is not so restrictive, the primary effect of further constraints is not to restrict the user but to make the system more comprehensible and manageable.

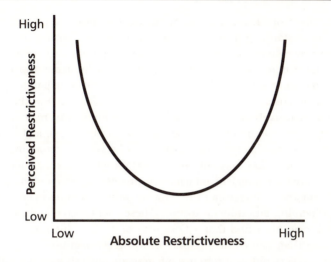

FIGURE 4.11 *Hypothesized relationship between absolute and perceived restrictiveness*

Of course, the turning point varies from user to user. Users who are very comfortable with computer-based systems have a threshold far to the left; the curve would be upward-sloping nearly everywhere. Users who are uncomfortable with DSS have a threshold far to the right, with the curve downward-sloping over a wide range of absolute restrictiveness. Other users lie somewhere between these two extremes.

Since restrictiveness, in general, is not a comparator, Figure 4.11 should not be interpreted as a plot of all DSS, but of any collection of DSS that can be compared and ordered in terms of absolute restrictiveness. Moreover, one should expect some perturbations of the basic U-shaped contour. We have seen that DSS components can restrict decision-making in many ways, so it should not be surprising if the effects of some of those constraints oppose the general U-shaped trend.

High- and Low-level Operators

Analyzing how the mix of high- and low-level operators in a DSS affects user perceptions helps explain the paradox of subjective restrictiveness. Objectively, a DSS consisting exclusively of many low-level primitives is not very restrictive; assuming a trivial rule set, users can combine the low-level operators to perform a wide range of information-processing activities. Such systems are far less restrictive than those comprising only a limited number of high-level operators such as statistical functions, mathematical programs, or choice rules. Increasing the number of low-level primitives further decreases the restrictiveness.

But users differ one from another. Some users harness the power of low-level operators, understanding how to combine primitives to perform more complex information-processing tasks and gladly expending any effort needed to do so. They appreciate being able to perform tasks that a limited set of higher-level operators would not support. They realize the benefit of expanding the set of primitives. These users' perceptions agree with the absolute view; they see a DSS that consists exclusively of low-level operators as minimally restrictive.

Many other decision makers will not agree with this assessment. These users take advantage immediately of the capabilities of a system containing only a few high-level operators. They may not care to exert the effort, or may not even possess the skills, to create equivalent information-processing by combining low-level primitives. For them, increasing the set of primitives simply makes the system more overwhelming and difficult to use. These users' perceptions conflict with the absolute view; they find that a DSS with only a few high-level operators is less restrictive than one consisting only of low-level operators.

Consider two very different systems: a regression analysis package and the APL language. Objectively, APL is the less restrictive, since it offers the power of a general-purpose programming language, while the regression analysis package only performs regressions. In particular, with a little knowledge of multivariate statistical analysis, one can easily program a regression operator in APL. Nonetheless, if running regressions is all a user wants, he or she may consider APL the more restrictive, because using it requires greater knowledge and effort.

Degree of Non-procedurality

Analyzing the degree of non-procedurality (Bonczek, Holsapple, and Whinston, 1981) of a DSS can also explain conflicts between objective and subjective assessments of restrictiveness. Consider, as a reference point, a DSS providing only procedural access to data and models. If one replaces procedural capabilities with non-procedural facilities, the absolute restrictiveness of the system increases. With the procedural capabilities, users had the power to define their own data retrieval operations and decision models, whereas using non-procedural facilities limits users to those retrievals and models that either have been predefined or are generated dynamically by the system. For some users, however, the system restrictiveness may decrease, because they may be better able to produce results using the non-procedural facilities than the procedural ones.

Ease of Use

Clearly, restrictiveness and ease of use are related. Casual analyses of the relationship, however, can lead to conflicting conclusions. One might quickly conclude that ease of use and perceived restrictiveness are negatively correlated, since making a DSS easier to use can make it seem less restrictive. But one might also argue that they are positively related, because increasing absolute restrictiveness can increase perceived restrictiveness while it makes a DSS easier to use.

Conflicting conclusions arise, in part, from the complex relationship between subjective and objective restrictiveness. Conflicts also appear because the term ''ease of use'' has different meanings in different contexts. For instance, ease of use sometimes refers to active ease of use, how easily the system can be used to perform a given task; other times it refers to passive ease of use, how easily the system's features can be operated. A careful analysis of the relationship between restrictiveness and ease of use leads to the following hypotheses:

- Keeping absolute restrictiveness fixed, increasing the ease of use of a system's features—for instance, improving the quality of the user interface—reduces the perceived restrictiveness.
- Keeping constant other factors that influence ease of use, increasing the absolute restrictiveness of a DSS makes that DSS less complex, hence easier to use in the sense of operating its features (passive ease of use).
- Keeping constant other factors that influence ease of use, increasing the absolute restrictiveness of a DSS can make that DSS either easier or more difficult for a user to apply to a given task, depending upon the user's preferred approaches to the task and the particular system components that have been restricted (active ease of use).

Summary

Owing to how they perceive the sets of possible and supported decision-making processes, users' assessments of system restrictiveness can differ significantly from absolute restrictiveness. Moreover, subjective restrictiveness varies from one user to another, making it difficult to generalize about the relationship between absolute and perceived restrictiveness. In some instances, users' subjective assessments align closely with objective restrictiveness, but in others, differences can be significant. Indeed, the relationship is sometimes anomalous: increased absolute restrictiveness can accompany decreased perceived restrictiveness. Analyzing the mix of high- and low-level operators and the degree of non-procedurality of the system can help explain the anomaly.

SOME EXAMPLES

To make the concept of system restrictiveness more concrete, I analyze and compare three different DSS that support the same multi-attribute decision-making task. The task might be renting an apartment, buying a car, or choosing a city in which to live. The three DSS are an advanced electronic spreadsheet package (call it AES), the Heuristic Elimination Support System (HESS), and the Elimination by Aspector (EBA). The systems all access the same database containing 100 alternatives, each rated with respect to 10 different attributes.

AES (not the name of a real system) is an advanced electronic spreadsheet package such as Lotus 1-2-3, SuperCalc 5, and Excel. In addition to the basic functions of an electronic spreadsheet package, AES has facilities for sorting tables of data by row or column, searching tables of data based on complex selection criteria, and generating simple business graphics. A template is provided that contains the database of alternatives and their attributes.

HESS is a computer-based system that implements a variety of process methods (heuristic elimination techniques) for solving multi-attribute problems: direct screening of alternatives, lexicographic sort, conjunctive elimination, and disjunctive elimination. These techniques can be used independently or in combination. HESS is a subset of MASS, a system developed originally as a pedagogic system to be used in an undergraduate Wharton School course in Decision Processes. The system functions effectively, however, as a DSS in its own right.

EBA implements a single choice rule, the "elimination by aspects" model studied by Tversky (1972). The EBA system described here is adapted from a more complex DSS, the Electronic Workbook of the College Board's Enrollment Planning Service, a system that supports recruitment planning decisions by colleges and universities.*

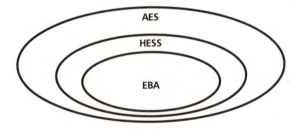

FIGURE 4.12   *Objective comparison of EBA, HESS, and AES*

An Objective Comparison

Objectively, EBA is more restrictive than HESS, which is more restrictive than AES. As shown in Figure 4.12, the decision-making processes supported by EBA are a proper subset of those supported by HESS, which are a proper subset of those supported by AES.

EBA supports only a single process, elimination by aspects, which is a sequential, conjunctive elimination rule. Although HESS does not explicitly support the

*The Electronic Workbook is described in greater detail in Chapter 6.

elimination by aspects choice rule as a menu item, the rule is emulated easily by using HESS's conjunctive elimination technique repeatedly. All of the processes supported by EBA, therefore, are supported by HESS. The converse is not true. HESS contains many decision rules whose effects cannot be achieved using EBA. Objectively, EBA is the more restrictive.

AES does not explicitly implement any of HESS's choice rules. But all choice rules supported by HESS can be emulated with AES by combining its sort and search commands, statistical functions, and general data manipulation and display facilities. Although AES may require more effort from the user, it supports all the decision-making processes supported by HESS. The converse is not true. AES can support scoring rules, such as the multi-attribute utility model, which are not found in HESS. Objectively, HESS is more restrictive than AES; by transitivity, so is EBA.

Although, in general, DSS cannot be ranked in terms of restrictiveness, we have just seen that these three can be. The analysis concentrated on the solution techniques they support, the operators and models they offer. One might wonder whether our ability to rank the systems is maintained when we consider other system components: sequencing rules, data, parameters, and visual representations. As shown in Table 4.2, the three DSS are ranked the same way when each of these other components is considered.

TABLE 4.2 *Comparing the restrictiveness of EBA, HESS, and AES*

System Component	EBA	HESS	AES
Solution techniques, operators, models	"Elimination by aspects" only	Several elimination techniques	Elimination techniques and others (scoring rules)
Sequencing rules	User can proceed in forward direction only	User can combine and order functions as desired; user can "back up"	User chooses how and when to use system functions
Parameter values	User supplies	User supplies	User supplies
Data	Predefined database only	Predefined database; user can modify or expand database; user can create new databases	Predefined database; user can modify or expand database; user can create new databases or import data
Visual representations	No user control; results are displayed in one format only; user cannot see raw database	Many display options under control of the user	User defines tabular displays and graphs

←————————Increasing restrictiveness ————————

Consider first the sequencing and combining of operators. EBA marches users through the elimination process; users cannot back up without starting from the beginning. In contrast, HESS is very flexible, allowing the four different elimination rules to be used in combination and in any order. Alternatives eliminated in HESS can often be reclaimed without beginning the process from scratch. And under AES, users have full control over how and when to combine the system's functions. Hence, from most to least restrictive, the ranking is EBA, HESS, AES.

Parametrization is a tie. All three systems allow users to define the parameter values that constitute the key judgmental inputs to the choice rules.

All three DSS reference the same database; nonetheless, they differ in their data-handling flexibility. Users of EBA are restricted to predefined databases provided with the system. Users of HESS have much more flexibility; they can modify or expand the predefined databases as well as create new databases of their own. Users of AES have the full power of an electronic spreadsheet package. As can HESS users, they can change existing values, add new alternatives, add new attributes, or use a different dataset (spreadsheet). They can also import data from other applications. Once again, EBA is most restrictive, AES least restrictive, and HESS falls between them.

Analyzing visual representations yields the same conclusion. In EBA users have no control over output formats; results appear in alphabetical order. Users are not able to view the raw database. In HESS, displays of data and results offer numerous options, all of which can be controlled by users. In AES, users can use the spreadsheet capabilities to define their own tabular displays and the business graphics capabilities to design their own plots.

Although the analysis of these three DSS shows that their relative restrictiveness is the same when evaluated with respect to different criteria, the analysis also highlights why, in general, we cannot use restrictiveness as a comparator. Since a system's restrictiveness is a function of constraints on a number of system components, making a simple statement about restrictiveness is not usually possible. Given two systems, for example, one might limit more significantly its operators and visual representations and the other might constrain more severely its data and sequencing rules. If so, we could not conclude which system was the more restrictive. What we could do, and this is the key to appreciating the restrictiveness attribute, is to describe *how* the two DSS differ in their restrictiveness.

Subjective Comparisons

One can easily imagine how individuals might arrive at different rankings of the three systems. Consider, first, differences in users' perceptions of appropriate decision-making processes. What matters to users is only the set of processes they would consider for solving the problem. If a user has a strong preference for elimination by aspects, he or she may have no reason to conclude that EBA is the most restrictive system; EBA does exactly what is wanted. Similarly, a user having a strong preference for one of the rules implemented by HESS may not find this system more restrictive than AES. Moreover, if a user has a strong preference for a rule not supported by any of the three DSS, he or she may feel equally restricted by them all.

Now consider users' perceptions of the processes supported by the three systems. Users may perceive only a subset of the supported processes if they are not fully aware of a system's capabilities, if they do not understand how to operate the capabilities, if they cannot apply the capabilities effectively to performing the task, or if they find the capabilities too demanding in terms of time and effort. Individual differences such as experience with particular systems, general computer skills, patience, and endurance may account for which limitations apply to given users.

These observations suggest that, contrary to the absolute view, many users might find AES more restrictive than HESS and, perhaps, than EBA. HESS and EBA offer users non-procedural access to high-level choice rules. Emulating these choice rules with AES requires constructing procedures that combine lower-level functions—among them, data search and sort. Search and sort are advanced spreadsheet features. Some users may not even know these functions are available in AES. Furthermore, in a number of spreadsheet packages, operation of the search and sort features is not intuitive and their documentation is not very clear. If this were true of AES, users might be unable to operate these capabilities properly. Even if users are able to operate the capabilities, lack of technical knowledge about AES or conceptual knowledge about multi-attribute techniques may prevent some of them from emulating HESS's choice rules. Lastly, some users may be able to perform the emulation, but may choose not to expend the considerable effort that is required. We should not be surprised if many users do not appreciate AES's capabilities fully and, therefore, assess it as very restrictive.

PRESCRIBING SYSTEM RESTRICTIVENESS

Having considered how DSS features *can* restrict decision makers' behavior, the next question to ask is, "How *should* a DSS restrict its users' decision-making processes?" While some DSS researchers—for instance, Sprague and Carlson (1982)—have advocated systems that tend toward one end or the other of the restrictiveness spectrum, others (Moore and Chang, 1983) believe the answer depends upon the design objectives. Indeed, in any given situation, DSS designers must trade off design objectives favoring greater restrictiveness against those favoring lesser restrictiveness. These objectives are summarized in Table 4.3.

Of the various design objectives that may apply to a given DSS effort, one objective is universally applicable and supersedes all others in importance: building a system that will be used! A DSS cannot achieve any of its other objectives if it is never used. Bennett (1983c) has observed that DSS users are often discretionary users, who may eschew systems that are not to their liking. Consequently, a system's

TABLE 4.3   Objectives affecting system restrictiveness

Objectives favoring greater restrictiveness	Objectives favoring lesser restrictiveness
Promoting use	Promoting use
Prescription of normative/preferred approaches for communication and consistency	Meeting unspecified needs
	Supporting changing decision-making environments
Proscription	Supporting multiple decision makers and tasks
Providing structure	Allowing users discretion
Promoting ease of learning and use	Fostering creativity
Fostering structured learning	Fostering exploratory learning

restrictiveness must be such that it promotes, rather than inhibits, use of the system.

Controlling system restrictiveness to promote DSS use is a double-edged sword, since either too much or too little restrictiveness may discourage would-be users from employing the system. How much restrictiveness constitutes too much or too little is situation-specific.

Consider, first, too much restrictiveness. If a decision maker has a preferred approach to solving a particular problem, and if that approach is not supported by the DSS, he or she may simply choose not to use the system. Moreover, since flexibility is often considered an important feature of DSS, users who ''feel'' too constrained by a DSS may avoid using it. For these reasons, designers must not make a system overly restrictive.

Now consider a DSS with too little restrictiveness. Such a system may overwhelm its users, providing them with so many different capabilities and options that they are unable to choose among or use the features effectively. Such a DSS may be difficult to use, and decision makers may quickly stop trying to make it work. To ensure that their intended users are both willing and able to use the DSS, therefore, designers may choose to make it more restrictive than they might otherwise.

In some organizational settings, DSS use is not truly discretionary. Pressure from peers, superiors, or competitors can impel a manager to employ a DSS. In such situations, DSS may be used even if their users see them as more or less restrictive than is desirable. Such organizational considerations may therefore play an important role in overcoming the danger of non-use.

The other objectives bearing on system restrictiveness address how a DSS will be used and, in particular, how that DSS is likely to affect the processes through which decisions will be reached. Each of these objectives tends to favor either greater or lesser degrees of restrictiveness, although a given DSS effort may include a mixture of objectives favoring greater and lesser restrictiveness.

Objectives Favoring Greater Restrictiveness

We often think of the user as the same person who purchases a DSS or commissions its creation. But frequently, the "client" who orders a DSS is distinct from the decision makers who use it (Moore and Chang, 1983). Managers commonly impose DSS on their subordinates, usually for the purpose of influencing the subordinates' decision-making behavior. When clients' motives or inclinations differ from those of users, restrictive DSS may be needed to ensure that the clients' objectives are achieved.

More generally, some objectives favoring greater restrictiveness are instances of trying to impose decision-making behavior that either designers or clients deem "good" or "desirable." Other objectives favoring greater restrictiveness, however,

TABLE 4.4 *Objectives favoring greater system restrictiveness*

Objective	Explanation/Illustration
Promoting use	Too little restrictiveness can make a DSS difficult to use effectively, leading some discretionary users to choose not to use it.
Prescription	DSS can be used to prescribe the use of normative decision-making techniques such as multi-attribute utility.
	DSS can be used to prescribe techniques that a manager prefers his or her subordinates to use. DSS can be used to prescribe the use of a common decision-making technique by different individuals/organizational units in order to promote consistency, coordination, and communication.
Proscription	DSS can be used to prevent users from following given decision-making processes. For instance, a DSS may proscribe the current decision-making process or one that contains systematic cognitive biases.
Providing structure	If a DSS implements very many operators that might be useful for addressing a task, decision makers may suffer from "operator overload" and be unsure how to solve their problem with the system. By restricting what users can do with a DSS, a designer may make the system more valuable by lending structure to the decision-making process.
Promoting ease of learning and use	Since too little restrictiveness can make a DSS complex and difficult to operate, increasing the restrictiveness may also increase the ease of learning and use.
Fostering structured learning	A DSS can train managers to use a particular decision-making technique by marching them through the steps they must follow.
	A DSS can take users on a "guided tour" of a database, systematically exposing them to particular pieces of information.

are instances of trying to help decision makers use DSS more effectively. For instance, Laurel (1986) suggests that system constraints "provide the security net that enables people to take imaginative leaps" and provide users with "increased potential for effective agency" (p. 80).

The objectives pertaining to how a DSS will be used that favor increased system restrictiveness can be placed into five groups (summarized below the double line in Table 4.4):

- prescription,
- proscription,
- providing structure,
- promoting ease of learning and use, and
- fostering structured learning.

Prescription

Perhaps the most obvious reason for building a restrictive DSS is to prescribe how decisions are made. Prescription can serve a number of purposes: to impose a "normative" decision-making process, to impose a "preferred" decision-making process even if it is not normative, or to impose a uniform decision-making process that meets organizational needs for communication, coordination, and consistency.

A decision-making technique is generally referred to as "normative" when that technique has been prescribed or established as the way a given task, or class of tasks, *should* be performed. For example, multi-attribute utility theory has been proposed as a normative approach to multi-criteria decision making. If a designer or client wants decision makers to adopt a normative approach, then a restrictive system that supports only that one approach may be appropriate.

Portfolio management provides a classic example. Normative portfolio theory asserts that acquisition and liquidation decisions be made by considering the entire portfolio, trading off risk and return, rather than by considering individual securities in isolation. But when analyzing the behavior of portfolio managers prior to designing his Portfolio Management System (PMS), Gerrity (1970, 1971) observed that the managers routinely violated normative theory. They examined individual securities and considered for whose portfolio to buy the security or from whose to sell it, rather than taking a portfolio-oriented approach. To force decision makers to adopt the normative approach, a designer might build a highly restrictive system that includes portfolio-oriented operators and excludes security-oriented ones.*

---

*Although Gerrity's intention was to move decision makers toward the normative model, he did not use restrictiveness in this manner. PMS supported both the current approach and the normative approach. I will address this design issue in Chapter 6 in the context of change agency.

Some DSS commentators may view prescribing normative approaches as antithetical to the traditional DSS approach, arguing that such systems replace rather than support decision makers. I disagree. Replacing decision makers requires both a well-defined process and the ability to perform that process without human intervention. But often, normative approaches only specify the decision-making technique (only structure the process), while humans provide the critical judgments (execute the process). For instance, although multi-attribute utility is viewed as a normative approach to decision making, the people who supply the weights and utilities play a crucial role in determining the outcome of the process. So a system prescribing a normative technique can still allow room for significant user discretion. Indeed, Phillips (1984) points to such a system—"MAUD" (Humphreys and Wisudha, 1979; Humphreys and McFadden, 1980)—as an example of "preference technology" that supports decision makers in forming preferences and making judgments. The restrictiveness attribute enables us to differentiate such systems from others that do, in fact, replace human judgment entirely with machine-generated solutions.

Managers sometimes prefer that their subordinates use a given decision-making technique even though it is not an established normative method. These managers can use restrictive DSS to impose their preferred techniques on their employees. For instance, Boynton and Victor (1989) propose that, in some situations, an information system can serve as a lever for managers to control the information-search behavior of their subordinates.

Similarly, consider the case of Western Electronics (Moore and Chang, 1983). Engineers, with little or no formal managerial training, were normally selected as general managers of the company's nearly one dozen integrated circuit production facilities. They reported to the corporate engineer, trained in both engineering and management, who was unsatisfied with their managerial planning in areas such as cost and productivity forecasting, scheduling, and asset and capital budgeting. Being preoccupied with major technical problems, the managers tended to adopt an informal "fire-fighting" approach to planning. The corporate engineer instituted a DSS for the purpose of facilitating a more formalized approach to facility planning by these managers. The case description does not provide details of the system's features, but it is reasonable to expect that the functionality included in the system would reflect those analytic techniques preferred by the corporate engineer.

Even when there is no most desirable method—either normative or preferred— for approaching a task, prescribing a single, uniform decision-making process may be necessary to meet an organization's needs for communication, coordination, and consistency. These needs are likely to be greatest in large organizations where decision making is decentralized.

In his study of 56 DSS, Alter (1980) observed that sharing a system can promote communication and consistency of decision making within an organization. Although Alter's study did not address system restrictiveness, sharing a restrictive

DSS that prescribes uniform decision-making methods should be especially useful in promoting consistency, coordination, and communication among individuals or organizational units.

Consistency often becomes important when numerous employees perform the same task in parallel. Approving loans, underwriting insurance, processing claims, and selecting vendors are but a few of many such tasks. In some instances, organizations automate these tasks. When automation is not possible or desirable, organizations may implement, instead, restrictive DSS that ensure consistency of decision-making approaches across employees.

Since decision making in organizations is usually hierarchical, with decisions at one managerial level constraining decisions at the next lower level (Emery, 1969), coordination between levels becomes an important concern. Restrictive DSS at lower levels can help implement higher-level decisions by constraining decision making in accordance with the higher-level decisions. Often the restrictiveness is achieved by limiting the parametrization of operators, with the values of key constraints passed down from higher-level decisions.

Prescribing normative, preferred, or uniform decision-making behavior does not necessarily mean that decision makers are limited to a single, fully specified process. Instead of specifying each step along the path to a decision, a restrictive DSS may prescribe a general approach to performing the task. Consider some examples: DSS that foster forward-looking rather than backward-looking planning allow more than one route to arriving at a decision, but whatever process is followed will be consistent with the forward-looking approach. DSS that force a reliance on external rather than internal data also need not impose a single process. By limiting access to data they ensure that whatever process is followed will reflect an external rather than an internal perspective. DSS for multi-attribute problems might prescribe a single technique, such as multi-attribute utility theory, but instead they might only limit decision makers to a class of methods such as "compensatory methods" or "elimination techniques."

Somewhere between systems that specify the decision-making process fully and those that prescribe a general problem-solving approach are ones that constrain a portion of the process. For instance, restrictive DSS can ensure that appropriate actions are taken when particular prespecified situations are encountered along the way to arriving at a decision. The regression analysis example illustrated this case, forcing a transformation when data are autocorrelated. So did the budget planning system that required decision makers to balance budgets showing deficits before proceeding with other activities.

Proscription

When designers do not have a specific process or approach to prescribe, they may nonetheless want to create a restrictive DSS that prohibits given decision-making behavior. Although there may be no one superior way to solve a given problem, one or more approaches may clearly be inferior. Here, restrictiveness is intended to prevent decision makers from using the DSS to support such processes.

A likely candidate for proscription is the current decision-making process. The purpose of a DSS intervention may be not so much to provide a new way to make decisions as to prevent decision makers from reaching decisions in their current, ill-advised manner.

As with prescription, a DSS may proscribe a complete decision-making process, a general approach to the task, or a portion of a process. Sometimes, when dealing with general approaches or partial decision-making processes, prescription and proscription may be two sides of the same coin. Fostering forward-looking planning can be recast as preventing backward-looking planning. Increasing reliance on external data decreases reliance on internal data. Prescribing a transformation of autocorrelated data can be seen as proscribing regression analysis on the original dataset.

In Chapter 1, I noted that researchers have identified many ways that human decision-making processes can be systematically biased. Debiasing, the use of DSS to reduce or eliminate the systematic cognitive biases to which human decision makers are prone, is a noteworthy instance of proscription. Designers might consider a number of ways of trying to reduce systematic biases by increasing restrictiveness: (1) building debiasing mechanisms into operators that elicit human judgment, (2) limiting human judgmental inputs, (3) excluding operators likely to promote biases, (4) compelling use of debiasing operators, (5) deliberately controlling access to data, and (6) preventing sequences of operators whose combined effects are likely to be biased. For example, Reneau, Wong-On-Wing, and Pattison (1984) found evidence in a laboratory experiment suggesting that users of information systems providing flexible data retrieval may be prone to a "confirmation bias"—a bias favoring information that confirms their initial hypotheses—in their information search behavior. Such a bias might be reduced by restricting users' abilities to search flexibly for information. Toward this end, Jacobs and Keim (1988) have experimented with a knowledge-based DSS that limits user discretion in data retrieval.

As another candidate for debiasing, consider the "wishful thinking" bias, where decision makers rely more on information associated with favorable or desirable outcomes. Very often, when a DSS includes a planning model, users are allowed to iterate through the model as often as they like, modifying inputs and examining outputs. The freedom to rerun the model facilitates evaluating different decisions as well as exploring the effects of uncertainty on decisions. The iterative capability can also be used by decision makers to "game" the system, however, wishfully producing (unrealistic) outcomes that they find desirable. Sequencing rules that restrict the ways in which decision makers can rerun models might be used to reduce the wishful thinking bias.

Providing Structure

Even when there are neither significant factors suggesting prescription nor compelling reasons for proscription, restricting information-processing activities just for the sake of providing structure to the process may be desirable. For the many tasks where no single, well-defined approach to decision making has been established, defining a problem-solving procedure may itself be an overwhelming task. If a DSS implements a large number of operators that are potentially useful for addressing the task, decision makers might suffer from ''operator overload,'' much as they sometimes suffer from information overload. By restricting what users can do with a DSS, a designer may make the system more valuable by lending structure to the decision-making process.

The benefits of providing structure can be twofold. First, the added structure can enable decision makers to use the system more effectively than they would a less restrictive system. Instead of struggling with the difficult meta-problem of selecting a decision-making process from the plethora of possibilities, users can more immediately put the system to constructive use in arriving at a decision. Second, the added structure can reduce the likelihood of dysfunctional outcomes following from ill-conceived decision-making processes that combine information-processing capabilities in unreasonable or inappropriate ways.

Restricting a DSS simply for the purpose of increasing structure poses special dangers. When prescriptive or proscriptive reasoning is used to restrict, significant attention presumably has been directed to the effects the DSS will have on the decision-making process and, ultimately, on the decision. When restrictiveness is not being used to advocate given decision-making behavior, however, which capabilities should be supported and which should be limited becomes less clear. If capabilities are arbitrarily eliminated, it is quite possible that such a system will foster bad decision making.

Promoting Ease of Learning and Use

The relationship between restrictiveness and ease of use has already been addressed more than once in this chapter: too little restrictiveness may lead to a complex system that is difficult to operate. To make systems easier to use, therefore, designers may make them more restrictive. In particular, increased restrictiveness can make systems easier to learn. For instance, in the domain of word-processing systems, Carroll and Carrithers (1984) used ''training wheels'' to constrain users and facilitate ease of learning.

This objective, ''ease of use,'' may appear to coincide with the preceding one, ''providing structure.'' Indeed, in both cases restrictiveness serves to make systems less complex, to offer fewer options, and to make systems less overwhelming. The distinction between the two objectives is the same as between active and passive understanding. Providing structure is the active case; increased restrictiveness makes the system less complex and more effectively applied to solving decision-making problems. Ease of use and learning is the passive case; increased restrictiveness makes the system less complex and more easily operated.

Fostering Structured Learning

In the systems he studied, Alter (1980) found that learning frequently was a by-product of DSS use, but that sometimes DSS were designed with the goal of fostering learning. Although system restrictiveness did not enter into the findings, it is easy to see how restrictive DSS can be used to implement structured learning experiences for decison makers. For instance, a restrictive system could train managers in the proper use of a given problem-solving technique by "marching" them through the sequence of steps they must perform. Similarly, a restrictive DSS could take users on a "guided tour" of a database, systematically exposing them to data elements that teach them lessons about their environment.

In a laboratory experiment, Dos Santos and Bariff (1988) studied the effect of restricting users' control over model manipulation on their ability to learn about their business through the use of a model-based DSS.* Subjects who used a system that forced them to follow a structured strategy for manipulating controllable variables subsequently performed better at problem finding and problem prioritization tasks than those who were given flexible access to the same model. Dos Santos and Bariff's results are consistent with an earlier, non-computer-based study (Lindberg and Brehmer, 1977) that found that, given freedom of choice, subjects do not adopt the preferred sequence of cue manipulations for learning cue–criterion relationships. These findings suggest that restrictive systems that structure model manipulation may be useful for fostering learning and greater understanding of the business environment, commonly cited benefits of DSS use.

Objectives Favoring Lesser Restrictiveness

As one of his six managerial objectives for DSS, Sprague (1980) asserted that a system should be process-independent and user-controlled. Many of the design objectives that favor lesser system restrictiveness can be seen as special cases of this general objective, often referred to as flexibility.† Most of Keen's (1980) arguments for adaptive DSS design can also be used to make a case for flexibility

---

*Dos Santos and Bariff (1988) refer to their more restrictive system as providing "system-guided model manipulation." In the terminology used here, this property is an aspect of "system restrictiveness" and should not be confused with "decisional guidance," a different system attribute discussed in Chapter 5.
†The term "flexibility" is used in different places in the DSS literature to refer to a number of different concepts. In particular, it often refers to the flexibility of the user interface, a concept related to the ease of use or convenience of operating the system. In many other places it is used as I am using it here, to refer to the freedom given the user to exercise discretion and choice while operating the system.

and lesser restrictiveness. The objectives pertaining to how a DSS will be used that favor lesser restrictiveness can be placed in the following categories (summarized below the double line in Table 4.5):

- meeting unspecified needs,
- supporting changing decision-making environments,
- supporting multiple decision makers and tasks,
- allowing users discretion,
- fostering creativity, and
- fostering exploratory learning.

TABLE 4.5 *Objectives favoring lesser system restrictiveness*

Objective	Explanation/Illustration
Promoting use	Discretionary users may choose not to use a system that does not allow them freedom to follow their own decision-making processes.
Meeting unspecified needs	Given the unstructured nature of the tasks being supported, designers and users are often unable to provide adequate functional specifications for DSS. One solution is to provide a broad collection of information-processing capabilities from which decision makers can choose as needed.
Supporting changing decision-making environments	Decision-making environments are dynamic. If a DSS is to have the longevity to continue to be useful as people, tasks, and organizations change over time, it cannot be very limited in its capabilities.
Supporting multiple decision makers and tasks	Because decision makers differ one from another, as do decision-making tasks, DSS that are intended to support multiple users or multiple tasks must be flexible enough to accommodate their varying styles and requirements.
Allowing users discretion	Most DSS aim to support or amplify human judgment, not to reduce or eliminate it. Consequently, a common DSS objective is to build a system that is minimally restrictive.
Fostering creativity	Support for idea processing and creativity is often seen as an important objective for a DSS. One means of facilitating creativity is by providing users with a free hand in studying the problem under consideration.
Fostering exploratory learning	Many have claimed that individual and organizational learning are important benefits following from the use of DSS. By experimenting with a nonrestrictive DSS and exploring its capabilities, decision makers can learn much about their decision-making problems.

I have endeavoured to identify conceptually distinct objectives, although in practice these goals often occur in combination.

Meeting Unspecified Needs

Keen (1980) notes that designers and users are often unable or unwilling to provide adequate functional specifications for DSS. Given the unstructured nature of the tasks being supported, specifying *a priori* what a decision maker's needs will be or what decision-making processes will be followed is neither easy nor usually possible. Instead of trying to predefine the data, models, analyses, and visual representations that a decision maker will want or need to use, therefore, one response to the problem of DSS design is to provide a collection of capabilities sufficiently broad that decision makers can choose for themselves which information-processing functions to employ in any given situation. This approach is consistent with Huber (1983), who argues that "DSS designs should enable their users to employ a variety of approaches to their decision tasks" (p. 575).*
Pursuing this objective leads naturally to building less restrictive systems.

Supporting Changing Decision-making Environments

Decision-making environments are not static. The people, tasks, and settings that constitute a decision-making environment all change with time.

People change. With experience, managers' understanding of their jobs and their decision-making problems evolve. In fact, Keen (1980) argues that DSS contribute to this change by shaping users' concepts of their tasks and situations. In addition to a given person's changing, the person holding a given position may change. The person sitting in front of the terminal today may not be the same one as next week, next month, or next year.

Decision-making tasks change. As the world changes, so do the problems managers confront. Short-run profit may give way to long-run market share as a goal. Cost reduction may yield to product differentiation. Interest rates, not inflation, may become the critical economic variable.

Organizational settings change. Changes in organizational culture, structure, or decision-making style often occur slowly, but takeovers and mergers as well as greatly intensified competition can lead to more rapid and radical organizational shifts.

If a DSS is to have longevity, to continue to be useful as the people, settings, and tasks it supports change, then that system must not lock users into a limited set of decision-making capabilities. Sprague and Carlson (1982) note that it is

---

*Huber's (1983) argument, presented in the context of cognitive style research and DSS design, can be used to support a number of the objectives favoring lesser restrictiveness, especially supporting multiple users and allowing users discretion.

widely known that DSS must be flexible to respond to the dynamic nature of decision-making environments. If supporting a changing environment is a design objective, then building a nonrestrictive DSS may be what is needed.

Supporting Multiple Decision Makers and Tasks

Sometimes, DSS are built to support a given decision maker performing a single task. More often, DSS support many different people, more than one task, or both. Even within the same organizational setting, people and tasks can vary greatly. Individuals differ one from another in many ways—cognitive style, propensity for risk, extroversion/introversion, experience, and education, among others—that may have a bearing on their use of DSS (Zmud, 1979; Sage, 1981; Huber, 1983). DSS tasks differ along a number of dimensions and may require different data structures, analytic tools, and visual representations. A restrictive DSS may be unable to support the various decision-making approaches demanded by multiple users or the assortment of capabilities required by multiple tasks. Consequently, less restrictive DSS may be appropriate when more than one person or task is involved.

Both prescriptive and descriptive DSS research comment on the need for less restrictiveness when a DSS is intended for use by more than one person. Carlson (1983a) argued that a DSS should not enforce or capture a particular decision-making pattern if it is to support several decision makers. Hogue and Watson's (1984) study of DSS in 18 organizations found that because the DSS tended "to support multiple users, they were designed to be flexible" (p. 122).

Allowing Users Discretion

A frequently mentioned reason for building DSS is to combine the best features of humans and machines. One human characteristic that we retain—in fact, that we emphasize—in the human–machine synergy is the ability to judge. Most DSS aim to support or amplify human judgment, not to reduce or eliminate it. In particular, many DSS are intended to allow free reign to human judgment, to allow decision makers maximal discretion, to constrain the decision-making process as little as possible. Consequently, a common DSS objective is to build a system that is minimally restrictive.

Fostering Creativity

One of the factors that makes managerial problem solving challenging is a need for creativity. Developing a new warehousing policy or naming a new product are examples of creative problem-solving activities. A number of authors (Young, 1989; Elam *et al.*, 1985; Weber, 1986; Elam and Mead, 1987, 1990) have stressed creativity and idea processing as important targets for computer-based support.

Although creativity can be supported by specific functional capabilities within a (restrictive or nonrestrictive) DSS, another means of facilitating creativity is by providing users considerable freedom to experiment with the system. When promoting creativity is a design objective, therefore, a less restrictive DSS may be appropriate.

Fostering Exploratory Learning

Keen (1980), Alter (1980), and Hurst *et al.* (1983), among others, have claimed that learning is an important benefit that can follow from building DSS. While restrictive DSS can teach structured lessons, less restrictive systems offer their users the potential for ongoing and significant exploratory learning and discovery. Decision makers can learn much about the nature of their decision-making problem, the broader context within which it exists, and various approaches to solving it by experimenting with a nonrestrictive DSS and exploring its capabilities. More specifically, managers can discover a great deal by freely analyzing the contents of databases as well as by constructing and executing their own models.

Summary

A DSS project will likely have a number of objectives, some of which may favor greater restrictiveness and others lesser restrictiveness. Objectives favoring greater restrictiveness tend to see the purpose of the DSS as improving decision making by influencing the decision maker's behavior in a way that has been deemed ''good' or ''desirable.'' Objectives favoring lesser restrictiveness see the purpose as improving decision making by providing a set of information-processing capabilities that are process-independent and under control of the user. When both types of objectives are present they must be traded off one against another. Moreover, if the DSS is to be employed by discretionary users, its restrictiveness must be within the range that is acceptable to them.

RESTRICTIVENESS AND DSS DESIGN

DSS design is a process that translates DSS objectives into DSS characteristics. We have, most recently, examined the way that system objectives influence the choice of appropriate DSS restrictiveness. Earlier we examined how DSS components restrict decision makers. Together, these two analyses form the basis for designing restrictiveness. The challenges for DSS designers are, first, to trade off conflicting objectives to determine appropriate restrictiveness and, second, to construct DSS components that realize the desired restrictiveness. Numerous obstacles, however, stand between the designer and meeting these challenges.

Trading off objectives is not easy. Behavioral objectives concerning how the system is to be used often conflict directly with the goal of getting the system used.

Behavioral objectives also frequently conflict one with another, some favoring greater and others lesser restrictiveness.

Once objectives are established, the design task can still be difficult, because perceived restrictiveness, not absolute restrictiveness, determines whether objectives are met. User behavior is determined by how restrictive the DSS is in practice, not in theory. Decision makers choose to use a system based on how restrictive it feels, not how restrictive it is. Users employ only those functions they are able and willing to operate, not the full set of capabilities.

DSS designers are in an uncomfortable position, since they control absolute, not perceived, restrictiveness. Building a DSS whose absolute restrictiveness *ought* to accomplish the desired objectives is not sufficient. They must construct a DSS whose restrictiveness *as perceived by users* accomplishes the objectives. The complex relationship between absolute and perceived restrictiveness hinders their efforts: since decreasing objective restrictiveness often increases subjective restrictiveness, designers can be trapped.

To make matters worse, designers have their own perceptions of reality. Designers' subjective assessments of a system's restrictiveness are likely to conform closely with the objective view, since most of the distortions—for instance, lack of skills or knowledge—do not apply to the designer. Unfortunately, what matters is not the designer's assessment of absolute restrictiveness, but the designer's perception of how the user will perceive the restrictiveness. This assessment sounds complex, looks complex (see Figure 4.13), and is complex.

In analyzing the designer, two additional subsets of decision-making processes must be considered. They are drawn with broken ellipses in Figure 4.13. The first new subset is the designer's perception of the set of user-perceived

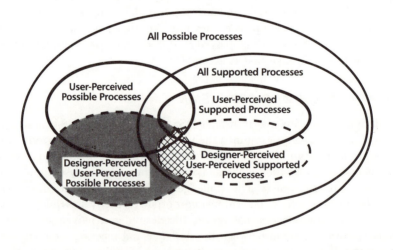

FIGURE 4.13   *The designer's perspective of user-perceived restrictiveness*

possible processes. We know that it is a subset of the full set of possible processes, but we do not know how it relates to the subset actually perceived by the user. Similarly, the second new subset is the designer's perception of the set of user-perceived supported processes. It must be a subset of the full set of supported processes, but again, we do not know how it relates to the subset actually perceived by the user. The contrast between the cross-hatched and shaded areas represents the designer's perceptions of user-perceived restrictiveness.

If the designer's expectations about a user's perceptions are inaccurate, the system may not accomplish its objectives. If the decision maker sees the system as much more or much less restrictive than the designer predicted, he or she may not use it, despite the designer's attempt to promote its use. Similarly, if the user does not recognize capabilities that the designer intended for him or her to employ, then the desired behavioral objectives may not be met. Discrepancies between user-perceived restrictiveness and designers' perceptions of the same, therefore, can stymie design efforts.

And it gets worse. Figure 4.13 depicts a single user. When a DSS is built for multiple decision makers the complexity, and the difficulty, are compounded. Each user has his or her own perceptions of the system's restrictiveness and these perceptions may not agree. The designer must assess and reconcile them all. If users' perceptions vary too greatly, satisfying the design objectives may not be possible.

What can DSS builders do to reduce perceptual differences and the design difficulties they cause? Three approaches long seen as important in DSS design and implementation may hold the key:

- training,
- user involvement in the design process, and
- adaptive design.

Training

Appropriate training in the use of a DSS can bring subjective restrictiveness into line with objective restrictiveness by helping decision makers appreciate more fully the processes the DSS supports. Training that provides passive knowledge of a DSS can alleviate users' being unaware of or unable to operate system features, while training that provides active knowledge can help users understand how to apply and combine operators to perform given decision-making tasks. Training in performing the task itself might reduce perceptual differences by expanding the set of possible processes considered by the decision maker. Such task-related training might make users aware of processes they never encountered, or convince them of the value of approaches they usually disregard.

User Involvement

Involving decision makers actively in the process of designing a DSS should help builders understand better how the users perceive the task and the system, thus alleviating the undesirable consequences of incorrectly assessing users' perceptions. Improving builders' perceptions may not be as beneficial as reducing variances in users' perceptions, but is still helpful. Involving users in design might also reduce users' perceptual differences by helping them understand better the system and the task.

Adaptive Design

Adaptive design (Keen, 1980) is an approach to DSS development where the user, builder, and system each adapt over time in response to feedback from the other two. Such adaptation may reduce the various differences in perceived restrictiveness, thus ameliorating the problems they engender. Let us consider how each of the three entities can adapt.

Designers can revise their understanding of the DSS and its users by observing decision makers while they use the system or by debriefing them later. Recognizing how users' perceptions of restrictiveness differ from what was predicted, builders can take two remedial actions: they can modify the system, changing its absolute restrictiveness, or they can edify the users, changing user-perceived restrictiveness. In terms of restrictiveness, one would say that designers' perceptions of users' perceptions have improved, allowing the designers to use system restrictiveness more effectively as a design variable. In the language of adaptive design, feedback from the user and the system to the builder has led to adaptation of all three.

Users can also adapt directly in response to their interactions with the system. Over time, decision makers may become increasingly proficient with the DSS, recognizing features they previously overlooked and using effectively features they originally found intractable. The subset of processes seen by the user as supported will expand, leaving a smaller gap between it and the full set of supported processes. After using the system, the set of decision-making processes users see as candidates may also grow, so the sets of possible processes perceived by users may include more of those supported by the DSS. These shifts reduce the differences between objective and subjective restrictiveness.

Finally, systems can be "self-adaptive," increasing or decreasing their own restrictiveness in response to their interactions with users. For instance, a DSS that supports searching for alternatives might become more restrictive over time by using exhibited user preferences to preclude searching certain regions. Similarly, research has demonstrated that, under certain conditions, paramorphic linear models derived from human judgments often outperform the same humans (Dawes and Corrigan, 1974). After an adequate sample of human judgments has been accumulated, this "bootstrapping" technique can be introduced in place of other operators that elicit judgments.

Systems can be designed to become less restrictive with use. This tactic might be appropriate when a DSS serves, in part, as a training device. At first the system can compel users to become acquainted with certain capabilities; later the full range of flexibility can be provided.

Adaptive design and system restrictiveness have a two-way relationship. We have seen that adaptivity can help overcome the perceptual problems associated with restrictiveness. But, even in the absence of perceptual problems, the system restrictiveness attribute can be a useful diagnostic within the adaptive design process, helping designers determine if and how a DSS should be modified. They may find that a DSS is not being used, or is not being used as planned, because the restrictiveness is inconsistent with design objectives.

Summary

System restrictiveness provides a powerful set of design considerations to DSS designers who must choose first how restrictive to make their systems and then how to make their systems restrictive. System restrictiveness must not be viewed as a design option, a feature of DSS that builders can choose to employ if they so desire. Whether or not a DSS designer considers system restrictiveness, the system he or she builds will intervene into existing decision-making processes and will in some way restrict those processes. DSS designers, therefore, must pay careful attention to this attribute.

Some builders will use system restrictiveness as the starting point for their designs. Others will consider it after much of the design is in place. Whichever approach one chooses, what is important is that at some point in the analysis and design process the DSS builder contemplates not just the individual functional capabilities but the broader issue of the restrictiveness of the system as a whole.

Because of the complexity of the issue, designing with restrictiveness is a challenge. Table 4.6 summarizes the obstacles one encounters, and three means of overcoming them. The decisional guidance attribute, presented in the next chapter, can serve as a fourth means of coping with these obstacles.

TABLE 4.6   DSS design and restrictiveness

Impediments to successful design
Conflicting objectives
Complex relationship between absolute and perceived restrictiveness
Designers' perceptions of users' perceptions of restrictiveness
Multiple users with differing perceptions of restrictiveness
Strategies to overcome impediments
Training
User involvement in design
Adaptive design

Chapter 5
DECISIONAL GUIDANCE

The outputs of a Decision Support System such as data displays, statistical analyses, modeling results, and graphs, are intended to support the human judgment involved in making decisions. But often those outputs are themselves produced from the judgmental inputs of the system's users. While interacting with a DSS, users may have numerous opportunities for exercising judgment and making choices. Some judgments concern what to do next: Should I run the same analysis again with different parameters? Should I peruse the database? Should I run a regression on the data? Other judgments are predictive: What will inflation be in the third quarter of this year? What is the likelihood that the prime interest rate will exceed 10% by year-end? How many units of my product will I sell this month? Still others are evaluative: Is this level of profit satisfactory? What is the trade-off between short-term profit and long-run market share? While the restrictiveness attribute tells us how much and what kind of judgmental discretion a DSS affords its users, understanding how a DSS is likely to affect decisional behavior also requires considering if and how that system guides its users as they exercise the judgmental freedom they are given.

Any interactive computer-based system must provide a means for users to communicate their judgmental inputs. Menus, command interpreters, fill-in tables, and question–answer dialogs are used widely for this purpose. When analyzing a DSS a key issue is whether these input mechanisms affect the substance of users' judgmental inputs. A related issue, equally important, is whether the system contains special mechanisms whose roles are to guide users' judgments. Consider some examples:

- Menus may lead to order effects. Because the order in which information is presented to human decision makers can affect its salience, users may tend to select the first and last items on menus.
- Context-sensitive help messages, commonly used to explain the options available to users, may provide users with information that helps them differentiate substantively the options they confront.
- Intelligence or expertise may be embedded in a system so that it can recommend actions and responses to its users.

This chapter is an extension of material originally published in Mark S. Silver, "Decisional guidance for computer-based decision support," *Management Information Systems Quarterly*, **15**(1), March 1991. Copyright 1991 by the Society for Information Management and the Management Information Systems Research Center at the University of Minnesota. All rights reserved.

Each example illustrates a different kind of guidance. In the first the guidance is a consequence—perhaps inadvertent—of using a traditional input mechanism. The second example's help facility, unlike many others that describe only the mechanics of selecting an input, provides its users with insight into the judgmental task. And in the third case a new mechanism has been introduced into the system for the purpose of advising the user. In each example the system guides the decision maker as he or she responds to its requests for judgments or choices.

If and how a DSS guides its users' judgmental inputs, intentionally or not, is clearly an important attribute of that system. I shall refer to this attribute as "decisional guidance," defined formally as follows:

Decisional Guidance: how a Decision Support System enlightens or sways its users as they structure and execute their decision-making processes—that is, as they choose among and use the functional capabilities of the DSS.

Several key points follow from the definition. First, the word "decisional" is significant. Most guidance deliberately built into DSS these days is better termed "mechanical" than "decisional," for its mechanisms, such as pull-down menus and help screens, are oriented more toward the mechanics of operating the system's features, often a matter of knowing when to push which buttons, than toward the decisional and judgmental tasks at hand. In contrast, decisional guidance helps users deal with the decision-making concepts involved in choosing among and interacting with a system's information-processing capabilities. For example, while a mechanical help screen might simply list each available option and how to invoke it, decisional guidance might identify the strengths and weaknesses of each alternative action.

Second, the term decisional guidance is not limited to instances where a designer purposefully includes guidance mechanisms in a system. Even when designers do not build guidance mechanisms into a DSS deliberately, the system's features may guide users in ways the designers never anticipated. Indeed, we can distinguish two kinds of decisional guidance: *deliberate* and *inadvertent*. Deliberate guidance, decisional guidance intentionally built into a system by its designers, is "meta-support" for judgmental activities, because it supports more effective use of a system that is itself intended to support more effective decision making. Help facilities that inform users and embedded intelligence that advises users exemplify this case. In contrast, inadvertent guidance is an unintended consequence of the system's design and is not planned by the system designer. Order effects not anticipated by a menu's designer illustrate this kind of guidance. It is probable that all DSS exhibit some decisional guidance; if they do not guide deliberately, then they likely guide inadvertently.

The third point is that even when guidance is deliberate, it is not necessarily intended to steer or lead decision makers in a given direction. The meta-support decisional guidance provides can be suggestive, making judgmental recommendations to users, but it may simply be informative, providing them with unbiased, pertinent information.

Fourth, the definition draws on Chapter 1's tree-like model of decision making to divide decisional guidance into two classes: guidance for *structuring* the decision-making process affects how users choose which operators to invoke and the order in which to invoke them; guidance for *executing* the process affects how decision makers perform the evaluative and predictive judgments necessary when executing the chosen operators.

Lastly, although people often confuse decisional guidance with system restrictiveness, their definitions differ significantly. Restrictiveness defines what users can do with a system; guidance describes, subject to what users can do, how the system affects what they do do. Decisional guidance is not independent of system restrictiveness. Since restrictiveness defines what users can and cannot do with a DSS, it also bounds what remains for the DSS to guide. Highly restrictive systems limit users' discretionary power, affording relatively few opportunities for significant guidance. Minimally restrictive ones, however, offer considerable opportunities for guiding decision makers. In general, as shown in Figure 5.1, the less restrictive a DSS, the greater the potential for the system to guide.

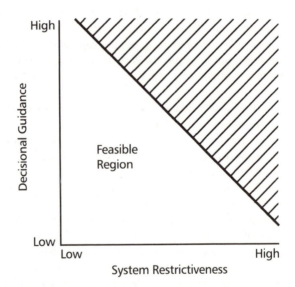

FIGURE 5.1   *Feasible combinations of restrictiveness and guidance. Note. Reprinted by permission, "Decision Support Systems: directed and nondirected change," Mark S. Silver, Information Systems Research, 1(1) (Jan.–Mar. 1990). Copyright (1990), The Institute of Management Sciences, 290 Westminster Street, Providence RI 02903. All rights reserved*

TABLE 5.1 A typology of deliberate decisional guidance

Targets
 Structuring the decision-making process (choosing operators)
 Executing the decision-making process (using operators)

Forms
 Suggestive guidance
 Informative guidance

Modes
 Predefined
 Dynamic
 Participative

Scope
 Short range
 Long range

Decisional guidance is a topic that has not been widely studied. Few researchers or designers have articulated prescriptions for or against deliberately building decisional guidance into DSS, and few studies have examined the effects of inadvertent guidance. Moreover, in today's DSS, deliberate decisional guidance is rare. Although a variety of recent projects have begun to develop decisional guidance mechanisms, the research to date is fragmented and mostly technologically oriented. Each project is independent of the others, with its own objectives, vocabulary, and methods. Most significantly, these projects tend to focus on developing guidance mechanisms rather than on examining their effects on decision-making behavior. We can expect to see more and more such efforts. Establishing a unified approach to studying guidance, one that recognizes the importance of both technological and behavioral issues, is therefore critical.

The structure of this chapter is similar to that of the previous one. I begin by examining how DSS can deliberately guide decision makers, first distinguishing different types of decisional guidance and then considering how each DSS component contributes to guidance. After presenting an integrated illustration of several guidance mechanisms, I turn to the questions of when and why a designer would deliberately build guidance into a system. I conclude by considering the effects and effectiveness of both inadvertent and deliberate guidance.

HOW CAN DSS GUIDE DELIBERATELY?

In this section I present a four-dimensional typology of the ways that designers can deliberately build guidance into DSS, deferring for the moment the questions of whether and why they should choose to do so. The typology, outlined in Table 5.1, is derived from analyses and extrapolations of approaches to decisional guidance proposed in the literature. Each dimension distinguishes types of guidance by posing a different question:

- What is the *target* of the guidance? What distinct aspect of decision making does the guidance enlighten or sway?
- What is the *form* of the guidance? What does the guidance offer decision makers that might enlighten or sway them?
- What is the *mode* of the guidance? How does the guidance mechanism work?
- What is the *scope* of the guidance? How much of the decision-making process does it guide?

Targets of Guidance: Structuring and Executing the Process

Just as a DSS supports the judgments required en route to making decisions, deliberate decisional guidance aims to support the judgments required in the course of operating a DSS. Before we can consider the content of such guidance—that is, how DSS can deliberately guide—we must be clear about what is being guided. What do users do with a DSS that could be affected by decisional guidance? What judgmental activities might designers aim to support? Chapter 1's tree-like model offers a natural response: DSS users structure and execute decision-making processes. Each of these requires human judgment; each can be the target of guidance.

Structuring the Decision-making Process

Guidance for structuring the decision-making process is support for "meta-choice," deciding how to decide, often the most difficult and critical activity in solving a problem. Sometimes the challenge is to choose among competing techniques, such as the many methods proposed for solving multi-attribute problems or the numerous models developed for forecasting time series. Other times, problems are less structured, and the task is to combine an amorphous set of capabilities into a coherent approach for reaching a solution. In either situation the system can guide its users in selecting and combining system functions. As systems become increasingly complex, with more operators, models, and datasets, such guidance becomes increasingly important.

Supporting meta-choice means more than just guiding users as they navigate through a complex system. It means helping users answer the decisional questions they confront when selecting capabilities. Given a specific multi-attribute problem, for instance, should a serial approach be used, where solutions are generated and evaluated one at a time, or should a parallel process be employed, where a set of competing alternatives is generated and evaluated as a whole? If the parallel approach is adopted, should a compensatory or non-compensatory rule be used to choose among the alternatives? Providing such guidance is not easy; it requires knowledge of the decisional properties of operators and the decisional relationships among them.

Decision makers' needs for guidance may be more or less specific. Speaking generally, decision makers must find an approach to solving their problem. When a DSS explicitly supports more than one problem-solving approach, decision makers may need assistance choosing among them. Or, in the absence of any well-defined approach, users may need help creating one from the capabilities the system offers.

More specifically, decision makers may need help choosing operators. They must decide what to do next, or, if they are just starting out, what to do first. This problem raises two questions: what do I need an operator to do, and which of several competing operators should I use to do it? For example, should I begin with a forecast, a graph of historical data, or a tabular display of my current position? Then, if I elect forecasting, which of a dozen different extrapolation methods should I use?

Executing the Decision-making Process

However difficult and important it may be, constructing the decision-making process is only one step toward reaching a solution. The chosen solution method must, of course, be executed. Here, too, decisional guidance has a place. The same DSS operators whose outputs (data displays, modeling results, statistical analyses, and graphic representations) support human judgment often require human judgments as inputs. The judgments might be predictions of future conditions (inflation rates, unemployment rates, sales, droughts, strikes, and so forth) or evaluations of preferences (acceptable profit levels, desirable warehouse locations, and trade-offs between costs and benefits, among others). A DSS might simply prompt users for these inputs, or it might guide users as they make the necessary judgments.

Consider DSS that support the elimination by aspects process. A simple system might prompt users to enter attributes and acceptable ranges for their values, producing a list of those alternatives satisfying the specified criteria. Although the system aids decision makers by performing the necessary database searches, it does not assist with the critical judgmental tasks of choosing and ordering attributes and defining acceptable ranges. Another system might provide such decisional guidance.

Forms of Guidance: Suggestive versus Informative

We are now prepared to ask, "How can DSS guide?" Regardless of whether the target is process structuring or execution, the answer is that decisional guidance can support users in two very different ways (Figure 5.2): "Suggestive guidance" makes judgmental recommendations (what to do, what input values to use) to the decision maker. In contrast, "informative guidance" provides pertinent information that enlightens the decision maker's judgment, without suggesting

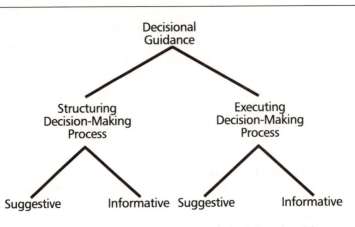

FIGURE 5.2   Targets and forms of decisional guidance

how to act. A DSS may contain instances of both forms of guidance. In fact, at any point of judgment, a system may offer suggestions, pertinent information, or both.

Suggestive Guidance

As its name suggests, ''suggestive guidance'' recommends how users can respond to the judgmental opportunities they encounter. For structuring the decision-making process, such guidance recommends which operators and inputs (data and models) to use. Recommendations might be a single operator (''use linear regression''), a small set of operators (''use linear regression or discriminant analysis''), or a rank-ordered list of operators (''linear regression is your best option, otherwise use discriminant analysis''). Alternatively, the DSS might recommend not using certain operators.

TABLE 5.2   *Examples of deliberate decisional guidance*

Suggestive guidance	Informative guidance
Structuring the process	
Recommended operator	Description/analysis of operators
Set of recommended operators	Comparison of operators
Ordered list of recommended operators	Map of relationships among operators
Set of operators not recommended	Record of behavior in similar contexts
	History of activity this session
Executing the process	
Recommended values	Definitions of required input values
Set of recommended values	Descriptions of how inputs will be used
Ordered list of recommended values	Tables, graphs, or analyses of data
Set of values not recommended	Record of behavior in similar contexts
	History of activity this session

For executing the process, suggestive guidance recommends parameter and other input values. The DSS might recommend a specific value ("set the inflation rate to 4.2%"), a set of (ordered or unordered) values ("set the inflation rate to 4.2%, 4.8%, or 5.4%") or a range of values ("set the inflation rate between 4% and 5%"). The guidance might also advise against using certain values.

The left-hand side of Table 5.2 summarizes the types of suggestions I have enumerated. The DSS literature describes a number of examples of these kinds of suggestive guidance:

Lee, Hurst, and Lee (1985) propose a "Third Generation Multiple Criteria Decision Support System (3G-MCDSS)," one of whose purposes is to guide decision makers in choosing among different approaches to solving multi-objective problems. Their prototype contains 13 different techniques—for instance, Goal Setting Support (Lee and Hurst, 1983), Surrogate Worth Trade Off (Haimes and Hall, 1974), Zionts–Wallenius (Zionts and Wallenius, 1976), and a number of variants of Goal Programming—that can be used to generate alternative solutions to multi-objective problems. The prototype embeds a small expert system that suggests a technique based on a combination of (1) user responses to specific questions (for instance, "Do you want to reach the final solution iteratively?"); (2) information about the problem already supplied by the user; and (3) rules predefined by the system's designers.

Wedley and Field (1984) describe a "Predecision Support System" that helps users structure their decision making by suggesting decision styles (autocratic, consultative, or group), methods (individual interactions, interacting group, nominal group, or delphi), and membership (expert, co-worker, or representative). Combining and adapting the findings of Vroom and Yetton (1973) and Stumpf, Zand, and Freedman (1979), the system asks its users as many as 10 questions about their problem before recommending one or more sets of styles, methods, and participants.

Kobashi (1984) discusses how suggestions might be useful in a computer-based decision aid for multi-attribute problems. Observing that some DSS march users step-by-step through the multi-attribute utility approach, he notes that experienced decision makers might benefit from more flexibility in interacting with the system and data. He proposes a decision aid for the multi-attribute utility method that allows all users more freedom in interacting with the data table, but that also makes suggestions to help novice users determine what to do next.

Collopy and Armstrong (1989) consider the meta-decision of choosing a forecasting technique for extrapolating time-series data. Statisticians have proposed numerous forecasting methods, such as deseasonalized simple regression against time, several varieties of deseasonalized exponential smoothing, and the Box–Jenkins method. Studies (Makridakis and Hibon, 1979; Hogarth, 1979; Makridakis *et al.*, 1982; Lopes, 1983) have found that the relative accuracy of the methods depends upon the interaction of the method with the series being forecast. For a given time-series, therefore, an important question is which method or weighted combination of methods should be used. Collopy and Armstrong used interviews and protocol analysis to develop an expert system addressing this problem. One might embed their system as a "mini-expert" within DSS that support many extrapolation techniques to provide suggestive guidance on which forecasting technique(s) to employ for a given set of data.

Stabell (1983) uses the term "decision channeling" to refer to the property of systems "that serves to both support and shift the decision process" (p. 251). He proposes "the presentation form for logical data structures, the nature of system defaults, a differential ease of transition between different system functions, and the structure of memory aids" (p. 251) as features that could foster decision channeling. Although Stabell uses the term to refer to features of the interface architecture, channeling can also be accomplished through suggestive guidance. The system would give users a choice of using features consistent with the old or new decision-making approaches, but would recommend those favoring the new one.

Informative Guidance

Without offering suggestions, "informative guidance" provides decision makers with pertinent information that enlightens their judgment and use of the system. Help screens are usually informative in nature, describing the available options without recommending any one of them. But most of the help screens we find today do not offer decisional guidance; they provide only information about the mechanics of choosing among options. What information could be provided that would help users with the judgments involved in making their selections?

For structuring the process, detailed analyses of the operators, including their advantages and disadvantages, might be pertinent information. Although currently less common than descriptions of individual operators, comparisons of operators with respect to their decisional properties can be particularly helpful. For example, if a user must select one of several choice rules, a table indicating which rules are elimination processes and which are scoring methods might be valuable.

For systems having complex relationships among their operators, users might be given a "map" that shows how operators are related one to another. For instance, such guidance could address the following questions: Which operators are logically consistent so that they can be used as part of the same coherent decision-making process? Which operators are substitutes? What are the precedence relationships that control the logical order in which operators are used?

For executing the process, informative guidance might include clear definitions of the required input values and a description of how they will be used by the operators. Tables, graphs, or statistical analyses of relevant data are also useful references for decision makers choosing input values for operators.

For both structuring and executing the process, a history of how the user, or other users, behaved in similar contexts in the past can be useful. Knowledge of what was done on previous occasions might motivate a user to behave in either the same or a different way in the current instance. The history would be even more informative if it included an indication of the concomitant outcomes; the more complete history might lead to different user behavior. Along the same lines, decision makers might be given a record of the path they traversed to reach their current location in the system. Knowing which operators they invoked and input values they supplied might influence their judgments on which operators and input values to use now.

The right-hand column of Table 5.2 summarizes the types of pertinent information described above. The DSS literature also reports on a number of examples of informative guidance:

Studer (1983) describes an adaptable DSS interface that supports selecting suitable operators for a given purpose, constructing more complex operators from those the system offers, and executing operators. Central to his approach is the concept of an "application model," which provides a graph-based description of the structure of a problem and the operators that can be used to solve it. In particular, the model identifies the relationships among components of the problem as well as those among different operators. The interface allows users (1) to navigate through the graphs as a way of seeing the application's structure and the operators available (navigation mode), (2) to acquire detailed information about components of the application (information mode), (3) to execute the operators and specify input data (execution mode), and (4) to create complex operators from more basic ones (operator definition mode). Each of these modes guides users by informing either their choice or use of operators.

Brennan and Elam (1986) identify a number of ways the modeling components of DSS are currently deficient, including their inability to help users uncover possibly interesting future analyses. Among the enhanced capabilities Brennan and Elam propose for model-based DSS is a generalized form of sensitivity analysis that might address "[w]hat to do next" by providing "clues as to interesting or important changes to the model structure or parameters" (p. 136). Such clues constitute informative guidance for structuring the decision-making process.

Modes of Guidance: Predefined, Dynamic, Participative

Speaking glibly about systems that guide their users with suggestions and pertinent information is easy. But how is the guidance generated? How do the guidance mechanisms arrive at the suggestions they offer the decision maker? How do they determine what information is pertinent for the judgment at hand? In short, how do the guidance mechanisms work?

Guidance mechanisms operate in one of three modes: predefined, dynamic, or participative. In the first case the designer *predefines* the specific suggestions or the particular information displays and builds them into the guidance mechanism. In the other two cases the designer constructs the guidance mechanism only; the mechanism then generates the suggestions and informational displays either itself by learning *dynamically* over time, or with the active *participation* of the decision maker.

Predefined Guidance

A guidance mechanism is referred to as "predefined" when the system designer prepares a set of recommendations or informational displays and embeds these directly into the system. The suggestions and information might be based upon the designer's own preferences, upon preferences of the client who commissioned the system, or upon normative views of experts and others who have studied the problem. For instance, given several options for graphing historical sales data, a designer might recommend a graph he or she finds especially useful, a graph the client is known to prefer, or a graph consistent with research findings on information display. Whatever his or her rationale, the designer has predefined the substantive content of the guidance. The help screens found in many systems today, for example, are mechanisms that typically function in this mode (although the guidance they offer is more mechanical than decisional).

Predefining the content of guidance does not necessarily mean that the same recommendations and information are always given. To be meaningful, guidance is likely to depend upon the context in which it is offered. After all, if a system provides meaningful assistance to users deciding what to do next, that assistance must reflect what they have done already. Similarly, if a DSS is to provide meaningful assistance to users responding to questions, that assistance needs to reflect how they have responded to previous questions. Consequently, the designer may need to anticipate the various contexts that may occur, prepare guidance for each, and create a mechanism that displays the appropriate predefined message in each context. Taken narrowly, context might be defined by the set of options the user confronts; taken broadly, context would include the path the user traversed through the system to reach this set of options. In this case the mechanism must track user behavior to determine the context and display the appropriate guidance.

Consider a simple example, a DSS organized by a main menu containing several operators. After an operator is executed, the user is always returned to the same main menu. Designers might predefine context-sensitive guidance that suggests which operator to use next, given which one was used last. Designers might predefine guidance that encourages users to try each operator, a different one on each iteration. Or they might predefine guidance that suggests running the same operator repeatedly, systematically varying its inputs.

Just as contextual information may be needed to determine which predefined guidance to present, some interaction with the user may be required to resolve which suggestions to make or information to display. The designer may embed logic in the guidance mechanism that asks the user key questions and then, based on the user's responses, determines and presents the appropriate guidance.

We have already seen examples of such guidance mechanisms. Lee, Hurst, and Lee's (1985) 3G-MCDSS asked users as many as 13 questions as the basis for suggesting a multi-objective method. Wedley and Field's (1984) Predecision Support System asked users as many as 10 questions to derive suggested styles, methods, and participants. In each system, designers predefined the logic that determined what would be suggested. But this logic required responses from the users.

Dynamic Guidance

By constructing adaptive mechanisms that "learn" as the system is used, designers can build decisional guidance into a DSS without predefining the content of that guidance. The suggestions offered and information displayed are generated by the mechanism dynamically, not by the designer in advance. A number of approaches have been proposed for developing these "dynamic" guidance mechanisms:

Fjelstad and Konsynski (1986) describe the "Spreadsheet Manager" to illustrate how cognitive responsibilities can be "reapportioned" from the user to the system. Among its capabilities the system assists users in selecting appropriate spreadsheet models or templates by guiding them through a structured query. To users, this guidance appears much the same as that offered by the 3G-MCDSS and the Predecision Support System. A distinctive feature of the Spreadsheet Manager, however, is that the knowledge base underlying the content of the guidance is not predefined by the designer, but is constructed dynamically by the system as its resources evolve—that is, as new spreadsheets are added to the model base or as existing spreadsheets are applied by users to new problems.

Liang and Jones (1987) propose a design for a self-evolving DSS, where the system records and analyzes user behavior to reset default policies and default values automatically in a way that optimizes some performance measure. In their example the system tracks whether decision makers use sensitivity analysis and which visual representation (bar chart, line chart, or table) they prefer. Based on the objective of minimizing expected user effort, the system derives default policies for these two options.

Liang and Jones's approach, intended to manage system defaults, can be applied to generating decisional guidance dynamically. The system can track user selections but, instead of resetting defaults, it can suggest that users select what they have selected most recently or most often. Or the system might recommend the option selected most often by some other user or by the full set of users. In contrast, the DSS might recommend an option the user systematically overlooks. If the DSS were also equipped with an ability to track outcomes, it might recommend the options that have been associated with the best performance in the past. As an alternative to these kinds of suggestive guidance, a DSS might analyze system use and display the analysis, without a recommendation, as informative guidance.

Manheim (1988) uses the term "active" systems to refer to DSS that provide decision makers with support independent of explicit user direction. He calls the subset of these systems that maintain a model of the user's cognitive processes to engage in a user–machine partnership "symbiotic" systems. His architecture for building symbiotic systems includes components for both user-directed and computer-directed information processing.

We can regard DSS with decisional guidance capabilities as a special, perhaps limited, case of active systems. More importantly, components of the symbiotic architecture can be useful for generating and delivering guidance. In a symbiotic DSS, a "history recorder" tracks all processing, noting, in particular, which input data generated which outputs. Based on a schematic model of human problem-working processes, a "history inference processor" maintains an up-to-date representation of the user's image of the problem. In terms of the architecture this representation is the basis for directing the computer to process information without explicit human involvement. But the recorder and inference processor also seem ideal for generating informative and suggestive guidance. Indeed, Manheim notes that the architecture can "provide information potentially useful to the user" (p. 363) and "make suggestions to the user about things she should consider doing" (p. 361).

Participative Guidance

Both predefined and dynamic mechanisms generate guidance with little direct input from, and no direct control by, the user. But designers can devise guidance mechanisms where users participate heavily in determining the content of the guidance they receive. These "participative" guidance mechanisms facilitate users' deriving their own recommendations or defining for themselves the information they need.

Suggestive guidance for meta-choice offers a good illustration. Consider a decision maker choosing among operators that can substitute one for another in terms of the functions they perform in a decision-making process. Perhaps these are choice rules, forecasting techniques, or solution generators. DSS can support the decision maker's meta-choice by providing a list of these operators and their associated properties. For instance, Kleindorfer, Kunreuther, and Schoemaker (1991) suggest that in different situations, different "legitimation criteria" are appropriate for justifying the choice of a problem-solving technique. In some situations optimality may be the dominant or only criterion, whereas in others understandability, defendability, simplicity, and accuracy may play important roles. Moreover, different problem-solving techniques may be justified by different

TABLE 5.3   An example of using legitimation criteria in decisional guidance

Operators	Legitimation Criteria				
	Optimality	Understandability	Defendability	Simplicity	Accuracy
Operator "A"	5	3	7	3	4
Operator "B"	4	3	8	8	6
Operator "C"	9	5	3	4	6
Operator "D"	8	8	8	2	7

Note: In the example, "A," "B," "C," and "D" are the names of the DSS's operators. In an actual DSS these might be "Multi-Attribute Utility," "Elimination by Aspects," "Lexicographic Sort," "LP Solver," "Regress," "Project," and so forth. The numbers in the cells rate each operator with respect to each criterion. In this example, the scale is from 0 to 10.

legitimation criteria. A linear program might rate high when judged in terms of optimality and accuracy, but not in terms of understandability and simplicity. A table, such as Table 5.3, that rates the problem-solving techniques with respect to legitimation criteria, could therefore guide decision makers.

By itself the table offers predefined, informative guidance. But if functions are added that empower users to manipulate the table, rank ordering the techniques or selecting one of them, the enhanced table becomes a participative, suggestive guidance mechanism. Compare it with predefined, suggestive guidance; the balance of responsibility for generating suggestions has shifted from the designer to the user. In the 3G-MCDSS and the Predecision Support System, the logic underlying the suggestions was predefined by the designers, with answers to some questions provided by the user; here, the designer provides some functionality and basic information, but the user determines how it is applied to generate suggestions. The balance can be shifted still further by increasing the user's participation in defining the table (being able to add techniques, add legitimation criteria, or change ratings).

Remarks

Some concluding comments motivated by the three modes of guidance are in order. First, since guidance frequently must be context-sensitive to be meaningful, even predefined guidance mechanisms can become quite complex. Second, although designers build the guidance mechanisms, they do not necessarily define the substantive content of the guidance the user receives—that is, the specific suggestions or information—since this may be generated dynamically or participatively. And lastly, guidance need not be a message or display that the system simply hands to the user; it may follow from active user participation.

Scope of Guidance: Short versus Long Range

The scope of decisional guidance can be either short or long range. Short-range guidance assists users with the choice they are confronting now: what to do next or how to respond to the question at hand. Long-range guidance supports a series of judgments, a larger portion of the decision-making process. The distinction is most important with respect to structuring decision-making processes, where users may want to structure the complete process, not just part of it. Structuring the process, therefore, is the case I shall concentrate upon here.

Most of the deliberate guidance we find today, mechanical or decisional, provides short-range assistance. Simple menus and context-dependent help facilities usually offer information concerning only the immediate choice of operators confronted by the decision maker. Look-ahead menus, which show users the options that follow from each current option, have slightly greater scope. In addition to enlightening the current choice by providing a glimpse of what might follow, they enable users to plan two steps of the decision-making process at once.

True long-range guidance would consider many steps together, helping users structure a significant portion of their decision-making process.

Long-range guidance is potentially more complex and more valuable than short-range, which provides only myopic support for meta-choice. Decision makers relying on short-range guidance must construct their decision-making processes as they proceed, since the guidance helps only with the immediate selection. But long-range guidance supports decision makers who wish first to create a plan of attack and then to pursue it. This approach is especially important when a DSS includes many operators, some of which are substitutes one for another and others of which are complements. By planning ahead, users can ensure that the operators they select are compatible and consistent throughout the process. Decision makers who plan their activities in advance are also more likely to understand the decision-making processes they follow and be able to replicate or defend them, if necessary.

Consider a DSS that includes several means of generating alternative solutions and several choice rules for selecting among alternatives. Suppose some alternative generators are not compatible with some choice rules, and suppose further that the decision maker prefers a given rule. By planning ahead, with the assistance of long-range guidance, the decision maker can be sure to use an alternative generator compatible with the desired choice rule.

Long-range guidance can play a special role in systems containing many low-level operators. Since decision makers may require significant technical or conceptual knowledge to piece the low-level operators together to perform higher-level functions, long-range guidance can provide the necessary information—and even some suggestions—for combining a sequence of low-level functions effectively.

Short- and long-range guidance can complement one another. A user might employ long-range guidance to develop a general plan of attack, relying on short-range guidance to decide exactly which operators to use at any given moment. Since the results of some information-processing activities may influence how a decision maker proceeds, even if long-range guidance was used to plan a detailed process, a decision maker may use short-range guidance to make minor changes in the plan.

Summary

In this section I presented a four-dimensional typology of how designers can build guidance into a system. Taken together, the targets (structuring and executing the process), forms (suggestions and information), modes (predefined, dynamic, and participative), and scopes (short and long range) define two dozen types of guidance. Note that although I presented numerous illustrations of these types of decisional guidance, the set of examples was a mixture of hypothetical features and prototype systems. An important research task that follows naturally from the foregoing analysis, therefore, is to develop (and test) guidance mechanisms of the various types. For designers the mechanisms may be useful candidates for inclusion in their systems; and for researchers the mechanisms represent tangible artifacts that can be studied.

In contrast with the individualistic, haphazard style of the past, we must now approach development systematically. The typology can organize our efforts. Moreover, given so many varieties of decisional guidance, we must also engage in a systematic program of examining the behavioral consequences of each type of guidance, understanding the effects they have on decision-making behavior and their effectiveness at accomplishing design objectives. In particular, we are interested in studying if and when a designer should consider building each type of guidance into a DSS. I will return to these topics shortly.

DELIBERATE DECISIONAL GUIDANCE AND DSS COMPONENTS

I have described how DSS can deliberately guide, but I have not identified the DSS components responsible for doing so. In Chapter 4 we found that three of the four components constituting the generic user view (operators, sequencing rules, and adaptors) determine a system's restrictiveness. All four components bear on decisional guidance. Since their roles depend upon whether guidance is aimed at structuring or executing the decision-making process (see Table 5.4), I will consider separately guidance for each of these targets. Thereafter, I will discuss how guidance is invoked, an issue common to both cases.

Structuring the Process

Navigational aids, the only DSS components not influencing restrictiveness, have primary responsibility for providing the guidance that supports meta-choice. This guidance for structuring the decision-making process is often a matter of helping users choose which *operators* to use.* Given the operators available in a given context, the navigational aids either offer suggestions or provide pertinent

TABLE 5.4   Deliberate decisional guidance and DSS components

Component	Guidance for structuring the decision-making process	Guidance for executing the decision-making process
Operators		***
Navigational aids	***	
Sequencing rules	***	
Adaptors	***	***

---

*Short-range navigational aids help users choose the next operator; longer-range aids might help choose a sequence of operators. Navigational aids can also help with the more general task of choosing an approach to solving the problem.

information for selecting among the operators. The operators themselves do not play a role in guiding; their selection is what is being guided.

Recall the important role that *sequencing rules* play in determining restrictiveness. The sequencing rules limit users by specifying which of the system's operators are available at any juncture in the decision-making process. Highly constraining sequencing rules, therefore, can obviate including navigational aids in a DSS, since users have few or no navigational choices.

From a design perspective one might be tempted to conclude that sequencing rules compete with navigational aids, since, at any point in the process, use of a given operator can be imposed by sequencing rules or suggested by navigational aids, but not both. But this is not the essence of the relationship. Although sequencing rules do constrain navigational aids, the two must function cooperatively in a well-designed system.

By limiting decision makers' options, strong sequencing rules can facilitate meaningful guidance. Creating navigational aids that offer worthwhile suggestions and information is much more difficult in systems with trivial rule sets, where users have a plethora of options, than in those where users choose among few alternative operators.

More importantly, sequencing rules specify when a given navigational aid is active. Just as sequencing rules define when operators are available, they also define when navigational aids are operative.* Since decisional guidance is context-dependent, each navigational aid may apply only to specific contexts, and the sequencing rules are responsible for ensuring that, in a given context, the correct navigational aids are available to decision makers. Managing the availability of the numerous navigational aids needed to offer substantial decisional guidance is a demanding chore.

Adaptors can also play a role in implementing guidance for meta-choice. Users can invoke the appropriate adaptive capabilities, if provided by the builders, to change the content of existing navigational aids or to create their own. If a DSS is being used by many people, for example, one of them may use an adaptor to provide guidance for the others.

Executing the Process

While guidance for structuring the decision-making process supports choosing among multiple operators, guidance for executing the process helps decision makers use the individual operators. Guidance for the predictive and evaluative judgments required by a DSS's *operators* can therefore be embedded within those operators.

---

*These two responsibilities of sequencing rules go together, since navigational aids support the choice among operators. The context defines both which operators are available and which navigational aids should be active.

Each operator is equipped with whatever guidance is to be offered for the judgmental inputs it accepts. *Navigational aids* and *sequencing rules* are not involved in this kind of guidance.

Adaptors can play the same role here as in the case of meta-choice. If builders provide the appropriate adaptive capabilities, users can change the definitions of operators to add to or alter the decisional guidance they offer.

Invoking Guidance

Deliberate guidance can be invoked two ways: users can request it explicitly, or DSS can provide it automatically. Either way, the sequencing rules manage the invocation of navigational aids, and the operators themselves handle the guidance they provide.

In general, guidance mechanisms are not inherently suited for one form of invocation or the other. Designers must choose in which situations they wish to use each approach. Some guidance, however, is most effective when invoked automatically. For example, status lines, maintained constantly on the display screen, provide pertinent information without users needing to ask for it. Similarly, warnings automatically caution users when dangerous or undesirable conditions occur.

Some systems contain (software) switches that change the method of invocation back and forth. Such switches might be controlled by the users themselves or might be accessible only by the DSS builders.

Giving users control of the switch recognizes that they may differ in terms of their preferences for guidance. Some users may always prefer to receive guidance automatically, some may always prefer to request it explicitly, and others may have preferences that vary with respect to the context or that change over time. For instance, some new users might prefer automatic guidance, but once they become more experienced they may want to turn the automatic feature off. In contrast, some users might prefer to explore a system first without being influenced by guidance and then to see how their processes and results would differ in light of the guidance the system provides.

When DSS builders control the switch, they can give different users different amounts of automatic guidance. For a given user, the switch lets builders adapt the system over time in response to changing circumstances.

System defaults, actions that are taken or values that are employed when users do not specify their own, can be seen as a special case of decisional guidance. Defaults represent suggestions rather than pertinent information; they are typically displayed automatically without users requesting them explicitly. In fact, some systems take the default actions or values without even notifying decision makers what those defaults are or that they are being used; many systems do give decision makers the option of using the defaults or providing alternatives.

AN ILLUSTRATION

In this section I describe a hypothetical DSS, HYPE, which illustrates many of the concepts discussed earlier in the chapter.* The system supports multi-attribute decision-making problems where users can supply their own data matrix consisting of as many as 200 alternatives and 15 attributes.

HYPE explicitly supports four techniques for solving multi-attribute problems:

- multi-attribute utility theory,
- conjunctive elimination,
- disjunctive elimination, and
- direct screening (elimination) by the user.

Each technique is implemented as a user-selectable operator, which can be used individually and, subject to some restrictions, in combination with the other operators. Users can apply these operators, together with additional operators that sort and display the data, to implement such solution techniques not offered by HYPE as the elimination by aspects process and various lexicographic rules.

HYPE is organized around the data matrix, which contains the alternatives and their attribute values. The rows are the alternatives; the columns are the attributes. All the major functions operate on the data matrix, transforming or displaying it in some way:

- The sort capability provides a multi-keyed sort of the alternatives (rows) based on the columns, including the original attributes plus any new fields defined by users. Lexicographic decision rules can be implemented by using the sort capability together with visual inspection of the results.
- The multi-attribute utility technique creates an additional column containing the score (utility) for each attribute. The sort capability can then be used to sort the alternatives with respect to the scores.
- Each elimination method–conjunction, disjunction, and direct screening— tags those alternatives (rows) that it eliminates. The display operators let users see the alternatives that remain, based either on a single method or on the combined effects of more than one elimination method. Operators can also be invoked that reinstate the alternatives eliminated by each method. The elimination by aspects process can be implemented by using conjunctive elimination repeatedly.
- Display operators allow users to see alternatives in original or sorted order and to see the full set of alternatives or those that remain after eliminations have been performed.

---

*The Multi-Attribute Software System (MASS) developed as a teaching tool at the Wharton School of the University of Pennsylvania implements many of the functional capabilities described here, but does not include very much of the decisional guidance, the focus of this example.

HYPE offers decisional guidance for formulating a problem-solving approach from these capabilities, as well as for executing some of the four basic techniques.

Structuring the Process

Guidance for structuring the process helps users to select among the basic techniques and, if desired, to combine them. HYPE offers both informative and suggestive guidance for these activities.

Informative Guidance

HYPE maintains a status line, which the user can switch on or off, at the bottom of the display screen. The status line, shown in Figure 5.3, keeps track of the methods that the decision maker has employed. An asterisk indicates that a given technique was used and a double asterisk identifies the most recently used method. For the elimination techniques the number of alternatives eliminated is shown in parentheses. If the data matrix has been sorted, the sort keys (identified by column numbers) are also indicated.

HYPE automatically generates warning messages when users attempt to combine methods in ways that may lead to inconsistent or confusing results. Warnings are generated when users attempt to mix compensatory and non-compensatory methods, to combine conjunctive and disjunctive eliminations, to sort on columns whose values are not independent, or to perform the same type of elimination repeatedly without first reinstating the eliminated alternatives. Although each of these actions might constitute deliberate behavior by the user, HYPE warns users of the potential problems that can be encountered. Users have the power to turn the warning facility off.

HYPE also provides an index of additional informative guidance from which users can choose. The index includes the following items:

- a description of each technique, including its advantages, disadvantages, and decisional properties;
- a snapshot of the most recent use of each technique, including the decision it produced and whether it was used in combination with other methods;

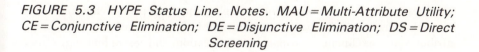

| MAU: * | CE: * (88) | DE: | DS: ** (7) | Sort Keys: 5 3 8 |

FIGURE 5.3 HYPE Status Line. Notes. MAU = Multi-Attribute Utility; CE = Conjunctive Elimination; DE = Disjunctive Elimination; DS = Direct Screening

- a comparison of the four basic techniques in terms of their decisional properties such as compensatory/non-compensatory; and
- recommendations for how the techniques can be applied and combined, including information on how the sort capability can be used to support various lexicographic rules, how conjunctive elimination can be used iteratively to support elimination by aspects, and how one might want to combine elimination and scoring methods first to eliminate some alternatives and then to score the remaining ones.

Suggestive Guidance

HYPE offers three types of suggestive guidance. The first guidance mechanism enters into a dialog with the decision maker, requesting information about the nature of the problem and his or her preferences for solving it. Based on (1) this information, (2) the decisional properties of the operators, and (3) if–then rules predefined by the system builder, HYPE generates one or more suggested approaches for solving the problem. The recommended approaches may be either single techniques or combinations of basic methods. This guidance capability must be explicitly invoked by the user.

HYPE's second suggestive guidance mechanism makes recommendations based on previous use of the system. By tracking all system activity, HYPE suggests the single most popular technique as well as the most popular combination of techniques. This form of guidance must also be requested explicitly.

A third suggestive guidance mechanism enables HYPE, in some contexts, to recommend automatically what the user should do next. For instance, after multi-attribute utility is used to create new columns containing composite scores for the alternatives, HYPE recommends sorting the data matrix on the new column. Similarly, after an elimination is performed, HYPE recommends displaying the set of alternatives that remain based on the most recent elimination. This guidance helps decision makers make better use of the basic system functions.

Executing the Process

HYPE embeds within several of its operators guidance for executing these operators. For instance, the multi-attribute utility operator includes guidance based on research in computer-based support for probability encoding and preference elicitation. Here, I will describe the support offered for the conjunctive elimination process.

The conjunctive elimination operator excludes any alternative not satisfying all the criteria set by the user, where a criterion is defined as an allowable range of values for a given attribute. For example, suppose a person choosing a city in which to live has a database containing 100 U.S. cities, each city rated on 10 attributes such as climate, transportation, education, and cost of housing. A user might require that a city have a score greater than 700 for climate and a rating less than 1200 for housing costs. So users of this operator must judge which attributes matter and, for each that does, which range of values is acceptable. Correspondingly, HYPE offers two types of decisional guidance: guidance for choosing attributes and guidance for defining acceptable ranges.

Choosing Attributes

The guidance HYPE offers for choosing attributes is of the informative variety and is provided at the request of the user. HYPE displays (textual) descriptions of the attributes, so decision makers can better judge which ones are of most importance to them. HYPE also reminds users of which attributes they selected, as well as the results that ensued, when they employed conjunctive elimination most recently. In addition, HYPE displays statistical analyses of the data matrix. Examining how the alternatives are distributed with respect to each attribute can help decision makers determine which attributes discriminate well among the alternatives. Studying the correlations among attributes can help decision makers choose one attribute in place of another.

Because HYPE is designed as a general-purpose system, which can function with many different datasets, it does not include suggestive guidance that recommends which attributes to use. A DSS that has knowledge of the attributes might engage users in a dialog to elicit the factors of importance to them and suggest which attributes most reflect their objectives.*

Setting Acceptable Ranges

Although its purpose is different, much of the guidance for selecting acceptable ranges of values is similar in content to the guidance for choosing attributes. For instance, HYPE also provides here a (textual) description of the attribute. Since each attribute is measured with respect to its own unique scale, an important component of the description is a detailed explanation of how the scale was derived and how it should be interpreted.

Here, too, HYPE provides a statistical summary of the distribution of alternatives with respect to the attribute. Such statistics as the low value, high value, median, 1st and 3rd quartiles, and mean are all potential endpoints for the range of acceptable values. For example, if the decision maker chooses all alternatives above the median value, he or she knows that half of the alternatives have been selected. Moreover, looking at the distribution of

---

*That HYPE displays descriptions of the attributes might suggest that it has knowledge about them. But this informative guidance mechanism simply displays on the screen predefined blocks of text that accompany the dataset. Suggesting which attributes to use would require significantly greater knowledge of the attributes.

alternatives with respect to the attribute may show natural break points in the data.

HYPE also enables decision makers to retrieve the attribute values for selected alternatives from the data matrix. For instance, a user might request the climate ratings for San Diego or Chicago. Decision makers familiar with some of the alternatives in the data matrix can use this capability to get a better feel for interpreting the attribute values. Furthermore, the retrieved values may serve as useful benchmarks for defining the range of acceptable values. A decision maker might specify only cities whose recreation score exceeds that of Boston.

PROVIDING DECISIONAL GUIDANCE: WHEN AND WHY

What do we know today about whether a system's designer should build decisional guidance into a DSS? Let us consider the opportunities, the motives, and the means for doing so.

Opportunity: Are there Significant Occasions for Providing Guidance?

A prerequisite for providing decisional guidance is having the *opportunity* to do so. Since restrictiveness constrains decision makers' discretionary power, it limits the occasions on which their judgment is called for, thereby limiting the opportunities for providing them with guidance. As shown earlier, in Figure 5.1, very restrictive DSS do not leave much room for decisional guidance. If a system supports few decision-making processes, then the opportunities for guiding meta-choice are minimal. If a system's operators require few judgmental inputs from their users, then the occasions for guiding predictive and evaluative judgment are limited. A prerequisite for meaningful guidance, therefore, is a reasonable amount of discretionary freedom.

Designers can treat the relationship between restrictiveness and guidance in two ways. The first way is as a sequential design process, where the builder initially determines how a DSS will constrain decision-making behavior and subsequently determines how much guidance will be provided within those confines. The second way determines restrictiveness and guidance jointly, with the designer choosing, for each judgmental opportunity, whether to restrict the decision-making process, to guide it, or to do neither.

Of the two, the sequential approach may be easier to follow, but the joint analysis is more advisable; as I discuss in Chapter 6, design trade-offs must be made between the two attributes. Moreover, considering restrictiveness independently of guidance is problematic; although guidance does not affect absolute restrictiveness, it can affect perceived restrictiveness. Increasing a system's guidance—informative or suggestive—can make the system easier to use, reducing its perceived restrictiveness for some users. To take account of this connection, the two design decisions are best considered together.

Motive: Why Should a System Guide?

Given the opportunity, what are the reasons for or against trying to provide decisional guidance? One can easily identify two sets of issues that affect the desirability of providing guidance: concerns about supporting decision makers and concerns about influencing decision makers. Each set of concerns can create a significant *motive* for providing decisional guidance but can also bring forth reasons for not doing so.

Supporting Decision Makers

One motive for providing decisional guidance is to build a more supportive DSS, one that helps users exercise judgment as they interact with the system and confront its complexities. As the frequency, complexity, and importance of the judgments demanded from them increase, decision makers may require—or, at least, desire—computer-based facilities that provide meta-support for the judgments they must make. The greater the needs of decision makers for this added support, the greater the motivation for providing guidance.

The need for decisional guidance is a function of both the system and its users. In general, the more complex a DSS and the less structured its users' perceptions of the decision-making task, the greater the need for guidance. More specifically, we can hypothesize that a number of factors contribute to the need:

- Some users require guidance more than others. Novices at making a given type of decision require more guidance than those who have confronted similar decisions many times in the past. Infrequent users of a DSS require more guidance than frequent users.
- The greater the degree of structure either inherent in the task or perceived by the decision maker, the less the required guidance. In particular:
  1. organizational environments that promote standard solution techniques need less structural guidance from their DSS;
  2. environments with well-defined objectives need less assistance in performing evaluative judgments;
  3. organizations facing less uncertainty and risk need less guidance for making predictive judgments.
- Systems composed of many high-level operators have different needs for guidance than those with predominantly low-level primitives. When a system has many high-level operators, the need for guidance is to help choose among competing solution techniques or among alternative methods of processing information. In contrast, when most operators are low-level primitives, guidance is needed to enable decision makers to piece these operators together to form an appropriate decision-making process.

While motivated by the objective of supporting decision makers better, decisional guidance may sometimes have the opposite effect. For example, decisional guidance might overload users with information, making the task of using the system more time-consuming and more difficult. Similarly, the guidance mechanisms may themselves make the system more complex, hence more difficult to learn and operate.

Influencing Decision Makers

The desire to influence users' decision-making behavior can motivate designers to provide decisional guidance, as when a system is intended to be an agent for directed change. While such a system allows its users the freedom to do as they please, the guidance can serve as a vehicle for encouraging given behavior. The objective might not be to point decision makers toward specific decisions, but only to influence the way they behave en route to reaching a decision. For instance, Elam and Mead (1987) suggest that a DSS whose purpose is to enhance creativity should provide feedback with ''depth and positive tenor'' to encourage prolonged alternative generation and delayed judgment. Such feedback could be in the form of decisional guidance.

We can hypothesize that many of the reasons for influencing decision makers through guidance are the same as those for building more restrictive DSS:

- to prescribe a given process or approach,
- to proscribe a given process or approach, or
- to foster structured learning.

Indeed, any decision-making process that can be imposed on users via a restrictive DSS might, instead, be recommended to decision makers by way of decisional guidance. For instance, to cause decision makers to refine their budget projections to bring deficits immediately into balance, the budget balancing operator could be the only one suggested after a deficit is projected.

I noted in Chapter 4 that debiasing decision makers is one reason for proscribing decisional behavior through restrictiveness. Just as restrictiveness might be used to reduce or eliminate decision makers' systematic cognitive biases, so too, might decisional guidance. Since many cognitive biases stem from decision makers' paying insufficient attention to critical information—for instance, their insensitivity to base rates—informative guidance might debias by confronting decision makers with the critical information they tend to bypass. And since biases may follow from such presentation effects as the order in which decision makers receive information, a DSS might warn users about the possible impacts of the sequence in which information is presented (Mason and Moskowitz, 1972). Similarly, informational messages could be displayed that caution users against falling into such other traps as the gambler's or sunk-cost fallacies.

Suggestive guidance might also be used for debiasing. For instance, decision makers often violate Bayesian Decision Theory by failing to consider prior probabilities when processing conditional probabilities.* But some systems have the information necessary to perform the Bayesian analysis themselves, and can then offer the resulting values as suggestions, thus reducing the likelihood of biased responses from the users.

That decisional guidance might influence decision makers' behavior is also a reason for excluding it from a system. If a system's objective is not to influence behavior, then fear of inadvertently biasing decision makers or unintentionally reducing their freedom might argue against providing decisional guidance.

Means: Can Decisional Guidance be Accomplished?

Given opportunity and motive, providing decisional guidance also depends on having the *means* to do so. Building decisional guidance into a DSS is much more difficult than providing mechanical guidance. Ironically, those systems offering the greatest opportunity and motivation are often the ones for which presenting meaningful guidance is the most problematic. For instance, in situations where DSS users are unclear how to proceed and need decisional guidance, DSS designers may be equally unclear how to guide them. Designers may find that incorporating many functional capabilities into a system is much easier than guiding a decision maker concerning their use.

Much of the difficulty follows from trying to provide guidance, especially suggestive guidance, that is both context-sensitive and of high quality. A complex, minimally restrictive DSS allowing its users to follow many paths and to choose among numerous options in arriving at a decision might present an excellent opportunity for decisional guidance, but the number of distinct contexts requiring support is vast. Imagine trying to anticipate so many different situations and produce well-suited guidance for each.

Finding a means to provide highly context-sensitive guidance is a formidable challenge for system builders. What modes are most likely to succeed? Having builders predefine guidance might be acceptable for simple systems or if only a limited number of contexts are to be supported, but it is at best an arduous task to provide such support throughout large or complex systems. Constructing participative mechanisms where users play a major role in defining their own guidance would be less difficult, but, by itself, how valuable would such guidance be? The most promising approach is to draw upon techniques from artificial intelligence to promote system learning as the basis for developing guidance dynamically as the DSS is used. The research by Fjelstad and Konsynski (1986), Liang and Jones (1987), and

---

*See Wright (1983) and Schocken (1985) for proposed computer-based methods for offsetting biases related to Bayesian analysis.

Manheim (1988), all cited earlier in this chapter, represent initiatives in this direction. Considerably more research is required to solve this problem.

Creating the content of the decisional guidance is only part of the problem. Means must also be constructed for delivering that guidance to the user. Although creating the guidance may be the more difficult task, tracking user behavior and ensuring that context-sensitive messages are presented at the correct junctures in the process are also non-trivial endeavors. Here, too, building intelligent mechanisms into the DSS could be advantageous.

For many systems today, providing meaningful decisional guidance may not be feasible because our knowledge of the means for constructing and delivering such guidance is limited. The prototype systems I have discussed, however, represent significant steps toward overcoming these barriers. As needed research proceeds on both the development and delivery fronts, the range of systems for which we are able to provide guidance should expand.

Summary

The foregoing analysis, outlined in Table 5.5, suggests that not all systems may be candidates for decisional guidance. Very simple or very restrictive systems may not present opportunities for offering decision makers meaningful guidance, whereas very complex systems may not be feasible for including guidance. Between these extremes, however, we find a significant middle range of systems for which decisional guidance might be appropriate. We need to understand better whether or not it should be provided in a given situation. Among the more prominent research questions are the following:

- When are decision makers' needs for guidance greatest? How great is the risk of degrading support by overwhelming users with too much guidance?
- When should a DSS designer act as an agent for directed change, using decisional guidance to influence the decision maker?
- When is it best to accomplish design objectives by restricting decision makers, by guiding them, or by doing neither?
- Given the difficulty of providing guidance, when does the cost of providing guidance exceed the benefits?

Some of these questions are ready for immediate investigation, but most depend on another set of research issues:

- What are the effects of decisional guidance, both inadvertent and deliberate, on decision-making behavior? How effective is deliberate guidance at accomplishing its objectives?

TABLE 5.5   Requirements for providing decisional guidance

Opportunity: Are there significant occasions for providing decisional guidance?

Motive: Why should a system guide?
   Supporting decision makers
   Influencing decision makers

Means: Can decisional guidance be accomplished?
   Creating guidance
   Delivering guidance

Clearly, the consequences of deliberate guidance are relevant for deciding whether to build decisional guidance into a system. But the effects of inadvertent guidance matter too. All DSS likely manifest some decisional guidance, since if they do not guide explicitly, they probably do so inadvertently. So deciding whether or not to provide guidance is essentially a choice between (1) guiding deliberately and (2) accepting the consequences of inadvertent guidance. Indeed, trying to offset inadvertent guidance effects may be the reason for choosing to guide deliberately.

THE EFFECTS AND EFFECTIVENESS OF DECISIONAL GUIDANCE

The effects of deliberate and inadvertent guidance must each be studied differently. For deliberate guidance, one focuses on the mechanisms designed specifically to guide. For inadvertent guidance, one looks at everything else—the functional capabilities, the interfaces to them, and how they are packaged—to see how users might be swayed unintentionally. In both cases, however, the studies are likely to draw heavily on findings about the limitations of human information-processing capabilities that lead to systematic biases in how people acquire and process information.

Inadvertent Guidance

Do DSS really guide inadvertently? If a system's features—say, its interface or its functional capabilities—foster systematic cognitive biases in their users, then those features may be responsible for the system inadvertently swaying its users' judgments. For example, not only might the order effects of menu items bias users' selections, but the common practice of highlighting the item chosen the last time a menu appeared may reinforce people's heuristic bias to rely on habit in decision making. Given the numerous cognitive biases reported in the literature—Sage's (1981) survey identifies no fewer than 27—empirical research is needed to study if and how DSS inadvertently sway decision makers.

Studying the inadvertent effects of DSS on users' judgmental inputs has significant implications for DSS design. If DSS designers understand how and when such guidance can occur, they can take steps to avoid the unintended consequences, perhaps by offsetting them with deliberate guidance. And, of course, studying the inadvertent effects is also central to understanding how DSS affect decision-making behavior. Were we to concentrate only on systems' intended consequences, we might misunderstand their impacts on decision-making performance.

Deliberate Guidance

Turning to deliberate guidance, we begin by asking what, if any, are the *effects* of deliberate guidance on decision-making behavior? How does decisional guidance affect the way people use the system and the way they make decisions? What are the consequences of providing decisional guidance? Are they positive, negative, or neutral, as seen from the perspectives of the decision maker, the system designer, and the organization? More specifically, consider the following research questions:

- When do decision makers find decisional guidance useful and when do they find it bothersome?
- When decision makers say they find decisional guidance useful, how do they use it? Does the guidance affect the operators they select, the responses they enter?
- How do decision makers process the information provided by informative guidance? How do they react to the recommendations made by suggestive guidance?
- Does decisional guidance affect how much time the decision maker spends using a system? Does guidance make a system easier to use? Does increased ease of use translate into increased frequency of use?
- When and how does decisional guidance bias decision makers? When are such biases desirable and when are they deleterious?
- And the bottom line: when does decisional guidance improve decision-making performance and when does it degrade it?

These questions require empirical investigation, but from existing studies of cognitive biases one can construct *a priori* arguments suggesting both positive and negative consequences of deliberate guidance. On the one hand, a guidance mechanism might foster cognitive biases, in which case the effect of the guidance would be to bias users' judgments systematically. On the other hand, a guidance mechanism might debias—that is, it might reduce or eliminate the effects of systematic biases—in which case the guidance leads to less biased judgments. Consider a few examples (see Hogarth (1980) for a review of the relevant studies):

- Informative guidance may present decision makers with information, in a unified and readily accessible form, for which they would otherwise have to search sequentially. Such guidance might reduce the "availability," "selective perception," and "confirmation" biases that lead to decision makers not acquiring or not weighting appropriately all relevant information. But the guidance might promote other biases that follow from order effects in the presentation of the information, from the mixing of quantitative and qualitative data, or from decision makers relying too greatly on the guidance to the exclusion of other relevant information.

- Decision makers who are asked to predict a series of values, say the Dow-Jones closing average for each of the next 10 weeks, often do so by beginning with a given point—an anchor—and adjusting it to create the remaining elements of the series. When using this "anchoring and adjustment" heuristic, decision makers often fail to adjust sufficiently; their predictions tend to be too close to the anchor. On the one hand, informative guidance might foster such biases by making such anchors (in the form of historical data) readily available. On the other hand, suggestive guidance might warn the decision maker of this bias and attempt to push him or her further from the anchor.
- Decision making is often strongly influenced by habit. If one time we make a decision in a given way and the results are acceptable, we may use the same approach repeatedly in the future, without studying whether this is in fact the best way to proceed. Providing guidance that simply reminds users of their selections on previous occasions, therefore, might foster such a bias. Providing users with more detailed analysis of, and feedback on, these decisions, however, might offset the bias of relying on habit.

Beyond answering questions about the full set of guidance's effects, we need to study the *effectiveness* of decisional guidance in achieving its objectives, such as being more supportive of decision makers or influencing their decision-making behavior. Does guidance succeed in accomplishing the objectives that motivate it? Does guidance cause negative side-effects that offset the benefits it produces? More specifically:

- How effective is each form of guidance at accomplishing each objective? We might expect that informative guidance would be most effective at supporting decision makers and suggestive guidance at influencing them. Is this so? Can carefully constructed informative guidance influence decision makers effectively? Can suggestive guidance make the DSS more effective at supporting decision makers?
- How effective is each mode of guidance (predefined, dynamic, and participative) at accomplishing each objective (supporting and influencing the decision maker)? Does mode interact with form of guidance (informative versus suggestive)? With target of guidance (structuring versus executing the decision-making process)?
- When do the costs of learning the guidance mechanisms exceed the benefits of using them?

These questions, too, require empirical investigation. The question of when to provide guidance, raised earlier, hinges on understanding the potential effects and effectiveness of guidance. And the development of successful guidance mechanisms relies on feedback from evaluating the performance of guidance mechanisms.

CONCLUSION

Today's DSS manifest relatively little of the deliberate decisional guidance I have discussed here. We find a few examples in prototype systems developed by researchers and even fewer cases in commercially available systems. And the DSS design literature pays relatively little attention to the issue of inadvertent decisional guidance. For DSS builders, therefore, decisional guidance represents a host of new design opportunities and a concomitant set of design issues. For researchers, the study of decisional guidance provides a coherent approach to a set of behavioral questions that are just now beginning to be addressed in a fragmented, technologically oriented manner.

Deliberately building decisional guidance into a DSS may overcome some of the obstacles to designing restrictiveness purposefully. One problem designers face is the difference between absolute and perceived restrictiveness; guidance can help reduce the gap by making systems easier to use, reducing perceived restrictiveness. Another difficulty is that a given DSS project may have several design objectives, each requiring a different level of restrictiveness; it may be that some of these competing objectives can be accomplished with guidance instead of restrictiveness, eliminating the conflict over restrictiveness. Indeed, the motives for providing guidance, influencing decision makers and being more supportive, line up well with many of the factors associated with restrictiveness. The relationship between decisional guidance and system restrictiveness is an important one. I shall say more about it in the next chapter, in the context of examining how DSS serve as agents for change.

Significant research is needed both in the behavioral aspects of decision making and the technological means for constructing guidance. Techniques from the field of artificial intelligence (AI), especially expert systems technology, should prove useful for providing guidance. Several of the prototype systems described here used embedded rule-based expert systems to generate suggestive guidance. Moreover, in discussing the requirements for guidance, the learning and inferencing techniques of AI were seen as important means for devising and delivering guidance. Indeed, advances in applying AI methods may be essential to providing meaningful guidance.

We have expended great effort during the past decade studying the individual functional capabilities that can support decision makers. Although more work still does need to be done in this area, the time has now come to devote attention to guiding decision makers in the use of these functional capabilities as well.

The more functional capabilities we develop for supporting decision makers, the more important it becomes to be able to choose among them.

I have presented many illustrations of decisional guidance from the recent DSS research literature. Some describe prototype systems; others describe concepts waiting to be implemented. Some are technology-driven ("How can I apply expert systems to DSS?"); others concentrate on a given problem domain. Only a few address the more general issue of supporting judgmental activities, without being limited to a specific technology or domain.

At first glance the various articles seem to have little in common. They use different terminology, cite different references, do not usually cite one another, and concentrate on different domains. Yet they have a great deal in common. They are all instances of deliberate decisional guidance, all attempts to provide meta-support for the various judgments that users of DSS are called upon to make. As technology advances further, we can expect to see even more research along these lines.

Each of these research efforts individually, and the field of computer-based decision support as a whole, would benefit from an integrated approach to addressing these issues. We could compare results, build a cumulative knowledge base of guidance techniques, and study the trade-offs among the various kinds of guidance. We could move more rapidly toward developing the means of creating and delivering meaningful, context-sensitive guidance. We could understand better how DSS affect decision making.

The study of decisional guidance as presented here *is* that integrated approach. It can unite the currently disparate research efforts. Guidance is not based upon a particular technology or focused upon a particular problem domain. It is oriented toward behavioral issues common to all DSS, namely, understanding the effects DSS can have on decision-making processes.

Chapter 6
CONCLUSION

In this final chapter I conclude some unfinished business. I begin by examining the implications of a central theme in much of the early Decision Support Systems literature, that DSS must be specific to the environments they support. One implication is that we must consider two additional system attributes—the precustomization and customizability of DSS. A second implication is that, when analyzing DSS, we must choose our frame of reference carefully, so we are clear which decision-making environment the system supports.

Once these concepts have been explored, I am prepared to "apply" the third descriptive tier. I do so in two ways. First, I use the system attributes to describe two existing systems: Lotus 1-2-3, an advanced electronic spreadsheet package, and the Electronic Workbook, a component of the College Board's Enrollment Planning Service. Second, I consider system restrictiveness and decisional guidance as design variables, analyzing the problem of how to construct DSS that serve as agents for directed or nondirected change. After analyzing three special classes of systems (Expert Systems, Executive Support Systems, and Group Decision Support Systems), I conclude by considering some further implications of this book for practitioners and researchers.

CUSTOMIZATION

A central concept in the research literature is that, to be successful, DSS must be tailored to the specific decision-making environments (the specific people, tasks, and settings) they support. The argument runs as follows: Environments are idiosyncratic, varying significantly in terms of the people who make the decisions, the decision-making tasks they confront, and the organizational settings within which they operate. Concomitant with differences in decision-making environments are differences in their needs for support. Most obviously, inherent differences in decision problems will lead to different information-processing requirements. Inventory management problems and merger/acquisition decisions, for instance, have significantly different support needs. Similarly, different individuals may approach the same problem in different ways. For example, one decision maker might choose among alternatives with a scoring method, while another might prefer a sequential elimination process. Finally, the organizational setting may influence the type of support needed. In some organizations, conforming with standard procedures might be the key criterion for choosing a decision-making strategy, whereas in others, political considerations might dominate. Given the great variance in needs, it is argued that systems truly supportive of decision makers will be responsive to the specifics of the environments they support.

The conventional interpretation of this claim is that the features of a DSS must be precustomized for the decision-making environment it will support. *Precustomization*, however, is only one way in which a system can be specialized to its environment. Another way is by designing a *customizable* system, one that allows its users to tailor it as needed to meet the needs of its environment.

These two approaches are not mutually exclusive; a DSS can be both precustomized and customizable. To see this, consider the possibilities for how users access data in a DSS. A system that provides access to predefined datasets is precustomized, but if users cannot change or augment those datasets, it is not customizable. And a system that allows users to create their own datasets is customizable, but if it provides no predefined data, it is not precustomized. A system would be both precustomized and customizable if it provides predefined datasets that users can modify and augment as needed.

In addition to data, various other features of DSS such as models, visual representations, and functional capabilities are subject to customization. For a given system, some of these might be precustomized (or customizable) and others might not. Moreover, a DSS might be precustomized with respect to some aspects of the environment (the people, tasks, or setting) but require further customization with respect to others. What matters, therefore, is not simply whether the system is precustomized, but how highly precustomized it is and how it is precustomized. Similarly, what matters is not simply whether the system is customizable but how highly customizable it is and how it is customizable.

Several factors suggest that DSS precustomization and customizability constitute two additional system attributes worthy of consideration: (1) that specialization is central to the notion of decision support, (2) that it is believed to affect a system's effectiveness, (3) that it is a characteristic of the system as a whole, (4) that it can be achieved by various combinations of precustomization and customizability, (5) that opinions differ among researchers as to how best to achieve it, and (6) that practice also varies widely in how it is achieved.

Precustomization

The precustomization attribute is defined formally as follows:

Precustomization: the degree to which, and the manner in which, at the time it is delivered to the user, some or all of the features of a Decision Support System have already been tailored to the specific decision-making environment it is intended to support.

In general, given two DSS, we cannot say which is *more* precustomized, because so many features (data, models, and so forth) might be precustomized and because the features might be precustomized with respect to so many aspects of decision makers, tasks, and settings. We can, however, always describe *how* two systems differ in precustomization.

One can distinguish systems that are precustomized for a unique decision-making environment from those that are precustomized for a class of environments. Some DSS are specifically designed for a particular person or set of people performing a particular decision-making task or tasks in a given setting. In such cases we have no expectation that the precustomized system would apply to other people performing the same decision-making task(s) in the same setting, to someone performing other decision-making task(s) in the same setting, or to someone performing comparable decision-making task(s) in other settings. For instance, a DSS might be designed to support John Smith as he constructs the monthly swivel-chair production schedule for the ABC Office Equipment Company. The system might reflect how Smith perceives his production problem, the techniques he prefers to use to solve it, the unique aspects of producing swivel chairs, the constraints imposed by ABC's organizational environment, and ABC's preferred solution strategy. Slightly less precustomized would be a system that addresses ABC's swivel-chair production schedule without regard to John Smith's particular decision-making style, or one that supports Smith's production management approach without being uniquely suited for the swivel-chair problem. Many of the early DSS were of these highly precustomized varieties. Such DSS require significant time and resources to build and, in general, are not transferable to other environments.

DSS that are precustomized for a given class of decision makers, tasks, or settings constitute less highly specialized systems. "Generalized DSS" (Ariav and Ginzberg, 1985), software systems that support a class of decision problems, such as scheduling and assignment decisions, are of this type. Systems suited for subclasses of these problems, such as assigning professors to courses or operators to shifts, would be more precustomized, but still of this variety. So would systems precustomized for a given type of organizational setting; for instance, Huber (1981) suggests that different decision aids are appropriate for rational, programmed, political/competitive, and "garbage can" organizational decision-making settings. Similarly, systems might be precustomized for the class of individuals with a given cognitive style.

That a DSS must be precustomized to achieve its objective of supporting decision makers is central to many views of DSS. Keen and Scott Morton (1978), for instance, assert that the DSS approach emphasizes "building systems for specific types of problems, tailored to specific decision situations and decision makers" (p. 6). Nonetheless, it is not universally agreed how precustomized a DSS needs to be, since customizability provides an alternative route to achieving customization. Several DSS commentators (Sprague and Carlson, 1982; Keen and Gambino, 1983) argue that for DSS to be multi-user systems, they must be sufficiently general to accommodate the varying styles of individual users. Similarly, systems that support multiple tasks or settings cannot be entirely precustomized. For these reasons, most commercially available DSS are not highly precustomized.

Customizability

The customizability attribute is defined formally as follows:

Customizability: the degree to which, and the manner in which, a Decision Support System empowers its users to specialize it as needed to fit the environment it supports.

The customizability attribute is a special case of the system restrictiveness attribute, since one way that systems restrict their users is by preventing them from modifying or extending system features: All else being equal, systems that are more customizable are less restrictive than others. As with restrictiveness (and precustomization), we are not always able to say which of two systems is the more customizable, because systems can be customizable in so many ways. We can, however, always describe *how* two systems differ in customizability.

Typical of highly customizable DSS are general- or multi-purpose support systems that users tailor to their environments by supplying environment-specific information such as data and models, by creating environment-specific operators and visual representations, or both. Classic examples of this type of customizable system are electronic spreadsheet packages and financial planning languages, content-free systems that allow users to define their own models and enter their own data, thus yielding a more specialized, content-laden system. In contrast, some customizable systems are not so generalized; users customize these DSS by modifying or extending the basic system features.

Highly customizable systems are attractive because they can achieve customization while requiring less effort by the builder than would constructing a precustomized system, since the user, not the builder, does the tailoring. Making a DSS customizable also facilitates system evolution, since users can modify or extend the DSS themselves as needed over time. Evolution is critical for DSS, since decision-making environments are dynamic, with people, tasks, and settings changing as time passes. Given Keen's (1980) argument that decision makers' understanding of, and approaches to, problem solving are likely to change through use of a DSS, coping with change is especially important; without an evolutionary capability the DSS might contribute to its own obsolescence.

Another argument for customizability is based on Keen's (1980) claim that DSS should support personalized use. Given differences among decision makers, changes in individual decision makers with time, and the unstructured nature of many decision-making activities, many believe that DSS should be flexible enough to support a variety of individualized approaches to problem solving. Here, too, customizability can provide the desired capability.

Several approaches to DSS design incorporate customizability. Moore and Chang (1983) propose an approach to DSS design featuring "expanding subsets of system capabilities," which permit "the easy definition of new operators, data constructs, or reports by the user without redesign or reprogramming. This is accomplished by building upon the existing operators, constructs, etc., in an extensible fashion" (p. 187). Carlson (1983a), in the ROMC approach, identifies control aids that "combine operations associated with one or more representations into procedures" (p. 27). And Donovan and Madnick (1977) describe ad hoc DSS that are designed specifically to be customizable, making it easy for different data and models to be pieced together rapidly in support of ad hoc decision-making needs. Each of these approaches emphasizes the ability to extend the DSS, creating new features by combining existing ones.

Precustomization and Customizability

DSS can be both precustomized and customizable. Most systems have so many features that might be specialized that some can be precustomized and others customizable. For example, a system may have datasets precustomized for an application, but may provide a modeling facility for users to construct their own models. Or a DSS might provide a highly precustomized forecasting model, but allow users to supply their own datasets. Moreover, DSS can be both precustomized and customizable because precustomizing a system does not, in general, preclude further customization. Indeed, precustomizing DSS and making DSS customizable can be complementary ways of facilitating system specialization. A DSS might include a predefined database, but users might be able to modify or extend it. A model might be built for a given task, but it might be further tailored for its users and setting. And a system's operators might be individually precustomized, but a macro facility might enable building new operators from the existing ones.

Although DSS can be both precustomized and customizable, a precustomized system may use up some degrees of freedom that would otherwise be available for customizability. Suppose a system contains a powerful facility for constructing new operators from existing ones, but is not otherwise customizable. If that system's existing operators are highly precustomized, the ability to combine them to form new operators does not increase significantly the system's customizability. If, however, the existing operators are generic, then the macro facility makes for a very customizable DSS.

Figure 6.1 positions systems in terms of how precustomized and customizable they are. Customization increases as one moves towards the upper right corner. The lower left corner contains information reporting systems; these standardized, prespecified reporting systems lack customization of either kind and therefore tend not to be highly supportive of decision makers.

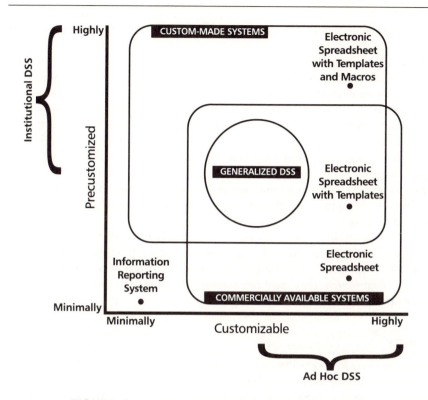

FIGURE 6.1   Precustomization and customizability

Custom-built systems, such as DSS developed for in-house use, might be located anywhere in the upper region of the grid. All are at least somewhat precustomized, many highly so. They vary widely with respect to whether they empower their users to customize them further. Commercially available software—that is, off-the-shelf DSS packages—might be located anywhere in the grid except for the leftmost and topmost portions. Since the packages are applied to many different environments, they cannot be highly precustomized and they must be at least somewhat customizable; usually, they are very customizable.

Electronic spreadsheet packages, such as Lotus 1-2-3, are a special case of commercially available systems. By themselves they are content-free and not very precustomized. Their functionality provides a potential for support, but they do not contain such customized entities as datasets, data structures (other than an empty matrix), or models. But these spreadsheet packages are very customizable, because they contain a facility for creating user-specified data and models. Electronic spreadsheet packages therefore fit in the lower right corner of the grid. Adding templates (predefined cell definitions) to the spreadsheet package moves the system higher in the diagram, and the further addition of macros (combinations of commands to form new features) raises the system even higher.

When I discussed DSS definitions in Chapter 1, I noted that Donovan and Madnick (1977) distinguish between two classes of DSS: "institutional DSS, which deal with decisions of a recurring nature, and ad hoc DSS, which deal with specific problems that are usually not anticipated or recurring" (p. 79). Institutional DSS tend to be far more precustomized than ad hoc systems, their value being their specialization for a given task, while ad hoc DSS are much more customizable, their value being their rapid adaptability to new needs. Institutional DSS will appear anywhere within the upper half of the diagram, because they will necessarily be precustomized and may or may not be customizable. Ad hoc systems will be anywhere on the right half of the grid, since they will necessarily be customizable and may or may not be precustomized.

The Generalized DSS that Ariav and Ginzberg (1985) describe are intermediate both in terms of precustomization and customizability, appearing, therefore, in the middle of the grid. They are precustomized for a class of problems, but not for a specific problem; they must be customizable enough to allow users to tailor them to particular problems.

Summary

Looking again at Figure 6.1, the precustomization and customizability attributes serve to distinguish many kinds of DSS. Indeed, while the DSS research community generally agrees that DSS need to be specialized for their environments, there is no agreement as to what combination of precustomization and customizability should be used to achieve this specialization. Each of these system attributes, precustomization and customizability, merits further attention, comparable to the treatments of system restrictiveness and decisional guidance in Chapters 4 and 5. Moreover, the trade-off between these two attributes requires special consideration, as does the relationship between them and system restrictiveness.

FRAME OF REFERENCE

We are witnessing a trend downward and to the right in Figure 6.1's grid, toward more customizable and less precustomized decision support software. The trend is fueled, in part, by the commercial availability of general-purpose packages for microcomputers that are fairly inexpensive, especially relative to custom-made systems. At the same time, the traditional line between system builders and system users is blurring. The blurriness follows from end-users' employing customizable software to accomplish what used to be the responsibility of system builders: making systems specialized. Moreover, customizability enables users to build systems on systems built on systems, further blurring role distinctions. While all this blurriness may not be a problem in practice, it is of great analytic concern because it can distort the frame of reference we adopt for describing systems. Moreover, it creates some confusion as to how to apply Sprague's (1980) framework. I will first address the frame of reference matter independent of Sprague's framework, and then I will turn to interpreting the framework and, in particular, the role of DSS Generators.

Builders and Users

Increasingly, the line between builders and users is blurring as end-user development replaces professional development for many decision support applications (Rockart and Flannery, 1983). And, as the line between builders and users blurs, so too can the distinction between development systems, the software that builders use to construct DSS, and the DSS themselves. The descriptive approach I presented in the preceding chapters is intended for analyzing DSS, not development systems. It is likely that development systems would best be described by a somewhat different set of characteristics. If we are unclear whether a person is functioning as a builder or a user, if we are unclear whether a system is functioning as a development system or as a DSS, then we may fail to perform the correct analysis. Consequently the frame of reference we adopt is exceedingly important; when we consider a system we must be sure we are analyzing it in its proper role, as DSS or as development system.

The fuzziness has two related sources: (1) professional developers and end-users using the same packages, but for different purposes; and (2) systems being built upon systems built upon systems. . . . I shall analyze each issue in terms of a simple abstract model of systems development, shown in Figure 6.2. As a starting point, consider the traditional development situation, where the "builder" and "user" are two distinct people. Suppose that person X employs system A to build system B for use by person Y. System A might be a package such as an electronic spreadsheet or it might be a programming language such as FORTRAN, BASIC, APL, or assembly language. System B is a DSS that can be used directly by a decision maker to support his or her problem solving. We traditionally refer to person X as the system builder and person Y as the user. Note, however, that

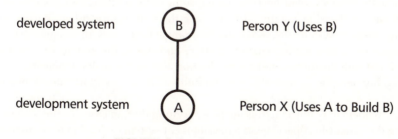

developed system   (B)   Person Y (Uses B)

development system   (A)   Person X (Uses A to Build B)

FIGURE 6.2   A two-level model

this statement implicitly adopts system B as our frame of reference. Both X and Y are users of systems: person Y is the end-user of the DSS (system B), but person X is the user of System A, the development system.

Builders and Users Employing the Same Systems

Many managers currently use customizable packages such as electronic spreadsheets and financial planning languages directly to support their decision making without employing information systems professionals to build precustomized DSS for them. Other managers, however, prefer to have someone else—an information systems professional, consultant, or staff assistant—build a precustomized DSS for them on top of the basic software package. In short, for some people the package functions as a decision aid, while for others it is a development system.

Figure 6.3 depicts the two situations. For concreteness, assume the system whose role is in question is an electronic spreadsheet package. The package is built by a team of analysts and programmers from the spreadsheet vendor's organization, using some programming language, say assembly language. So the development team is a user of assembly language and is the builder of the spreadsheet package. This much is common to both cases (a) and (b) in the figure.

Figure 6.3(a) shows the case of a management consultant using the spreadsheet package to develop a precustomized DSS for a manager. The consultant is the user of the empty spreadsheet package and is the builder of the precustomized system that comprises spreadsheet package, template, and macros. The manager is the user of the precustomized system. In this case the empty spreadsheet package is functioning as a development system. Analyzing it in terms of the three-tiered descriptive approach would not be necessary for understanding the effects of the DSS on the manager. The precustomized system, the spreadsheet package with template and macros, is the system that is delivered to the manager. This is the system whose effects on decision-making behavior are of interest. This is the system that should be studied with the three-tiered approach.

Figure 6.3(b) illustrates the case where a manager uses the spreadsheet package directly. The manager takes advantage of the customizability of the system to develop a spreadsheet—a model, some data, perhaps some macros—to aid his or her decision making. In this case the empty spreadsheet package is the information system delivered to the manager. This is the system whose effects on decision-making behavior matter, and this is the system that should be analyzed with the three-tiered approach. Note that here, the development system is assembly language, and the system builder is the vendor's development team.

Some readers may object to this analysis, arguing that, in case (b), the manager is using the spreadsheet package as a development system to develop for himself or herself a precustomized system comprising spreadsheet package, spreadsheet model,

(a) Consultant Develops Customized DSS for Manager

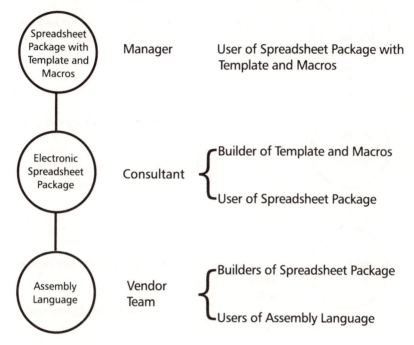

(b) Manager Uses Spreadsheet Package Directly

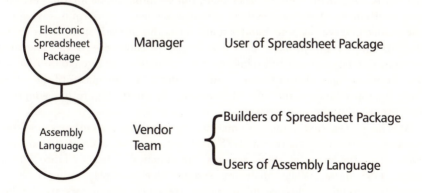

FIGURE 6.3 The blurring of builders and users

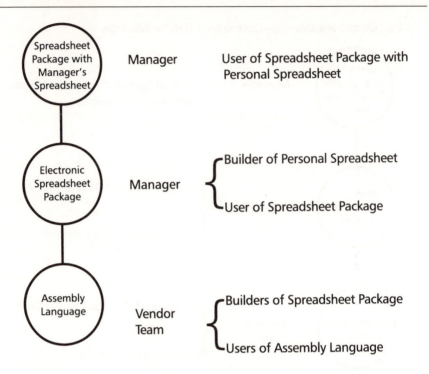

FIGURE 6.4 An alternative interpretation of the manager as spreadsheet user

data, and macros, and that he or she subsequently uses this precustomized system as a decision aid. This interpretation is rendered in Figure 6.4. By itself this alternative argument appears acceptable, but its implications for studying DSS and their effects on decision-making behavior are not. The harm in saying that the manager serves as both builder and user is that it leads us to focus on the customized system—package plus customized spreadsheet—as the system of interest. But the computer-based information system that was given to the manager was the empty spreadsheet package, and *its* effects, not the effects of the system built on top of it, are the ones that matter. In short, Figure 6.4 adopts an inappropriate frame of reference.

We have seen that some systems—in the example, an empty spreadsheet package—can function either as DSS development systems or as customizable DSS. And the users of those systems can function either as DSS builders or as DSS users. When analyzing systems that can play either role, we must be careful to choose the frame of reference that allows us the best analytic leverage for understanding the effects of the system on the decision maker.

Systems Built on Systems

A second, related, frame-of-reference problem occurs when systems are built upon systems built upon systems . . ., an increasingly common phenomenon. Here the distinction between user and builder becomes even fuzzier. Consider what happens if the manager in Figure 6.3(b), the one who used the empty spreadsheet package directly, passes the spreadsheet he or she created to another manager, Manager B, as a template. Viewing the first manager, Manager A, as a system builder and the template (together with the spreadsheet package) as a distinct DSS is now perfectly appropriate, because this DSS is the system delivered to Manager B. To Manager B, this is the only system of interest.

The situation is depicted in Figure 6.5(a). Manager A clearly uses the empty spreadsheet package. Depending on the frame of reference we select, however, we may see Manager A either as the user of a DSS (the empty spreadsheet package) or as the builder of a DSS (the one passed to Manager B). Both interpretations are acceptable, because Manager A has played both roles. Likewise, we may regard the empty spreadsheet package as either a DSS development system or a customizable DSS, because it has served both functions. The appropriate

(a) Manager A Gives Spreadsheet to Manager B

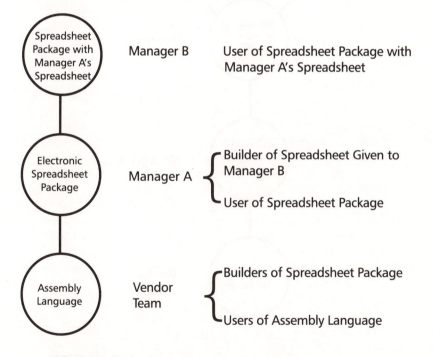

FIGURE 6.5(a) *Systems built on systems built on . . .*

(b) Extending the Chain

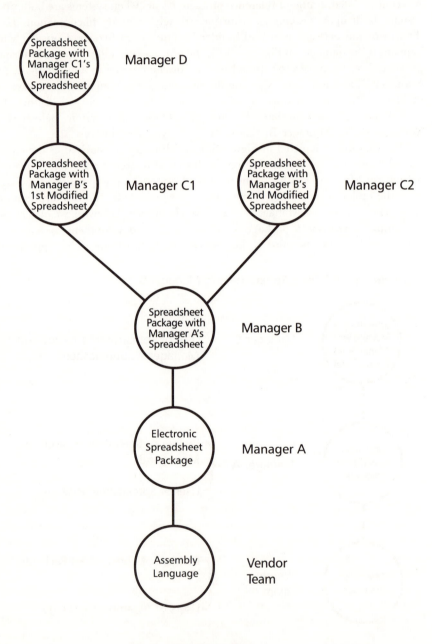

FIGURE 6.5(b)

interpretation depends upon which system's effects are being analyzed—that is, upon whether the frame of reference is the decision support that the empty spreadsheet package gives Manager A, or the support the package plus template afford Manager B.

The situation can easily become more complex, as seen in Figure 6.5(b). Manager B might modify the template and pass it to Manager C1, then modify it again and pass it to Manager C2. And Manager C1 might make further modifications, passing the revised template to Manager D. Indeed, as the figure shows, we could have a collection of systems built one on top of the other. The person who uses each intermediate system can be seen as both user and builder.

What conditions are necessary to grow such a collection of systems? Each system must be customizable, so its users can employ its adaptive capabilities to create the next-level system. The chain might continue indefinitely, but it will end if a noncustomizable system is produced. In the spreadsheet example, simply adding more macros and modifying cell definitions will not inhibit customizability, but building a master macro that traps the user and prevents him or her from modifying the template and macros will end the chain.

Interpreting Sprague's Framework

In the preceding discussion I carefully avoided using the term "DSS Generator" (Sprague, 1980), because the trend toward customizable systems and the blurring of the roles of builder and user has led to some confusion over how to interpret this term and Sprague's influential framework (reprinted earlier as Figure 2.7 and shown again here as Figure 6.6). The DSS community interprets Sprague's framework in two very different ways. The first interpretation, which I personally prefer, sees the framework as a descriptive and prescriptive approach to designing DSS. Indeed, the title of his article, "A framework for the development of Decision Support Systems," emphasizes DSS development. The approach is descriptive, because it characterizes successful efforts such as the GADS Project, and it is prescriptive, because Sprague proposes it as the way DSS should be constructed. The key element of the framework is the DSS Generator, which constitutes the middle technological level. Sprague recommends that, rather than developing each new DSS—Specific DSS, in his language—from scratch, directly using basic software tools, we build an intermediate, more advanced system from the tools, a DSS Generator, which we can then use repeatedly to build specific systems. Sprague's approach is compelling conceptually, and is supported by ample evidence of its successful application.

The framework reflects the traditional distinction between builders and users. Builders are associated with the middle level and decision makers with the top level. Sprague notes that financial planning languages can function as DSS Generators (electronic spreadsheet packages were not yet widely visible in 1980), but given the extensive list of criteria Sprague and Carlson (1982, Chapter 11)

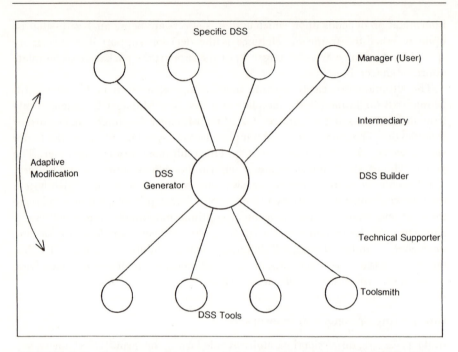

*FIGURE 6.6   Sprague's framework for the development of DSS. Note.
Reprinted by special permission from the MIS Quarterly, 4(4) (Dec. 1980).
Copyright 1980 by the Society for Information Management and the
Management Information Systems Research Center at the University of
Minnesota. All rights reserved*

put forth for a desirable DSS Generator, we must conclude that financial planning
languages and electronic spreadsheet packages are, at best, ''embryonic'' (Sprague
and Carlson, 1982) Generators.

Unfortunately, a second interpretation of Sprague's framework is probably more
widespread. This interpretation borrows Sprague's vocabulary without adopting his
developmental approach, and in the process leads to much confusion. Consistent
with the first interpretation, precustomized systems are called Specific DSS. But
customizable systems such as electronic spreadsheet packages and financial
planning languages, which *can* function as (embryonic) DSS Generators, are
universally branded ''Generators,'' even when used directly by decision makers.
Implicitly, and sometimes explicitly, this interpretation defines the DSS used by
decision makers as falling into two categories: Specific DSS and DSS Generators.

But this is not the distinction Sprague was making. He distinguished not two
types of DSS, but Specific DSS from one kind of development system used to
produce them (DSS Generators). Indeed, his purpose was to distinguish two
approaches to building Specific DSS: DSS Generators and traditional tools.

Looking again at Figure 6.6, we are reminded that Generators are associated with builders and Specific DSS with decision makers.

Today, systems such as electronic spreadsheet packages and financial planning languages sometimes function as Generators, development systems used by builders, and sometimes function as actual DSS, systems used directly to support decision making. By universally labeling such systems "DSS Generators," irrespective of how they are used, we risk confusing development systems with actual DSS. Yes, we must distinguish empty spreadsheet packages from spreadsheet packages coupled with specific spreadsheet models. But when these systems are being considered in terms of how they support decision makers directly, the difference is not the roles they play (DSS Generator versus Specific DSS) but their system attributes (customizable versus precustomized).

Clarifying the current terminologic confusion requires three steps:

- We must recognize that systems such as electronic spreadsheet packages and financial planning languages can play two different roles, and we must analyze them according to the role they are playing.
- When talking about systems decision makers use, we should employ the precustomization and customizability attributes, rather than the Specific DSS/DSS Generator distinction.
- We must recognize that Sprague's framework, as a descriptive and prescriptive framework from 1980, may not describe all cases today. We should expect to find

  1. cases where there are more levels above the Specific DSS level, as systems are built upon systems; and
  2. cases where software tools are combined to form not a DSS Generator used by builders, but a customizable DSS used by decision makers.

DESCRIBING EXISTING DSS WITH SYSTEM ATTRIBUTES

To make the descriptive approach more concrete, I use the four system attributes—system restrictiveness, decisional guidance, precustomization, and customizability—to analyze two very different DSS: Lotus 1-2-3, a popular electronic spreadsheet package, and the Electronic Workbook, a system that supports enrollment planning decisions for colleges and universities.

Lotus 1-2-3

Lotus 1-2-3 is the most popular of a class of microcomputer-based systems known as electronic spreadsheets.* The system provides three primary facilities: a

---

*This section describes Version 2.2 of Lotus 1-2-3.

spreadsheet capability for building, modifying, displaying, storing, retrieving, and manipulating spreadsheet-based representational models; a graphics capability for displaying spreadsheet data graphically in softcopy or hardcopy; and a data management capability for sorting, searching, and summarizing tables of data. The spreadsheet capability includes, but is not limited to, simple and complex mathematical functions, statistical functions such as mean and standard deviation, and financial and accounting functions such as net present value and internal rate of return. The system can perform multiple regression analyses and solve systems of simultaneous linear equations. A macro facility empowers users to store sequences of operators that can be invoked easily with a single command and to create more sophisticated programs.

In the analysis that follows, I describe Lotus 1-2-3's attributes from the frame of reference of a decision maker using the empty spreadsheet package directly as a DSS.

System Restrictiveness

Objectively, Lotus 1-2-3 is a minimally restrictive system. Although it may not offer the full power of high-level programming languages such as FORTRAN, Pascal, or APL, it does provide its users with significant abilities to construct their own representational models, to execute the models repeatedly, and to perform whatever other calculations they desire. Users can define their own tables of data, fill them with data imported from operating system files, search them, sort them, graph them, and analyze them statistically. Users can invoke 1-2-3's functional capabilities in any order they choose. The primary restriction imposed by the system is the spreadsheet format; the spreadsheet (two-dimensional array) is the basic structure for all models and data.

Some users may perceive Lotus 1-2-3 to be more restrictive than it is objectively. Because users of the empty spreadsheet package must create their own spreadsheets from basic functions and must combine low-level functions to accomplish many information-processing tasks, some users may be limited in what they can or will accomplish with Lotus 1-2-3. For instance, some users may be unable to make individual functions work properly or, more likely, may be unable to combine basic functions to perform more complex tasks. And some users may be unaware of, or unable to use effectively, some of the advanced features such as data management, multiple regression, and macro construction. Other users may choose not to expend the time and effort necessary to use low-level operators to perform complex information-processing tasks. For example, the various choice rules for multi-attribute problems can be executed in Lotus 1-2-3, but doing so would require extensive use of the ''/DATA SORT'' and ''/DATA QUERY'' commands, which may be too difficult for some users and too tedious or time-consuming for others. So, despite its minimal restrictiveness from an absolute perspective, Lotus 1-2-3 may be significantly restrictive for some of its users.

Precustomization and Customizability

Like all spreadsheet packages, Lotus 1-2-3 is minimally precustomized but highly customizable. As a content-free system, it is hardly tailored for the decision-making environments it supports. At most, 1-2-3 contains a few functions—such as net present value and internal rate of return, for financial problems—that reflect the particular domains to which it will be applied. But 1-2-3 does provide users with the capability to tailor the system to their needs, defining their own models, data tables, and graphics displays. Moreover, the extensive macro facility empowers users to customize further the system by creating new functions from combinations of existing ones.

Customizability is a special case of absolute restrictiveness. That Lotus 1-2-3 is highly customizable contributes to its being minimally restrictive. And precustomization interacts with perceived restrictiveness. That Lotus 1-2-3 is minimally precustomized may be why some decision makers find accomplishing their information-processing tasks with it difficult, tedious, or impossible, perceiving it to be more restrictive than it objectively is.

Decisional Guidance

Lotus 1-2-3 provides relatively little in the way of decisional guidance either for structuring decision-making processes or for executing them. The system includes fine look-ahead menus and an extensive context-sensitive help facility, but these mechanisms support primarily the mechanical task of operating the system and not the decisional aspects of structuring a coherent decision-making process and making predictive and evaluative judgments.

The absence of decisional guidance might be attributable to the lack of precustomization. Since the empty spreadsheet package has little decisional content, developers of spreadsheet packages have little basis for offering meaningful decisional guidance. The developers of the package do not know how the system will be applied, so they cannot offer guidance for using it. Ironically, because decision makers must customize the system themselves, a process that may entail many decision-related judgments, decisional guidance that helps them tailor the system to their needs might be extremely valuable. For instance, guidance that helps decision makers construct spreadsheet models might be greatly beneficial. Such guidance could also counter any perceptions of restrictiveness that follow from the difficulty of using a content-free system. But finding a means of providing such guidance is not an easy task.

Remarks

I have been describing 1-2-3 from the frame of reference of decision makers who use the empty spreadsheet package directly to support their decision making.

Many users of Lotus 1-2-3 do not fit into this category, because they use it as a clerical system to perform nondecisional tasks, because they use it as a development system for building customized DSS, or because they use it augmented by a template someone else has constructed for them. Even excluding these people, however, a large population of managers are using Lotus 1-2-3. How do the system attributes help us understand its popularity?

One factor is certainly cost. Since Lotus 1-2-3 is not precustomized and is customizable, literally millions of people can use the same system, making its cost for any one user very reasonable. A precustomized system would be far more expensive. Furthermore, a given user can employ the system repeatedly, customizing it anew for each new decision-making problem that is encountered, further increasing the cost savings over customized software.

Lotus 1-2-3 may also be popular because the high customizability and low restrictiveness can be assets in the eyes of many decision makers who are happy to define their own models and their own procedures for manipulating these models. These people may appreciate the ease with which they can change or extend their models. It has been argued (for instance, Bloomfield and Updegrove, 1982) that a major benefit of modeling is the insight that follows from the process of building the model. If this is so, then constructing their own models using a customizable system may be more valuable to many managers than running a model someone else built for them.

In contrast, people who perceive 1-2-3 to be very restrictive because it does not provide them with specialized capabilities will find its lack of precustomization a liability. Such people require a more customized system; augmenting Lotus 1-2-3 with templates and macros might meet their needs. Indeed, although I have been concentrating on decision makers who use the empty spreadsheet directly, I would be remiss if I did not mention those who use Lotus 1-2-3 coupled with templates and macros provided by others. These users often get the best of both worlds. They get the nonrestrictiveness and customizability of Lotus 1-2-3, and they get the precustomizaton afforded by the template and macros. In some cases the template and macros even include some decisional guidance.

We are starting to see customizable packages that are a bit more precustomized appearing on the market. Examples of these are systems that are suited for a class of problems—the Generalized DSS that Ariav and Ginzberg (1985) describe—and systems that implement one or more specific decision-making techniques.* For instance, a number of systems (Arborist, Expert Choice, Lightyear, and Supertree, among others) that implement one or more choice rules for multi-attribute problems are now available for microcomputers. It will be interesting to see how these products compete with the spreadsheet packages. We should expect, in the

---

*See Golden, Hevner, and Power (1986) for a review of more than a dozen "Decision Insight Systems" for microcomputers, many of which are examples of highly customizable systems that are also somewhat precustomized by including one or more specific decision-making techniques.

long run, to find an integration of the two. Already these packages tend to pass data easily to and from Lotus 1-2-3, and some are implemented not as stand-alone systems but as Lotus 1-2-3 templates or "add-ins." As spreadsheet vendors continue to expand the functionality of their systems, we might see some of these precustomized features built directly into the spreadsheet packages.

The Electronic Workbook

The Electronic Workbook (EWB) is a component of the Enrollment Planning Service, a service offered by the College Board to its member institutions.* The service and the EWB are both based on a conceptual model of student choice of colleges and universities (Zemsky and Oedel, 1983), developed by researchers at the University of Pennsylvania's Institute for Research on Higher Education. The service and system help college and university officials plan their enrollment recruiting strategies through use of a "market segment model" that identifies 304 geographic markets throughout the nation and characterizes SAT test takers (prospective applicants) as belonging to one of four market segments.

Subscribers to the service receive stylized printed reports of aggregate data, derived by analyzing raw SAT score submissions according to the conceptual model. Some elements of the database contain institution-specific information, whereas others contain market data common to all colleges and universities. In addition to the printouts of the aggregate data analyses, subscribers receive a workbook that follows a six-step recruitment planning process devised by the research team that developed the market segment model.

The EWB is a microcomputer-based support system that helps recruitment planners take advantage of the richness of the Enrollment Planning Service's data, analyses, and planning process in ways that exceed what would be feasible with the manual workbook. More specifically, the EWB helps planners study the data provided by the service, identify their institutions' strengths and weaknesses, and determine a recruitment strategy that includes selecting the geographic markets to receive increased attention in the recruitment process. The EWB is organized as a sequence of six steps, following fairly closely the logic of the manual worksheets. In fact, the system's main activity menu is formatted to appear identical to the schematic diagram of the planning process depicted in the paper workbook (see Figure 6.7).

System Restrictiveness

The EWB operates in two modes: Structured and Flexible. In Structured Mode the system is, by design, extremely restrictive. Users are compelled to execute the six steps in order, and the basic data, display formats, and algorithms are all

---

*This section describes Version C.1 of the Electronic Workbook.

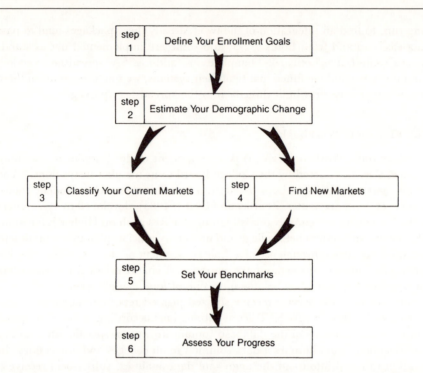

FIGURE 6.7   *The Enrollment Planning Service. Note. Reprinted from the Enrollment Planning Service User Guide, by permission of the College Entrance Examination Board. Copyright (1985) by the College Entrance Examination Board. All rights reserved*

predetermined by the EWB. Moreover, several steps do not offer users any opportunities to exercise discretion. For these steps, users control only the pace at which they move through the predefined displays and the determination of which of these displays are printed. Although other steps afford users more control, even they are somewhat restrictive. For example, Step 4 implements an elimination by aspects approach to selecting new markets for development, but since the system predefines the first two selection criteria, the solution space has already been constrained before users have a chance to express their preferences.

In Flexible Mode the EWB is less restrictive, but here, too, the system is designed to be quite constraining. Users are given more discretion in how each step is executed, and since users now can influence the outcome of each step, they are also given opportunities to backtrack and repeat previous steps. Nonetheless, the sequence of steps is still constrained, because users are not permitted to skip any steps when moving forward through the system.

In Step 1 of Flexible Mode, users can choose a subset of the database as input to the planning process, rather than being forced to use the entire database, as in Structured Mode. Similarly, users define the values of several key parameters that affect subsequent steps in the process. The basic display format, however, is the same as in Structured Mode and cannot be altered.

Step 3 of Flexible Mode also expands users' opportunities to exercise judgment. Whereas in Structured Mode the system executes a predefined algorithm to produce a list of markets for intensified recruitment, in Flexible Mode the users make their own selections via an elimination by aspects approach. Nonetheless, users are still restricted to this one choice rule, and to attributes contained in a particular subset of the database. Similarly, in Step 4 of Flexible Mode users are less constrained by the system because the two selection criteria predefined in Structured Mode are removed.

Several features make the EWB slightly less restrictive than it would otherwise appear. For instance, users can define up to 10 new data items for use as attributes in the elimination by aspects approach of Steps 3 and 4. Users cannot, however, employ these data elsewhere in the system.

Version C.1 of the software added a "free-form" option that allows users to bypass the six steps entirely, executing instead an elimination by aspects process to select from among *all* markets using *any* attributes in the database. This option, added in response to feedback from users of earlier versions, makes the EWB less restrictive (1) by not requiring users to engage in the six-step process, (2) by allowing users to select from among all markets at once (the six-step process limits users to considering different subsets of markets in each of Steps 3 and 4), and (3) by allowing users to employ any combination of attributes in the database (the six-step process limits users to considering different subsets of attributes in each of Steps 3 and 4). Not all modifications to the EWB, however, have reduced its restrictiveness. A goal-setting operation has been added that must be performed prior to executing the six-step process.

Decisional Guidance

The EWB offers small amounts of decisional guidance. The guidance is limited, in part, because the restrictiveness of the EWB eliminates many opportunities for including meaningful guidance within the system.

The EWB includes some common forms of guidance for navigating through its capabilities. For instance, the system interacts with its users through look-ahead menus, and a status line is constantly displayed and updated at the bottom of the screen. Moreover, when users must choose which of 26 maps to display or print, the EWB recommends the ones that are likely to be the most interesting based on an analysis of the relevant data.

The elimination by aspects choice rule embedded in Steps 3 and 4 includes some, but not all, of the guidance described in Chapter 5 for HYPE's conjunctive elimination method. When selecting attributes, users interact with the EWB via a hierarchy of menus that organize the numerous candidate attributes, thus facilitating choosing among them. To enlighten users as they define acceptable ranges for attribute values, the EWB displays several statistics (including the low, high, median, and mean values) both for the full set of markets and for those remaining at any point in the elimination process.

One might also consider Structured Mode as a form of guidance for Flexible Mode. By operating first in Structured Mode, as the EWB encourages them to do, users can regard the system's actions as suggestions to be accepted or rejected when they execute the corresponding steps in Flexible Mode. Indeed, by executing Structured Mode through all six steps, users can see the consequences of the system's actions before making their own decisions in Flexible Mode. Moreover, since users may switch from Structured to Flexible Mode after any step in the process, they can begin the planning process by following the system's actions, and then override the system beginning whenever they see fit.

Precustomization and Customizability

The EWB is highly precustomized. Not only is it designed for the specific task of recruitment planning for colleges and universities, but it implements a particular process for performing this task tied to a specific model of the problem. Furthermore, each subscribing institution is delivered a version of the system precustomized with its own institution-specific data.

The EWB is minimally customizable. For displays, users can choose between two color palettes. Before beginning the six-step process, users can specify which geographic regions (the database is divided into six) are to be included in the analysis; and, for use in the elimination by aspects process, users can supply as many as 10 additional data elements characterizing the geographic markets.

Remarks

The EWB's attributes are consistent with the objectives that motivated its creation. The system was intended to complement the printed data reports and analyses produced by the Enrollment Planning Service with an interactive computer-based system that would (1) provide a means for recruitment planners to handle effectively the voluminous data produced by the service, (2) help planners interpret their data in a manner consistent with the conceptual model that produced it, (3) assist planners in integrating the data into their institutions' planning, and (4) encourage planners to follow the six-step recruitment planning process. The EWB, therefore, is highly precustomized and highly restrictive to take advantage of, and to enforce, the conceptual model, the complex data structures, and the six-step planning process created by the Enrollment Planning Service researchers. In the language of Chapter 4, the restrictiveness reflects several design objectives, including prescription, providing structure, and fostering structured learning. Recognizing that too much restrictiveness may be undesirable, however, the system includes both Structured and Flexible Modes. And, despite the restrictiveness, human judgmental inputs still play important roles in key stages of the planning process.

The system design reflects significant interactions among the four system attributes. The operators, data structures, models, and displays are *precustomized* to support uniquely the six-step planning process, compliance with which is enforced by the high degree of *restrictiveness*. The limited *customizability* follows directly from the high degree of *restrictiveness*, which also limits the opportunities for users to make judgments and thus the opportunities for providing meaningful *guidance*. The *decisional guidance* that is present—for instance, guidance in using elimination by aspects—is facilitated by having precustomized operators; the guidance can be tailored to the characteristics of these specialized operators.

*DSS AS CHANGE AGENTS: DESIGNING WITH SYSTEM ATTRIBUTES**

In the preceding section, I used the system attributes to describe existing DSS. In this section I apply the system restrictiveness and decisional guidance attributes in a different way. Here I discuss their roles as design variables, using them to describe alternative strategies for designing the features of DSS intended to serve as agents for directed or nondirected change.

The section is divided into two parts. First, I introduce the important concept of DSS as change agents, examining what the literature has to say about two different approaches to change agency (directed change and nondirected change); then, I consider design strategies consonant with each approach, drawing heavily upon the restrictiveness and guidance attributes.

DSS and Change Agency

The concept of change agency has long been recognized as important for understanding DSS. Ginzberg (1978) found in a study of 29 systems that DSS require a substantially greater degree of individual change to be successful than do other types of information systems. Alter (1980), in his study of 56 DSS, noted that "implementation of a decision support system always constitutes some kind of change in a work environment" (p. 143). Keen and Scott Morton (1978) argue that the DSS designer must adopt the role of a "clinical, facilitative change agent" (p. 210). Barki and Huff (1985) found that users more extensively used "those DSS that bring change than DSS that do not result in substantial changes" (p. 261).

Although one finds general agreement in the literature that DSS cause change in the processes through which decisions are made, and that causing such individual

---

*The text, figures, and table contained in this section, with a few minor differences, were published previously. Reprinted by permission, "Decision Support Systems: directed and nondirected change," Mark S. Silver, *Information Systems Research*, **1**(1) January–March 1990. Copyright (1990), the Institute of Management Sciences, 290 Westminster Street, Providence, RI 02903. All rights reserved.

and organizational change is a proper function of a DSS, no consensus exists concerning what the appropriate role of the change agent* should be. Change agency comes in two varieties, reflecting two different attitudes on the part of the DSS designer. On the one hand, when designers comprehend that change will occur and deliberately attempt through a DSS to force the direction of that change, we have an instance of "directed" change. On the other hand, when designers understand that change will occur but do not try to influence the direction of that change, allowing it to be determined instead by the decision maker through DSS use over time, we have a case of "nondirected" change. By default, when designers do not recognize their roles as change agents, a nondirected change situation follows.

Each of these two views of change agency—directed and nondirected change—is advanced and supported by prominent elements of the DSS research literature. The coexistence of these opposing philosophies raises numerous research questions, among them, "When should each view be adopted?" and "What is the relationship between a system's role as a change agent and its design features?" The first question is outside the scope of this book; here, I focus on the second one. More specifically, I am concerned with how one's view of change agency in a given situation is reflected in the features of the DSS he or she produces. Should there be systematic differences between the features of DSS implementing directed change and those implementing nondirected change?

The DSS research literature says very little about this issue. The studies explicitly addressing the use of DSS and change agency have concentrated on the connections among *implementation processes*, system success, and organizational/individual change, not upon the relationship between DSS *design features* and change agency. Moreover, scarcely any attention has been paid to the conflict between directed and nondirected change. In fact, the literature hardly notes that conflicting views exist. Papers presenting one or the other of the two positions do not even acknowledge the presence of an alternative perspective on DSS and change agency. Stabell (1983) stands alone in explicitly identifying the conflict, and even he devotes only a few paragraphs to its discussion. Boynton and Victor (1989) observe a related but different dichotomy in the literature on information search support. Moore and Chang (1983) address a closely related topic in their discussion of "meta-design considerations" for DSS, but they do not comment on the underlying tension in the literature.

Although the literature does not address the issues I raise here, it is not silent on the topic of change agency. Either explicitly or implicitly, much of the current DSS literature rests upon the notion of DSS as agents for change. And both the

---

*A large body of research literature discusses the role of human change agents in affecting the behavior of individuals, groups, and organizations. Here, however, I discuss a different kind of change agent: a computer-based system whose introduction into a decision-making environment causes change by intervening in the processes through which decisions are made.

directed change and nondirected change viewpoints can be seen prominently. The terms "directed" and "nondirected" change do not appear often, but the underlying concepts do.

Directed Change

In one of the early DSS research efforts, Gerrity (1970, 1971) introduced an approach to DSS design and implementation that was subsequently endorsed by Keen and Scott Morton (1978) and expanded upon by Stabell (1975, 1983). The key components of this approach were normative, descriptive, and functional modeling, as illustrated in Figure 6.8. Under this scheme the designer develops a normative model of how the decision "should" be made and a descriptive model of how the decision is currently being made. The functional model specifying the DSS is then defined as some point between the descriptive and normative models, intended to move the decision maker in the desired direction. The underlying attitude is clearly one of directed change.

Gerrity and the Portfolio Management System (PMS) he created provide a classic example of a designer viewing his role as that of an agent for directed change. Normative portfolio theory requires that a decision maker evaluate portfolios as a whole, trading off risk and return for the entire portfolio. Gerrity observed that portfolio managers were violating prescriptive theory by evaluating individual securities and searching for appropriate portfolios, rather than examining portfolios and searching for appropriate securities. An important component of his system design, therefore, was to provide portfolio-oriented operators, thus encouraging the managers to move from security-oriented to portfolio-oriented analysis.

Nondirected Change

Sprague and Carlson (1982) identify six performance objectives for DSS. The fifth item on their list is the following:

> To support a variety of decision-making processes but not be dependent on any one. In other words, to provide support that is process independent and under full control of the user. (p. 95)

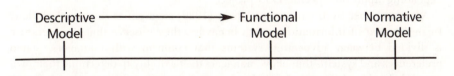

FIGURE 6.8 *Schematic interpretation of Gerrity's decision-centered design approach. Note. This figure is an interpretation of the approaches presented in Gerrity (1970, 1971), Keen and Scott Morton (1978), and Stabell (1983).*

This assertion forms the foundation for a view of DSS as agents for nondirected change, with the user assuming responsibility for controlling the direction of any changes that occur. In essence, the DSS builder provides information-processing capabilities that are potentially valuable for performing the task, and the decision maker decides if and how to make use of these capabilities. Contrast this process-independent DSS philosophy with Gerrity's approach, where the system is intended to move the decision maker in a given direction.

Sprague and Carlson point to the Geodata Analysis and Display System (GADS) as a DSS that implements their philosophy. GADS provided its users with capabilities to access, display, and analyze data in making geographically oriented decisions such as allocating policemen to beats. The purpose of the system was to improve the effectiveness of professionals by giving them access to useful, graphically oriented, computer-based facilities, but not to impose any particular decision-making process on them. Studies indicated that processes changed and decisions improved with the use of GADS, while individual decision makers varied in terms of how they used the system to arrive at decisions.

Other well-known DSS development approaches can also be seen as reflecting a nondirected view of change agency. For instance, Stabell (1983) makes the following collective observation concerning evolutionary, middle-out, and adaptive design as presented by Moore and Chang (1983), Hurst *et al.* (1983), and Keen and Gambino (1983), respectively:

> They say little about the direction or content of the changes to be achieved. The guidelines presented are consistent with the view of the DSS builder as an agent for nondirected change. It is the user who is responsible for defining the content of the change. The builder is merely a facilitator for user-directed change. (p. 225)

A Broader View of Change

Some DSS researchers have moved toward less extreme positions on change agency. The first step in this direction is to recognize the existence of both the directed and nondirected philosophies of change. Rather than dogmatically adopting a single perspective on change agency, this more enlightened viewpoint accepts the legitimacy of each approach and sees the choice between them depending upon the specific DSS project.

A recent paper by Boynton and Victor (1989) exemplifies this point of view. In the context of information-search behavior, they observe that the literature is divided between advocating systems that conform with managers' stated preferences and systems that allow managers the flexibility to determine their own search behavior. Acknowledging that in some situations these approaches may be appropriate, they argue that in other situations a completely different strategy may be more desirable: designing an information system that directs or controls users' search behavior. Such controls may be needed, for instance, to avoid a mismatch between the search propensities of a manager and the search requirements of his or her task and organizational role. Empirical research is in progress to understand better when directed and when nondirected search is appropriate.

A second step from the extreme positions not only recognizes the legitimacy of each philosophy of change, but sees a given DSS project as an opportunity for combining the two philosophies. That is, a system may be designed to direct some decision-making changes and to allow for other, unplanned changes, as well. From this mixed viewpoint the fundamental design issue is not choosing between directed and nondirected change, but deciding how much of each underlying philosophy should be reflected in the system.

Keen and Gambino's (1983) prescriptions for DSS design illustrate this second step. Although Stabell has tagged their view with the nondirected-change label, in fairness, they appear to advocate a mixture of the two agency views. In particular, their approach incorporates the descriptive and prescriptive mappings suggested by Gerrity. When described elsewhere (Keen, 1980), the adaptive design approach again appears to combine both points of view.

Stabell has also branded Moore and Chang's (1983) "evolutionary approach" as nondirected change. In the same article, however, Moore and Chang characterize the nature of DSS interventions by defining a continuum of designs, with "strong" designs at one extreme and "weak" designs at the other. A "strong" design deliberately attempts "to shape or refine the user's decision-making process," while a "weak" design follows "the user's current preferences and existing capabilities" (p. 174). The "strong" and "weak" endpoints map nicely into directed and nondirected change, respectively. The interior points must then represent mixed approaches.

Here, I take only the first step in the direction of a broader view of DSS and change agency, studying closely—but independently—the cases of directed change and nondirected change. Taking the second step, a combined approach, would be premature at this time. While strategies combining directed and nondirected change constitute a topic worthy of research in the future, we must have a much better understanding of the two extreme cases before we will be in a position to consider points between them.

Design Strategies: Applying Restrictiveness and Guidance

A natural question to ask is "What DSS features are logically consistent with which points of view?" The discussions of system restrictiveness and decisional guidance in Chapters 4 and 5 suggest that each of these attributes has a role to play in answering this question. Moreover, we must keep in mind the relationship between the two attributes: the greater the restrictiveness, the less opportunity for guidance.

Analyzing the system features consistent with each of the two philosophies—directed change and nondirected change—yields a separate set of design strategies,

TABLE 6.1   Strategies for directed and nondirected change

Directed Change	Nondirected Change

Intuitive Strategy DC
  Highly Restrictive DSS
	Intuitive Strategy NDC
	  Minimally Restrictive DSS

Alternative Strategy DC-A
  Highly Restrictive DSS with organizational
  mechanisms to promote use
	Alternative Strategy NDC-A
	  Not-so-minimally Restrictive DSS

Alternative Strategy DC-B
  Not-so-highly Restrictive DSS with
  Decisional Guidance
	Alternative Strategy NDC-B
	  Minimally Restrictive DSS with
	  Decisional Guidance

Alternative Strategy DC-C
  Not-so-highly Restrictive DSS with
  training/coaching
	Alternative Strategy NDC-C
	  Minimally Restrictive DSS with
	  training/coaching

	Alternative Strategy NDC-D
	  Minimally Restrictive DSS with
	  organizational mechanisms to
	  promote use

as shown in Table 6.1. The principal component of all these strategies is the judicious design of system restrictiveness and decisional guidance. Ideally, we would like a design strategy to be based entirely on system features such as restrictiveness and guidance. But by themselves, system attributes such as restrictiveness and guidance are not always sufficient to realize the desired type of change. Often another ingredient is necessary. Indeed, computer-based systems are complex interventions, consisting not only of the systems themselves but of organizational policies and procedures as well (Kling and Scacchi, 1982). Therefore, while some of the strategies I consider here are ''pure'' in that they consist only of choosing restrictiveness and guidance appropriately, others complement careful design of the system's features with a set of implementation tactics, such as training and coaching, that are external to the system.

I focus on *design strategies*—that is, on designing system features consonant with change-agency objectives. Of course, a complete *implementation strategy* for a DSS will include many other items, such as involving users in design or acquiring top-management support. Important as these other items are, the discussion here concentrates on the features of the system itself and not on the full implementation strategy. I reference implementation tactics in the discussion of design strategies only as they are needed to complement the roles played by the restrictiveness and guidance attributes.

Directed Change

Most of the design objectives favoring greater restrictiveness—prescription, proscription, providing structure, and fostering structured learning—are very much in the spirit of directed change. Indeed, when a philosophy of directed change is adopted, a natural starting place may be to contemplate a highly restrictive DSS, one that includes the desired processes, excludes undesirable processes, and minimizes the number of other processes that might divert users from the desired ones (Strategy DC in Table 6.1). In particular, the current decision-making process might be excluded to force a change in problem-solving methods. In some directed-change situations, simply implementing a highly restrictive DSS may be a successful strategy for achieving the design objectives. For example, in order to direct users to use multi-attribute utility theory, a plausible approach is to build a DSS whose capabilities are limited to multi-attribute utility models. Similarly, to force managers to consider more external information and less internal data in planning, the amount of internal data accessible through a DSS might be constrained. Likewise, to prevent decision makers from following their current processes, functions central to those processes might be excluded from a DSS.

In other instances of the directed-change philosophy, however, one or more objectives favoring lesser restrictiveness may also be present. For example, a DSS may be intended both to cause specific changes in decision-making behavior and to foster creativity and exploratory learning. One objective particularly likely to favor lesser restrictiveness is system use, since there is a significant danger that a highly restrictive DSS will be eschewed by discretionary users. In situations where too much restrictiveness will inhibit DSS use, or leave other objectives unsatisfied, an alternative strategy must be adopted.

If system use is the only problem, then a possible solution is to implement the highly restrictive DSS together with organizational mechanisms that promote its use (Alternative Strategy DC-A). A likely mechanism is a policy of mandatory use. Such a policy might be instituted by a manager who is implementing a DSS for the purpose of changing his or her subordinates' decision-making behavior. Alter (1980) warns us, however, that a potential pitfall associated with mandatory use is "half-hearted" use. Half-hearted use of a DSS might fail to lead to the desired changes in decision-making behavior. Other organizational mechanisms to promote use, such as pressure from peers or competitors, might therefore be considered.

A much different design strategy for directed change would be to reduce the restrictiveness of the system, an approach aimed at overcoming the problem of nonuse as well as satisfying other objectives that favor lesser restrictiveness. The danger here is that without the restrictiveness to enforce the desired changes in decision-making processes, these changes may never take place.

Gerrity's (1970, 1971) Portfolio Management System (PMS) offers a case in point. Recall that Gerrity's objective was to move portfolio managers from a security-oriented approach toward the normative portfolio-oriented approach to decision making. PMS included security-oriented operators as well as the portfolio-oriented operators Gerrity hoped portfolio managers would eventually use. Unfortunately, a follow-up study conducted by Stabell (1974, 1975) several years after Gerrity's study revealed that, although PMS was still being used, the desired changes in decision making had not been realized. Evidently, given the opportunity to use either the old or new approaches, portfolio managers remained with their original decision-making methods.

The portfolio management example reinforces the concern that a reduced restrictiveness strategy may lack the means to bring about desired changes in decision-making behavior. Two solutions are possible here, one involving only system features and the other requiring activities external to the system. First, we can now introduce decisional guidance into the picture, since the lessened restrictiveness provides the opportunity and the directed-change philosophy constitutes the motive (Alternative Strategy DC-B). Without actually forcing users to follow certain processes, as restrictiveness would, guidance, especially of the suggestive variety, might nudge users in the desired direction. Such guidance would be an instance of the "decision channeling" advocated by Stabell (1983), which "serves to both support and shift the decision process" (p. 251). Further research is required to identify the means for providing this form of guidance.

Instead of compensating for reduced restrictiveness by building decisional guidance into a DSS, a second reduced-restrictiveness approach attempts to direct change by training or coaching decision makers (Alternative Strategy DC-C). Training would emphasize using the system in a manner consonant with the desired changes in decision-making processes. Ongoing coaching might be used instead of or in addition to training in order to foster the desired decision-making behavior. This approach may be necessary or desirable given the difficulty of building meaningful, context-sensitive decisional guidance into a DSS. Given current technology, a human trainer or coach may be better able to channel a user's decision-making behavior than can any features we embed in the system. A key drawback of employing human coaches rather than computer-based guidance, however, is that managers may use the DSS in the coaches' absence, with no mechanism present to direct system use.

Huber (1983) suggests a similar approach in the context of cognitive style research and DSS design. Noting that it might be dysfunctional to build DSS that are restricted to their users' cognitive styles, and that it might be equally undesirable to build systems that only complement their users' styles, he envisions building more flexible DSS that incorporate both decision aids consonant with and aids complementary to decision makers' styles. Users would then be free to choose appropriate aids as required by particular tasks. Through training and coaching, decision makers can be educated to choose the most appropriate aid in a given situation. This approach need not be limited to cognitive style considerations; in many

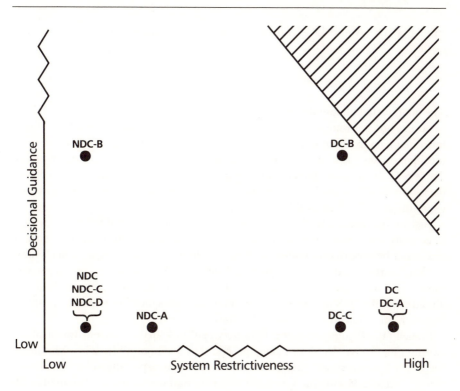

FIGURE 6.9 Strategies for directed and nondirected change. Notes.
Strategy DC-A adds organizational pressures for use, whereas DC-C adds
coaching or training. Strategy NDC-C adds coaching or training, whereas
Strategy NDC-D adds organizational pressures for use

cases, flexible DSS can be built that support users' decision-making processes as
well as alternative processes, with desired behavioral changes fostered by training
and coaching.

The four strategies associated with directed change are positioned with
respect to their restrictiveness and guidance on the right half of Figure 6.9.
When the intuitive strategy (DC) of simply building a highly restrictive DSS
is not appropriate, an alternative is formed by modifying system features,
introducing external influences, or both. In Alternative Strategy DC-A,
restrictiveness and guidance are unchanged, but pressure to use the system is
added. In contrast, Alternative Strategies DC-B and DC-C reduce system
restrictiveness and compensate by adding decisional guidance and training/
coaching, respectively. Two of the strategies (DC and DC-C) are pure, in the
sense that they involve only the design of system features, whereas the other two

strategies (DC-A and DC-B) involve both system features and implementation tactics.

Nondirected Change

The nondirected philosophy of change expects change in decision-making behavior to occur, but does not try to influence the direction of that change. Since users must be given freedom to choose their own decision-making processes, the most intuitive strategy is to implement a minimally restrictive DSS (Strategy NDC in Table 6.1). Presumably, such a DSS will include facilities to support the current decision-making process as well as offer sufficient leeway for users to explore and experiment with other problem-solving approaches.

Just as the agent for directed change could not necessarily succeed with a maximally restrictive DSS, an agent for nondirected change might not wish or might not be able to build one that is minimally restrictive. The designer's hope is that, without advocating specific decision-making changes, changes will nonetheless occur over time and that they will be for the better. Simply building a nonrestrictive DSS that supports the current process together with many others, however, may fail to accomplish this basic objective.

Stabell (1983) suggests that a DSS may lead to "further entrenchment of the existing, ineffective decision-making process that it supports" (p. 228). Minimally restrictive systems supporting existing processes seem especially vulnerable to this threat. Indeed, Moore and Chang (1983) note that unless the user is highly self-motivated, such systems may lead primarily to higher decision-making efficiency but not to greater decision-making effectiveness. Worse yet, we can imagine a very nonrestrictive DSS allowing users to move to a process inferior to their current process, "hanging themselves," as it were, with all of the rope the designer gives them. For instance, a minimally restrictive DSS allows more room for systematic cognitive biases and other decision-making weaknesses to creep into the process.

Another concern is that minimally restrictive DSS may prove to be very difficult for decision makers to use effectively. In providing users with a great deal of flexibility to define their own decision-making processes, those decision makers may be overwhelmed by the many options they confront, suffering from operator or information overload. Decision makers may also combine functional capabilities in unproductive ways. Moreover, decision makers may find it difficult to retrace their steps and to describe to others how decisions were reached.

These potential problems with nonrestrictive systems suggest that the simple strategy may need to be modified. One possibility is to increase somewhat the restrictiveness of the DSS in order to preclude entrenchment in the current process, proscribe potential decision-making errors, or reduce the overload of options suffered by users (Alternative Strategy NDC-A). In keeping with the philosophy of nondirected change, the increased restrictiveness serves not to impose a new decision-making process on users but to facilitate their effective use of the system as they determine for themselves how best to proceed.

Instead of increasing restrictiveness, another possible strategy is to seize the opportunity the minimal restrictiveness provides to add a significant amount of decisional guidance to the system (Alternative Strategy NDC-B). Unlike the ''decision-channeling'' guidance employed in the case of directed change, here the guidance is intended only to make the system more usable and to help users overcome the difficulties associated with nonrestrictive systems. The guidance tends to be more ''informative'' and less ''suggestive,'' although different specific motives will likely lead to different forms of guidance. Avoiding entrenchment in the current process and preventing decision-making blunders are motives that may entail suggestive guidance, while helping users cope with complex systems favors informative guidance.

Yet another possible strategy provides human trainers and coaches to counter the problems posed by nonrestrictive DSS (Alternative Strategy NDC-C). As in the case of directed change, training/coaching external to the system is seen as a substitute for decisional guidance embedded in the system. But just as the nature of guidance for nondirected change differed from that for directed change, so too does the nature of training and coaching. Here, the role of trainers and coaches is simply to enable users to appreciate the system's capabilities and use them effectively, not to indoctrinate decision makers concerning the proper way to make decisions with the system.

Minimally restrictive DSS may create another problem. Recall that, with respect to system use, restrictiveness is a double-edged sword: either too much or too little restrictiveness can lead to nonuse. There is a danger, therefore, that the minimally restrictive DSS will not be used. The three modifications already proposed—increased restrictiveness, the addition of decisional guidance, or the provision of training/coaching—could potentially solve this problem. Alternatively, if nonuse is the only concern, then the minimally restrictive system can be augmented by organizational pressures, as already described for directed change, to encourage or require system use (Alternative Strategy NDC-D). Caution must be observed, however, since this approach addresses only the problem of nonuse and not the underlying problem of overloading the decision maker with capabilities.

The left half of Figure 6.9 positions the strategies for nondirected change in terms of their restrictiveness and guidance. When the intuitive strategy (NDC) of building a minimally restrictive DSS is not appropriate, the system design features can be modified either by increasing the restrictiveness as in Alternative Strategy NDC-A or by adding decisional guidance as in Alternative Strategy NDC-B. Instead of modifying system features, another possibility is adding training or coaching as in Alternative Strategy NDC-C. To promote use of the system, the intuitive strategy can be augmented by organizational pressures for its use, forming Alternative Strategy NDC-D. Of the five strategies, three (NDC, NDC-A and NDC-B) are pure strategies, while the other two (NDC-C and NDC-D) include implementation tactics.

Remarks

We have seen the roles that system restrictiveness and decisional guidance can play in the process of designing a DSS to achieve given objectives. The analyses identified nine design strategies, four for directed change and five for nondirected change. The proposed strategies need to be studied empirically to determine their effectiveness individually and in comparison one with another. The better we understand system restrictiveness and decisional guidance, the better we should be able to understand the relative merits of the various design strategies. Conversely, studying the strategies should provide additional insights about restrictiveness and guidance. In particular, studying the strategies provides an opportunity to comprehend better the relationship between the two attributes. For example, if one's objective is to avoid overloading decision makers with information, what is the trade-off between using increased restrictiveness and informative guidance?

We should not be surprised that there is an interplay between these system attributes and design objectives. Causing directed or nondirected change are design objectives that are directly related to the effect of the DSS on the decision-making behavior of its users, and system restrictiveness and decisional guidance are system attributes that capture how systems affect their users' decision-making behavior.

DESCRIBING SEVERAL SUBCLASSES OF DSS

In Chapter 1, I adopted a broad definition of DSS, one that encompasses all computer-based information systems that affect or are intended to affect how their users make decisions. In this section I consider briefly how the system attributes can help us understand three identifiable subclasses of DSS that are currently receiving much attention from researchers and practitioners: Expert Systems, Executive Support Systems, and Group Decision Support Systems.

Expert Systems

Expert Systems have been defined many ways. Some define Expert Systems as computer-based information systems that perform problem-solving tasks at the level of experts in the field. Others define them as computer-based information systems that solve problems by mimicking or emulating an expert in the field. Still others define them in terms of their underlying technology, and without reference to human expertise, as computer-based information systems that solve problems by using knowledge bases, symbolic processing, and inferencing techniques. Other definitions abound.

No matter which definition one adopts, a recurring question is "What is the relationship between Decision Support Systems and Expert Systems?" Adopting narrow definitions of DSS and of Expert Systems leads one to conclude that these are two different types of systems. For instance, while not necessarily adopting this position themselves, Turban and Watkins (1986) explain how and why one might wish to distinguish DSS from Expert Systems. And Luconi, Malone, and Scott Morton (1986) do distinguish DSS from Expert Systems, arguing that each is used to address a different type of problem. Viewed narrowly, DSS support, but do not replace, human problem solving, whereas Expert Systems, using their knowledge bases and inferencing capabilities, generate solutions without human intervention. Just as a narrow definition of DSS excludes operations research models, where mathematical algorithms produce optimal decisions for the decision maker, it also excludes Expert Systems, where inference engines generate solutions for the decision maker.

Because I have adopted a broad definition of DSS, I view the relationship differently; since Expert Systems are clearly instances of computer-based information systems that affect or are intended to affect how their users make decisions, they are certainly instances of DSS. The essential question then becomes, ''What are their unique characteristics as DSS?'' To answer this question, distinguishing two types of systems is useful. First, we have stand-alone Expert Systems, computer-based systems that take facts from the user and, by invoking their inference engine and knowledge bases, produce solutions for him or her. These are the kinds of systems that Luconi *et al.* referred to as Expert Systems when they distinguished Expert Systems from DSS. Second, we have computer-based support systems that have embedded within them Expert Systems or expert systems (inferencing) technology. These systems, which Luconi *et al.* call Expert Support Systems, are the ones that Turban and Watkins describe when they examine the integration of DSS and Expert Systems.

As DSS, we can describe the systems of each type in terms of their system attributes. The first type, stand-alone Expert Systems, are systems that are highly precustomized and highly restrictive, since they are designed to solve a particular problem and since user control is usually limited to providing facts and to asking simple questions such as ''Why?'' and ''How?'' The second type of system, those that have expertise or inferencing capabilities embedded among their other capabilities, vary in their designs. The expertise or inferencing might be embedded restrictively, so that the conclusions drawn by the embedded Expert System are imposed on the decision makers and constrain their use of the system's features. Or the expertise might be embedded as suggestive decisional guidance, recommending to the decision makers how to proceed in using the system. In short, embedding expertise in a DSS raises the design trade-off between system restrictiveness and decisional guidance.

Executive Support Systems

A second set of systems currently receiving much attention are Executive Support Systems (ESS)—sometimes called Executive Information Systems (EIS; Rockart and Treacy, 1982)—defined by Rockart and DeLong (1988) as follows:

the routine use of a computer-based system, most often through direct access to a terminal or personal computer, for any business function. The users are either the CEO or a member of the senior management team reporting directly to him or her. Executive support systems can be implemented at the corporate or divisional level. (p. 16)

According to this definition, the defining characteristic of an ESS is not the system's functions or features, but who its users are. Who the users are, in turn, determines the system's features. In other words, the features of the system reflect the unique needs of executives. This approach appears to be compatible with the spirit of Chapter 3, where I advocated developing a mapping from the characteristics of decision-making environments to the features of DSS. But Rockart and DeLong go on to emphasize that "[t]o understand what an ESS is, one must differentiate it from the older DSS concept"—that is, from DSS narrowly defined—noting that "[c]onfusion between executive support and decision support systems is significant because a narrow or hazy view of ESS will limit the potential of ESS for top management" (p. 18). Since I have adopted a broad definition of DSS, however, treating ESS as a special class of DSS seems perfectly reasonable. We can then enlist the system attributes to describe how the features of ESS may differ from other DSS.

Most early ESS provided executives primarily with "status access" (Rockart and Treacy, 1982), the ability to retrieve easily predefined (and often highly stylized) displays of current data that provide a snapshot of the organization's key status indicators. Such systems have much in common with the information reporting systems (IRS) that predated DSS, both providing users with predefined reports and not affording them flexibility in defining the information being displayed. But the ESS differed from the reporting systems in several significant ways: (1) their data were more current, since ESS were constantly being updated whereas IRS were periodic reports; (2) the ESS contained key status indicators and were tailored to the needs of executives, whereas IRS were not focused on any particular managerial need; and (3) the ESS provided easy, on-line access to the relevant display, whereas the IRS provided hardcopy that needed to be laboriously searched by hand. So although IRS and early ESS were comparable in their lack of customizability, the ESS were significantly more precustomized.

The distinctive attribute of the many ESS that provide only status access is their restrictiveness. These systems are highly restrictive in two ways: they do not provide modeling capabilities, and they provide access only to predefined data displays. This restrictiveness is generally by design (see, for instance, Houdeshel and Watson, 1987), and is based on the contention that such limitations are appropriate, and even necessary, for systems that will be used by top executives. The argument is that adding modeling capabilities and more flexible data access risks making the system more complex and difficult to use, thus reducing the likelihood that the senior executives will use it at all.

Increasingly, however, we are finding that ESS are expanding beyond status access to include querying and analytic capabilities. Moreover, Rockart and DeLong emphasize the importance of communication capabilities, such as electronic mail, within ESS. These trends reflect a significant lessening of restrictiveness as the adopting of ESS becomes more widespread. In terms of the system features it appears that the distinguishing characteristics of ESS may be their functional capabilities, the particular mix of information-processing functions that are needed by executives. ESS also differ from other DSS in terms of non-system characteristics such as their implementation and support requirements.

Group Decision Support Systems

A third set of information systems currently generating great interest are those that support groups of people working together. This class of systems now has a variety of names, among them, Group Decision Support Systems (GDSS; Huber, 1984; DeSanctis and Gallupe, 1987), Computer-Supported Cooperative Work (CSCW; Greif, 1988), Electronic Meeting Systems (EMS; Dennis, George, Jessup, Nunamaker, and Vogel, 1988), Groupware (Johansen, 1988), and Coordination Theory (Malone and Crowston, 1990). This class includes such technologies as electronic mail, decision rooms (Gray, 1983), and teleconferencing. As a whole, these systems suport groups of people as they interact ''any place, any time''—that is, no matter whether they are co-located or dispersed and no matter whether they communicate synchronously or asynchronously. Any given system, however, is likely to support some subset of the possible cases, such as synchronous communication among geographically distant people. In particular, the term GDSS has been applied most often (though not exclusively) to systems that support co-located, synchronous groupwork, where all participants convene together in a specially equipped decision room. For overviews of the findings of such GDSS research, see Gray (1987) and Nunamaker (1989).

The same issues that apply to other forms of information-systems support for managerial activities apply to computer-based support for groups of people working together. Among these issues, analyzing system restrictiveness appears to be especially important. Galegher and Kraut (1990) identify a continuum of technologies for supporting intellectual teamwork that range from ''prescriptive'' through ''permissive.'' The continuum aligns well with system restrictiveness; technologies at the prescriptive end are highly restrictive, whereas those at the permissive end are highly flexible. Galegher and Kraut illustrate the contrast between prescriptive and permissive systems by comparing generic electronic mail systems, which afford users much flexibility of message content, with ''The Coordinator'' (Flores *et al.*, 1988), a system that imposes much structure on electronic conversations. They also consider the design trade-off between permissive and prescriptive technologies, noting that it reflects both ideological and practical choices. Many of the factors they identify as influencing these choices—such as concern that casual users will not adopt a prescriptive technology—correspond with those I discussed in Chapter 4 for restrictiveness.

Restrictiveness also comes into play when analyzing GDSS of the decision room variety. Consider the following:

- DeSanctis *et al.* (1989) hypothesized that restrictiveness in the delivery of heuristics to decision-making groups would reduce decision time and would, depending upon the comprehensiveness of the heuristic, either enhance or reduce consensus. While their laboratory experiment did not confirm their specific hypotheses, the results raised a number of interesting questions concerning the effects of restrictiveness in the delivery of heuristics.
- Galegher and Kraut (1990) observe that some GDSS are "prescriptive" in that they are designed to impose a particular model of group discussion (wherein individualistic idea generation precedes discussion and feedback) on group members.
- Decision rooms that employ human facilitators to moderate the group sessions present a unique twist on the system restrictiveness–decisional guidance trade-off: What should be the "attributes" of the facilitator? The facilitator (1) might be restrictive, forcing the group to use particular tools in a specific order; (2) might guide the group, suggesting that particular tools be used in a specific order; or (3) might be passive, providing neither restrictiveness nor guidance.*

Summary

We see that these three classes of systems—Expert Systems, Executive Support Systems, and Group Decision Support Systems—are special cases of computer-based information systems that affect decision makers, raising the same issues as the full set. Two such issues are especially important: First, we must describe systems carefully and systematically, understanding how they are similar and how they vary; second, we must study systems not just in terms of their features, but in terms of their effects on the behavior of their users.

IMPLICATIONS FOR PRACTICE

Strong prescription based on the three-tiered approach to describing DSS would be premature at this time. Considerably more research, both descriptive and prescriptive, is required. A long-term goal of such research is to construct a prescriptive mapping from the characteristics of decision-making environments to the features of DSS. Although such a mapping is still distant, the descriptive

---

*These three cases are similar, but not identical, to the three modes of interaction (chauffeured, facilitated, and user-driven) studied by Dickson *et al.* (1989).

mechanism and the discussions that accompanied its presentation introduce a set of design considerations that can be of immediate value to DSS designers.

Defining Objectives

One of the first activities in any systems development project is defining objectives. Two key questions to be asked at this stage are the following:

- Which decision-making environment(s) is the system intended to support?
- Which philosophy of change underlies this project?

The Decision-making Environment

A number of questions need to be asked to identify the nature of the decision-making environment(s) being supported: Is the system to support a single, unique environment—that is, a given individual or individuals facing a given task or tasks in a given setting? If so, what is this environment and what are its characteristics? If not, is the system intended to support (1) a small number of similar environments, varying, perhaps, only in one of the environmental characteristics (the decision maker, the task, or the organizational setting); (2) a broad class of environments; or (3) any and all decision-making environments? In each case of multiple environments, what do the environments have in common and how do they differ?

Philosophy of Change

Here, too, a number of questions need to be asked: Is the objective to direct change—that is, to foster specific changes in the processes through which decisions are being made—or is the objective to facilitate but not direct change, allowing decision makers to determine for themselves the nature of the changes that take place? If the objective is directed change, what are the intended changes? And if the objective is nondirected change, what aspects of the process are likely to change?

Using the Three Tiers

Once the intended environment and attitude toward change are defined, the three-tiered analysis can be used to design the system's features. When used to describe existing systems the analysis proceeds sequentially, in a bottom-up direction, since each tier builds on the descriptive information of its predecessors. But when used for system design the order is less straightforward. We begin with the big picture, using the third tier to determine the attributes of the system as a whole. Then we proceed bottom up, first defining the functional capabilities (first tier) and how they are packaged (second tier).

The Third Tier: System Attributes

Among the first design decisions to confront are how precustomized and how customizable the system should be.* These decisions should be made jointly, taking into account the following considerations:

● Whether a single or multiple environments are being supported. The more environments being supported, the more customizable and the less precustomized the system should be.
● If multiple environments are being supported, how greatly the environments vary one from another. The more variance across environments, the more customizable and the less precustomized the system should be.
● How dynamic or volatile the environments are—that is, how rapidly the people, tasks, and settings are likely to change. The more volatile they are, the more customizable the system should be.
● How greatly the development team is expected to remain involved after the system is delivered. The less involvement expected, the more customizable the system should be.
● How skillful the prospective users are likely to be at employing the system. The less skillful they are, the more precustomized the system should be.

The next design decisions are how restrictive and how guiding to make the system. These attributes, too, should probably be considered jointly, since whether to restrict or to guide the decision maker is often a key trade-off. Here, the following considerations should be taken into account:

● The underlying attitude toward change, directed or nondirected. For each attitude a number of combinations of restrictiveness and guidance are viable, as discussed earlier in this chapter.
● The various factors identified in Chapters 4 and 5 as favoring or opposing restrictiveness and guidance.
● The need to promote system use. With respect to system use, restrictiveness is a double-edged sword; too much or too little may inhibit use. Guidance that makes a system easier to use may promote use.
● The differences between objective and perceived restrictiveness. When system builders deliberately use system restrictiveness as a design variable, they must keep in mind that individuals may differ one from another and from the absolute perspective in perceiving the restrictiveness of a system. And, in most cases, it is the perceived restrictiveness that is responsible for the system's effects on decision-making behavior. Decisional guidance that makes a system more

---

*In the brief discussion here I focus on the degree of precustomization, customizability, restrictiveness, and guidance. A related, more difficult part of the design decision is the manner of precustomization, customizability, restrictiveness, and guidance.

accessible to decision makers might help to bring users' perceptions of the system's restrictiveness more in line one with another and with the objective view.

- The design decisions concerning precustomization and customizability. Increasing customizability reduces absolute restrictiveness, and increasing precustomization is likely to reduce perceived restrictiveness. Increasing precustomization is likely to make providing decisional guidance easier, but decreasing precustomization may make providing decisional guidance more important.

The First Two Tiers

The attributes provide a context for the remainder of the system design. At the first tier, builders define the particular functional capabilities to be included in the system. Which capabilities are included may be constrained by prior decisions about restrictiveness, and how generalized the capabilities are is influenced by prior decisions about precustomization. Moreover, proposed capabilities should be analyzed with respect to the decisional needs they are intended to meet. Once the basic capabilities have been defined, the builder moves to the second tier, defining how the capabilities will be packaged. All four attributes play a role in determining how the system appears to its users. For instance, restrictiveness is a major determinant of the sequencing rules, customizability influences the design of adaptors, decisional guidance is often implemented through navigational aids, and precustomization is reflected in how tightly data, models, and representations are linked to operators.

IMPLICATIONS FOR RESEARCH

The three-tiered approach to describing DSS raises numerous research issues. Some questions address the approach itself, exploring and extending each of the three analytical levels. Other questions apply the descriptive approach to studying current research issues in the field. The discussion that follows is not intended to be an exhaustive survey of DSS research issues; it consists of some major research issues related to the descriptive approach.

The Three Tiers

Our understanding of each of the three descriptive tiers can benefit from additional research. At the first tier, which describes systems in terms of their functional capabilities, the chief research effort is matching computer-based capabilities with decision makers' needs. Ideally, one wants to develop an ever-expanding catalog of decision makers' needs and associated computer-based support functions. Two activities can contribute to this effort. One is studying the needs of decision makers that are likely candidates for computer-based decision support. In particular, we must consider how needs vary with decision-making environments—that is, how different people, tasks, and settings manifest different needs for support. These needs should be organized in a hierarchy, moving from more general to more specific needs, because the same general need might apply to many environments but vary in its specifics from one class of environment to another.

A second activity is studying the computer-based methods for meeting these needs, which includes both matching existing capabilities with needs and inventing new capabilities to meet needs not currently being met adequately. We must be as specific as possible in describing computer-based techniques so that builders can easily take such methods "off-the-shelf" and apply them in the contexts of the particular DSS they are constructing. Matching existing and new computer-based methods with decision-making needs is not primarily a developmental (technological) research task; it is one that requires empirical investigation of the effects of the computer-based aids on decision-making behavior.

Research at the second tier, which describes how a DSS appears to its users, integrates technological and behavioral issues. One challenge is to devise new DSS components—for instance, new navigational aids or sequencing rules—that can be used to accomplish particular design objectives. Another challenge is to understand better the trade-offs among alternative configurations of components. For example, what are the relative merits of embedding data and models in operators versus keeping them as separate entities?

Much research effort is needed at the third tier, the level that tells most about how a DSS affects the decision-making processes of its users. In Chapters 4 and 5, I discussed how DSS *can* restrict and how they *can* guide; we need more empirical studies of how DSS *do* restrict and how they *do* guide. We need to study more fully how restrictiveness and guidance affect decision-making behavior. I also discussed in those chapters factors favoring greater and lesser restrictiveness and factors favoring including and excluding guidance. Within these discussions were many propositions that require empirical testing. Of special importance is understanding when and how restrictiveness and guidance promote system use, inhibit system use, or have no effect on whether a system is used. Lastly, we need to study the technological means of providing restrictiveness and guidance in those situations where designers choose to do so. In short, system restrictiveness and decisional guidance require further descriptive, prescriptive, and developmental research.

Earlier in this chapter I presented briefly two additional system attributes: precustomization and customizability. Both of these require treatments similar to those received by restrictiveness and guidance. These attributes, too, require descriptive, prescriptive, and developmental studies. Moreover, there is no claim that the four attributes considered here form a complete set; we need to search for additional attributes that may have a bearing on how computer-based information systems affect decision-making behavior.

How DSS Affect Decision Making

One reason for developing the systematic approach to describing and differentiating DSS was to facilitate studying the effects DSS have on the decision-making behavior of their users. Studying these effects also requires a means of describing how processes can be affected. Typically, empirical and conceptual studies of DSS have described the effects of DSS using a variety of informal phrases: decision makers consider more alternatives, decisions are made more quickly, more information is considered in the decision, more timely information is considered in the decision, and so forth. But just as systematically studying the effects of DSS requires a method for describing and differentiating systems, it also requires a method for describing and differentiating the effects. In Chapter 1, I presented two ways of categorizing the effects of computer-based systems on decision-making processes. The first considers whether DSS amplify or attenuate the existing strengths and weaknesses of a decision-making process. The second considers whether DSS affect the structure or the execution of the process. These are only two components of describing the effects; we need to complement them with a means of describing how the structure of the decision-making process is affected. To do so, we may wish to draw on the phase models (for instance, Simon, 1960, 1977) that have been so popular in the DSS literature (see Silver, 1986, Chapter 1, for one such approach). Developing such a descriptive mechanism must be a high priority for DSS research.

DSS do not deterministically impose effects on decision-making processes; consequences emerge from the interaction of the system with its environment over time (Markus and Robey, 1988; Poole and DeSanctis, 1989). Studying the effects, therefore, also requires a means of describing decision-making environments; and it requires process-oriented rather than outcome-oriented studies. We are just now beginning to see a movement in this direction.

Cognitive Biases

As I have discussed several times, behavioral decision theorists have observed that, due to humans' limited capabilities to process information, human decision makers often resort to simplifying heuristics that can lead to systematic misprocessing of information, referred to as systematic cognitive bias. Literally dozens of cognitive biases have been reported (for overviews and surveys see Tversky and Kahneman, 1974; Slovic, Fischhoff, and Lichtenstein, 1977; Hogarth, 1980; Sage, 1981; Hogarth and Makridakis, 1981; and Kahneman, Slovic, and Tversky, 1982). Several researchers have raised the question of if and how computer-based decision support is related to systematic cognitive bias (Mason and Moskowitz, 1972; Sage, 1981; Kydd and Aucoin-Drew, 1983; Wright, 1983; Reneau, Wong-On-Wing, and Pattison, 1984; Schocken, 1985; Remus and Kottemann, 1986; Jacobs and Keim, 1988; and Kydd, 1989). In Chapter 1, I suggested one way of viewing the relationship: a DSS can improve decision making by attenuating such biases, or it can degrade decision making by amplifying them.

System restrictiveness and decisional guidance may play key roles in determining which consequences are obtained. On the one hand, a designer might try to "debias" users by deliberately restricting or guiding decision makers in ways that prevent the biased processing of information. On the other hand, designers might inadvertently restrict or guide users in ways that foster biased information processing. The relationships among system restrictiveness, decisional guidance, and systematic cognitive biases merit further attention. In particular, just as studying design strategies for causing directed and nondirected change raised questions concerning the trade-off between restrictiveness and guidance, so too does examining design strategies for avoiding or eliminating systematic cognitive biases. For example, Remus and Kottemann (1986) propose using artificial intelligence techniques to reduce the cognitive biases of decision makers performing statistical analyses. Many of their proposed techniques could be implemented either restrictively, by imposing analyses on the user, or through guidance, by suggesting such analyses.

A Prescriptive Mapping

The descriptive approach proposed here represents a critical step on the path toward a prescriptive mapping from decision-making environments to DSS, but considerably more research is needed before we can offer significant prescriptions concerning the type of system to be built for a given type of decision-making environment. We must first find a satisfactory way of describing and differentiating the elements of decision-making environments: the people, tasks, and organizational settings. Only then can we approach the mapping.

Describing Decision-making Environments

Several of the research tasks I have described depend on being able to describe and differentiate decision-making environments. Building a prescriptive mapping from environments to systems, describing how the interactions of systems and environments affect decision-making behavior, precustomizing systems for classes of decision-making environments, and matching decision-making needs with environments all require being able to describe environmental characteristics. A number of characteristics such as the decision maker's cognitive style (among other individual differences), the structure of the task, the functional domain of the task, and the decision-making style of the organization have been proposed for differentiating decision-making environments, but most have not been studied in detail in the context of DSS. We need now to describe systematically and differentiate decision makers, decision-making tasks, and decision-making settings. The descriptive mechanism for DSS may play a valuable role in evaluating characteristics proposed for describing decision-making environments. Those environmental characteristics shown to have meaningful implications in terms of the three-tiered analysis might be seen as the most promising ones to pursue.

Development Systems for DSS

A number of different software approaches can be used to develop DSS. One means of implementing DSS is by using general-purpose languages such as FORTRAN and APL. Alternatively, Sprague (1980) advocates "DSS Generators," packages of related hardware and software capabilities that enable builders to construct DSS quickly and easily. Since the three-tiered approach is used to describe specific DSS, not the development systems from which they are created, two important research questions are (1) how to describe the characteristics of development systems, and (2) how the characteristics of development systems are reflected in the DSS they produce. More specifically, the second question asks how the functional capabilities, user views, and system attributes of a DSS are influenced by the characteristics of the software system that produced it. One component of this research is purely descriptive, but a second component is developmental; devising DSS development systems that incorporate the three-tiered approach and that designers can easily use to produce DSS with given features—for instance, DSS with non-trivial sequencing rules or with extensive guidance—would be useful.

Directed and Nondirected Change

Earlier in this chapter I presented four DSS design strategies for directed change situations and five for nondirected change situations, each of which employed restrictiveness and guidance as design variables. As I noted then, each strategy needs to be studied individually and, within each type of change, the relative merits of each strategy need to be assessed. Change agency raises another question, one which does not involve the descriptive approach directly, but which logically precedes the issue of design strategies: Which view of change agency, directed or nondirected change, should be adopted? Although some DSS researchers and practitioners universally embrace one philosophy or the other, a broader perspective of DSS recognizes the legitimacy of both positions, with the choice between them situation-specific. We must study which views apply in which situations.

Generalizing the Attributes Beyond DSS

System attributes were defined in the context of DSS as reflecting how the system as a whole affects the decision-making behavior of its users. One may wonder, however, whether the system attributes can be generalized to computer-based information systems other than DSS and to tasks other than decision making. More generally, an attribute could reflect "how the system as a whole affects the task performance of its users." The precustomization and customizability attributes would generalize immediately; their definitions do not reference decision making, so changing "DSS" to "computer-based information system" in the definitions is all that is needed.

The definition of system restrictiveness does refer to decision-making processes, but could be generalized to include decision making as well as other information-processing activities such as communication, document preparation, and transaction processing, and to refer to other kinds of systems beyond DSS:

System Restrictiveness: the degree to which, and the manner in which, a computer-based information system constrains the information-processing activities of its users.

A number of information systems researchers (Silver *et al.*, 1988) recently explored this generalization to see how well it applies to such systems as electronic communication systems, computer-aided software engineering (CASE) tools, information retrieval systems, and interorganizational systems. For each type of system, restrictiveness was seen as a relevant concept for understanding the system, and factors favoring or opposing restrictiveness were identified, many similar to those presented in Chapter 4 for DSS restrictiveness. Understanding the general properties of restrictiveness and how the concept varies across system types appears to be a fruitful endeavor. One might want to do the same with decisional guidance, generalizing it in a similar fashion to "task guidance."

CONCLUSION

Description is an important activity for both practitioners and researchers. DSS designers need to describe what they are trying to accomplish (alternative system designs and intended effects on decision-making processes) and what they have accomplished (systems built and effects produced). Researchers need to describe the entities and relationships they are studying. The three-tiered descriptive approach can help meet the needs of both groups. Moreover, it can be used both before the fact, to describe alternative designs for systems, and after the fact, to describe systems already constructed.

The system itself plays the pivotal role in the process of supporting decision makers with computer-based systems; it serves both as the output of the developmental processes and as an input to the process of system use, thereby intervening in the process of decision making. Not surprisingly, in many DSS research studies the key variable is the DSS itself. Sometimes the DSS is the dependent variable, as in the question "Do different development systems systematically produce different types of DSS?" Other times the DSS is the independent variable, such as when we ask, "Are some types of DSS more likely to be used than others?'' Addressing the former question demands being able to describe systematically if and how a collection of DSS differ one from another. And answering the latter requires being able to vary systematically the features of DSS. The three-tiered descriptive mechanism offers researchers both of these analytic capabilities.

Although describing and differentiating DSS is necessary for much DSS research, it may not be sufficient. Means are also required for systematically describing and differentiating the characteristics of decision-making environments, and for systematically describing and differentiating the effects of DSS on the decision-making processes of their users. Such a threesome of descriptive mechanisms would constitute a solid foundation for DSS research and practice.

BIBLIOGRAPHY

Ackoff, Russell L. (1967) "Management misinformation systems," *Management Science*, **14**(4) (Dec.), 147–156.

Alter, Steven L. (1977a) "Why is man–computer interaction important for Decision Support Systems?", *Interfaces*, **7**(2) (Feb.), 109–115.

Alter, Steven L. (1977b) "A taxonomy of Decision Support Systems," *Sloan Management Review*, **19**(1) (Fall), 39–56.

Alter, Steven L. (1980) *Decision Support Systems, Current Practice and Continuing Challenges*, Addison-Wesley, Reading, Massachusetts.

Alter, Steven L. (1981) "Transforming DSS jargon into principles for DSS success," in Donovan Young and Peter G. W. Keen (eds), *DSS-81 Transactions*, Atlanta, Georgia, 8–10 June, pp. 8–27.

Anthony, Robert N. (1965) *Planning and Control Systems: A Framework for Analysis*, Graduate School of Business Administration, Harvard University, Boston, Massachusetts.

Applegate, L. M., Konsynski, B. R., and Nunamaker, J. F., Jr (1986) "A Group Decision Support Sysytem for idea generation and issue analysis in organization planning," *Proceedings of the Conference on Computer-Supported Cooperative Work*, Austin, Texas, 3–5 Dec., pp. 16–34.

Ariav, Gad, and Ginzberg, Michael J. (1985) "DSS design—a systemic view of decision support," *Communications of the ACM*, **28**(10) (Oct.), 1045–1052.

Barki, Henri, and Huff, Sid L. (1985) "Change, attitude to change, and Decision Support System success," *Information and Management*, **9**(5) (Dec.), 261–268.

Beach, Lee Roy, and Mitchell, Terence R. (1978) "A contingency model for the selection of decision strategies," *Academy of Management Review*, **3**(3) (July), 439–449.

Benbasat, Izak (1984) "An analysis of research methodologies," in F. Warren McFarlan (ed.), *The Information Systems Research Challenge*, Harvard Business School Press, Boston, Massachusetts, pp. 47–85.

Benbasat, Izak, and Nault, Barrie R. (1990) "An evaluation of empirical research in Managerial Support Systems," *Decision Support Systems*, **6**(3) (Aug.), 203–226.

Bennett, John L. (1974) "Integrating users and Decision Support Systems," *Proceedings of the Sixth and Seventh Annual SMIS Conference*, San Francisco, California, 11–13 Sept., pp. 77–86.

Bennett, John L. (ed.) (1983a) *Building Decision Support Systems*, Addison-Wesley, Reading, Massachusetts.

Bennett, John L. (1983b) "Overview," in John L. Bennett (ed.), *Building Decision Support Systems*, Addison-Wesley, Reading, Massachusetts, pp. 1–14.

Bennett, John L. (1983c) "Analysis and design of the user interface for Decision Support Systems," in John L. Bennett (ed.), *Building Decision Support Systems*, Addison-Wesley, Reading, Massachusetts, pp. 41–64.

Blanning, Robert W. (1979) "The functions of a Decision Support System," *Information and Management*, **2**(3), 87–93.

Blanning, Robert W. (1989) "Model Management Systems," in Ralph J. Sprague, Jr, and Hugh J. Watson (eds), *Decision Support Systems: Putting Theory into Practice*, 2nd edn, Prentice-Hall, Englewood Cliffs, New Jersey, pp. 156–169.

Blanning, Robert W., Holsapple, Clyde W., and Whinston, Andrew B. (eds) (1991) *Model Management Systems*, IEEE Computer Society Press, Washington, DC.

Bloomfield, Stefan D., and Updegrove, Daniel A. (1982) "Modeling for insight, not numbers," *EDUCOM Bulletin*, **17**(3) (Fall), 5–9.

Bonczek, Robert H., Holsapple, Clyde W., and Whinston, Andrew B. (1980) "The evolving roles of models in Decision Support Systems," *Decision Sciences*, **11**(2) (Apr.), 339–356.

Bonczek, Robert H., Holsapple, Clyde W., and Whinston, Andrew B. (1981) *Foundations of Decision Support Systems*, Academic Press, New York.

Boynton, Andrew C., and Victor, Bart (1989) "Information system design and the control imperative: a modest proposal," Darden School Working Paper Series.

Brennan, J. J., and Elam, Joyce (1986) "Enhanced capabilities for model-based Decision Support Systems," in Ralph J. Sprague, Jr, and Hugh J. Watson (eds), *Decision Support Systems: Putting Theory into Practice*, Prentice-Hall, Englewood Cliffs, New Jersey, pp. 130–137.

Brooks, Frederick P., Jr (1975) *The Mythical Man-Month*, Addison-Wesley, Reading, Massachusetts.

Carlson, Eric D. (1979) "An approach for designing Decision Support Systems," *Data Base*, **10**(3) (Winter), 1–15.

Carlson, Eric D. (1983a), "An approach for designing Decision Support Systems," in John L. Bennett (ed.), *Building Decision Support Systems*, Addison-Wesley, Reading, Massachusetts, pp. 15–39.

Carlson, Eric D. (1983b) "Developing the user interface for Decision Support Systems," in John L. Bennett (ed.), *Building Decision Support Systems*, Addison-Wesley, Reading, Massachusetts, pp. 65–88.

Carlson, Eric D., Grace, Barbara F., and Sutton, Jimmy A. (1977) "Case studies of end user requirements for interactive problem-solving systems," *MIS Quarterly*, **1**(1) (Mar.), 51–63.

Carroll, John M., and Carrithers, Caroline (1984) "Training wheels in a user interface," *Communications of the ACM*, **27**(8) (Aug.), 800–806.

Churchman, C. West (1968) *The Systems Approach*, Dell, New York.

Clemons, Eric K. (1980) "Data base design for decision support," Working Paper 80-10-02, Department of Decision Sciences, the Wharton School, University of Pennsylvania.

College Board, The (1985) *Enrollment Planning Service User Guide*, New York.

Collopy, Fred, and Armstrong, J. Scott (1989) "Toward computer-aided forecasting systems: gathering, coding, and validating the knowledge," in George R. Widmeyer (ed.), *DSS-89 Transactions*, San Diego, California, 12–15 June, pp. 103–119.

Cyert, Richard M., and March, James G. (1963) *A Behavioral Theory of the Firm*, Prentice-Hall, Englewood Cliffs, New Jersey.

Davis, Gordon B., and Olson, Margrethe H. (1985) *Management Information Systems: Conceptual Foundations, Structure, and Development*, 2nd edn, McGraw-Hill, New York.

Dawes, Robyn M., and Corrigan, Bernard (1974) "Linear models in decision making," *Psychological Bulletin*, **81**(2), 95–106.

Dearden, John (1972) "MIS is a mirage," *Harvard Business Review*, **50**(1) (Jan.–Feb.), 90–99.

Dennis, Alan R., George, Joey F., Jessup, Len M., Nunamaker, Jay F., Jr, and Vogel, Douglas R. (1988) "Information technology to support electronic meetings," *MIS Quarterly*, **12**(4) (Dec.), 591–624.

DeSanctis, Gerardine (1984) "Computer graphics as decision aids: directions for research," *Decision Sciences*, **15**(4) (Fall), 463–487.

DeSanctis, Gerardine, and Gallupe, R. Brent (1987) "A foundation for the study of Group Decision Support Systems," *Management Science*, **33**(5) (May), 589–609.

DeSanctis, Gerardine, D'Onofrio, Marianne J., Sambamurthy, V., and Poole, Marshall Scott (1989) "Comprehensiveness and restrictiveness in group decision heuristics: effects of computer support on consensus decision making," in Janice I. DeGross, John C. Henderson, and Benn R. Konsynski (eds), *Proceedings of the Tenth International Conference on Information Systems*, Boston, Massachusetts, 4–6 Dec., pp. 131–140.

Dickson, Gary W., Robinson, Lora, Heath, Richard, and Lee, Joo Eng (1989) "Observations on GDSS interaction: chauffeured, facilitated, and user-driven systems," *Proceedings of the Twenty-Second Annual Hawaii International Conference on System Sciences*, vol. III, pp. 337–343.

Donovan, John J. (1976) "Database system approach to management decision support," *ACM Transactions on Database Systems*, **1**(4) (Dec.), 344–369.

Donovan, John J., and Madnick, Stuart E. (1977) "Institutional and ad hoc DSS and their effective use," in Eric D. Carlson (ed.), Proceedings of a Conference on Decision Support Systems, *Data Base*, **8**(3) (Winter), 79–88.

Dos Santos, Brian L., and Bariff, Martin L. (1988) "A study of user interface aids for model-oriented Decision Support Systems," *Management Science*, **34**(4) (Apr.), 461–468.

Elam, Joyce J., and Mead, Melissa (1987) "Designing for creativity: considerations for DSS design," *Information and Management*, **13**(5) (Dec.), 215–222.

Elam, Joyce J., and Mead, Melissa (1990) "Can software influence creativity?" *Information Systems Research*, **1**(1) (Jan.–Mar.), 1–22.

Elam, Joyce, J., Henderson, John C., Keen, Peter G. W., Konsynski, Benn, Meador, C. Lawrence, and Ness, David (1985) "A vision for Decision Support Systems," unpublished manuscript.

Elam, Joyce J., Huber, George P, and Hurt, Mimi E. (1986) "An examination of the DSS literature (1975–1985)," in Ephraim R. McLean and Henk G. Sol (eds), *Decision Support Systems: A Decade in Perspective, Proceedings of the IFIP WG 8.3 Working Conference*, Elsevier Science Publishers B.V., North-Holland, Noordwijkerhout, The Netherlands, June, pp. 1–17.

Emery, James C. (1969) *Organizational Planning and Control Systems: Theory and Technology*, Macmillan, New York.

Emery, James C. (1974) "Cost/benefit analysis of Information Systems," in J. Daniel Couger and Robert W. Knapp (eds), *System Analysis Techniques*, John Wiley & Sons, New York, pp. 345–425.

Emery, James C. (1987) *Management Information Systems: The Critical Strategic Resource*, Oxford University Press, New York.

Fjelstad, Oystein D., and Konsynski, Benn R. (1986) "The role of cognitive apportionment in information systems," in Leslie Maggi, Robert Zmud, and James Wetherbe (eds), *Proceedings of the Seventh International Conference on Information Systems*, San Diego, California, 15–17 Dec., pp. 84–98.

Flores, Fernando, Graves, Michael, Hartfield, Brad, and Winograd, Terry (1988) "Computer systems and the design of organizational interaction," *ACM Transactions on Office Information Systems*, **6**(2) (Apr.), 153–172.

Fripp, J. (1985) "How effective are models?" *Omega*, **13**(1), 19–28.

Galegher, Jolene, and Kraut, Robert E. (1990) "Technology for intellectual teamwork: perspectives on research and design," in Jolene Galegher, Robert E. Kraut, and Carmen Egido (eds), *Intellectual Teamwork: The Social and Technological Bases of Cooperative Work*, Lawrence Erlbaum, Hillsdale, New Jersey, pp. 1–20.

Geoffrion, A. M. (1989) "Integrated modeling systems," *Computer Science in Economics and Management*, **2**, 3–15.

Gerrity, Thomas P., Jr (1970) "The design of man–machine decision systems," unpublished Ph.D. dissertation, Massachusetts Institute of Technology, Cambridge, Massachusetts.

Gerrity, Thomas P., Jr (1971) "Design of man–machine decision systems: an application to portfolio management," *Sloan Management Review*, **12**(2) (Winter), 59–75.

Gibson, David V., and Ludl, E. Jean (1988) "Group Decision Support Systems and organizational context," in Ronald M. Lee, Andrew M. McCosh, and Piero Migliarese (eds), *Organizational Decision Support Systems, Proceedings of the IFIP WG 8.3 Working Conference*, Elsevier Science Publishers B.V., North-Holland, Como, Italy, June, pp. 273–285.

Ginzberg, Michael J. (1978) "Redesign of managerial tasks: a requisite for successful Decision Support Systems," *MIS Quarterly*, **2**(1) (Mar.), 39–52.

Ginzberg, Michael J. (1981) "DSS success: measurement and facilitation," Working Paper Series #20, GBA 81–28 (CR), New York University, Graduate School of Business Administration, Computer Applications and Information Systems.

Ginzberg, Michael J., and Ariav, Gad (1986) "Methodologies for DSS analysis and design: a contingency approach to their application," in Leslie Maggi, Robert Zmud, and James Wetherbe (eds), *Proceedings of the Seventh International Conference on Information Systems*, San Diego, California, 15–17 Dec., pp. 46–56.

Ginzberg, Michael J., and Stohr, Edward A. (1982) "Decision Support Systems: issues and perspectives," in Michael J. Ginzberg, Walter Reitman, and Edward A. Stohr (eds), *Decision Support Systems*, North-Holland, Amsterdam, pp. 9–31.

Golden, Bruce L., Hevner, Alan R., and Power, Daniel J. (1986) "Decision insight systems for microcomputers: a critical evaluation," *Computers and Operations Research*, **13**(2/3), 287–300.

Gorry, G. Anthony, and Scott Morton, Michael S. (1971) "A framework for Management Information Systems," *Sloan Management Review*, **13**(1) (Fall), 55–70.

Grace, Barbara F. (1977) "Training users of a prototype DSS," in Eric D. Carlson (ed.), Proceedings of a Conference on Decision Support Systems, *Data Base*, **8**(3) (Winter), 30–36.

Grajew, Jakow, and Tolovi, Jose, Jr (1978) *Conception et Mise en Oevre des Systemes Interactifs d'Aide a la Decision: L'Approche Evolutive*, Third Cycle Doctoral Thesis, Institut d'Administration des Entreprises, Université de Grenoble II.

Gray, Paul (1983) "Initial observations from the decision room project," in George P. Huber (ed.), *DSS-83 Transactions*, Boston, Massachusetts, 27–29 June, pp. 135–138.

Gray, Paul (1987) "Group Decision Support Systems," *Decision Support Systems*, **3**(3) (Sept.), 233–242.

Greif, Irene (ed.) (1988) *Computer-Supported Cooperative Work: A Book of Readings*, Morgan Kaufmann, San Mateo, California.

Hackathorn, Richard D., and Keen, Peter G. W. (1981) "Organizational strategies for personal computing in Decision Support Systems," *MIS Quarterly*, **5**(3) (Sept.), 21–27.

Haimes, Yacov Y., and Hall, Warren A. (1974) "Multiobjectives in water resources systems analysis: the surrogate worth trade-off method," *Water Resources Research*, **10**(4), 615–623.

Hamilton, Scott, and Ives, Blake (1982) "Knowledge utilization among MIS researchers," *MIS Quarterly*, **6**(4) (Dec.), 61–77.

Henderson, John C. (1987) "Finding synergy between Decision Support Systems and Expert Systems research," *Decision Sciences*, **18**(3) (Summer), 333–349.

Hogarth, R. (1979) "Discussion of the paper by Professor Makridakis and Dr. Hibon," *Journal of the Royal Statistical Society*, Series A, **142**(2), 136.

Hogarth, Robin M. (1980) *Judgement and Choice*, John Wiley & Sons, Chichester.

Hogarth, Robin M., and Makridakis, Spyros (1981) "Forecasting and planning: an evaluation," *Management Science*, **27**(2) (Feb.), 115–138.

Hogue, Jack T., and Watson, Hugh J. (1984) "Current practices in the development of Decision Support Systems," in Leslie Maggi, John Leslie King, and Kenneth L. Kraemer (eds), *Proceedings of the Fifth International Conference on Information Systems*, Tucson, Arizona, 28–30 Nov., pp. 117–127.

Houdeshel, George, and Watson, Hugh J. (1987) "The Management Information and Decision Support (MIDS) System at Lockheed-Georgia," *MIS Quarterly*, **11**(1) (Mar.), 127–140.

Huber, George P. (1980) *Managerial Decision Making*, Scott, Foresman, Glenview, Illinois.

Huber, George P. (1981) "The nature of organizational decision making and the design of Decision Support Systems," *MIS Quarterly*, **5**(2) (June), 1–10.

Huber, George P. (1983) "Cognitive style as a basis for MIS and DSS designs: much ado about nothing?" *Management Science*, **29**(5) (May), 567–579.

Huber, George P. (1984) "Issues in the design of Group Decision Support Systems," *MIS Quarterly*, **8**(3) (Sept.), 195–204.

Humphreys, Patrick, and McFadden, Wendy (1980) "Experiences with MAUD: aiding decision structuring versus bootstrapping the decision maker," *Acta Psychologica*, **45**, 51–69.

Humphreys, Patrick C., and Wisudha, Ayleen D. (1979) "MAUD—an interactive computer program for the structuring, decomposition, and recomposition of preferences between multiattributed alternatives," Technical Report 79–2, Uxbridge, Middlesex; Decision Analysis Unit, Brunel University.

Humphreys, Patrick C., and Wisudha, Ayleen D. (1987) "Methods and tools for structuring and analysing decision problems," Technical Report 87–1, Decision Analysis Unit, London School of Economics and Political Science, vols 1 and 2.

Hurst, E. Gerald, Jr, Ness, David N., Gambino, Thomas J., and Johnson, Thomas H. (1983) "Growing DSS: a flexible, evolutionary approach," in John L. Bennett (ed.), *Building Decision Support Systems*, Addison-Wesley, Reading, Massachusetts, pp. 111–132.

Hurt, Mimi E., Elam, Joyce J., and Huber, George P. (1986) "The nature of DSS literature presented in major IS conference proceedings (1980–1985)," in Leslie Maggi, Robert Zmud, and James Wetherbe (eds), *Proceedings of the Seventh International Conference on Information Systems*, San Diego, California, 15–17 Dec., pp. 27–45.

Ives, Blake (1982) "Graphical user interfaces of business information systems," *MIS Quarterly*, Special Issue, 15–47.

Jacobs, Sheila M., and Keim, Robert T. (1988) "An experimental study in overcoming hypothesis-confirming search strategies in computerized information retrieval systems," in Janice I. DeGross and Margrethe H. Olson (eds), *Proceedings of the Ninth International Conference on Information Systems*, Minneapolis, Minnesota, 30 Nov.–3 Dec., pp. 81–89.

Janis, Irving L., and Mann, Leon (1977) *Decision Making*, Free Press, New York.

Jarvenpaa, Sirkka L. (1989) "The effects of task demands and graphical format on information processing strategies," *Management Science*, **35**(3) (Mar.), 285–303.

Jarvenpaa, Sirkka L., and Dickson, Gary W. (1986) "Myths vs. facts about graphics in decision making," *Spectrum*, **3**(2) (Feb.), 1–4.

Jarvenpaa, Sirkka L., and Dickson, Gary W. (1988) "Graphics and managerial decision making: research based guidelines," *Communications of the ACM*, **31**(6) (June), 764–774.

Johansen, Robert (1988) *Groupware: Computer Support for Business Teams*, Free Press, New York.

Kahneman, Daniel, Slovic, Paul, and Tversky, Amos (1982) *Judgment Under Uncertainty: Heuristics and Biases*, Cambridge University Press, Cambridge.

Keen, Peter G. W. (1975) "Computer-based decision aids: the evaluation problem," *Sloan Management Review*, **16**(3) (Spring), 17–29.

Keen, Peter G. W. (1976) " 'Interactive' computer systems for managers: a modest proposal," *Sloan Management Review*, **18**(1) (Fall), 1–17.

Keen, Peter G. W. (1980) "Adaptive design for Decision Support Systems," *Data Base*, **12**(1/2) (Fall), 15–25.

Keen, Peter G. W. (1981) "Value analysis: justifying Decision Support Systems," *MIS Quarterly*, **5**(1) (Mar.), 1–15.

Keen, Peter G. W., and Gambino, Thomas J. (1983) "Building a Decision Support System: the mythical man-month revisited," in John L. Bennett (ed.), *Building Decision Support Systems*, Addison-Wesley, Reading, Massachusetts, pp. 133–172.

Keen, Peter G. W., and Scott Morton, Michael S. (1978) *Decision Support Systems: An Organizational Perspective*, Addison-Wesley, Reading, Massachusetts.

Keeney, Ralph L., and Raiffa, Howard (1976) *Decisions with Multiple Objectives: Preferences and Value Tradeoffs*, John Wiley & Sons, New York.

King, John L. (1983) "Centralized versus decentralized computing: organizational considerations and management options," *Computing Surveys*, **15**(4) (Dec.), 319–349.

Kleindorfer, Paul R., Kunreuther, Howard C., and Schoemaker, Paul J. H. (1991) *Decision Sciences: An Integrative Perspective*, Cambridge University Press, Cambridge.

Kling, Rob, and Scacchi, Walt (1982) "The web of computing: computer technology as social organization," *Advances in Computers*, **21**, 1–90.

Kobashi, Yasuaki (1984) "The use of suggestions in a tables-oriented decision aid," in Leif B. Methlie and Ralph H. Sprague, Jr (eds), *Knowledge Representation for Decision Support Systems, Proceedings of the IFIP WG 8.3 Working Conference*, Elsevier Science Publishers B.V. North-Holland, Durham, U.K., 24–26 July, pp. 221–225.

Kottemann, Jeffrey E., and Remus, William E. (1987) "Evidence and principles of functional and dysfunctional DSS," *Omega*, **15**(2), 135–143.

Kydd, Christine T. (1989) "Cognitive biases in the use of computer-based Decision Support Systems," *Omega*, **17**(4), 335–344.

Kydd, Christine T., and Aucoin-Drew, Leslie (1983) "Strategies for reducing cognitive bias in the design and implementation of Decision Support Systems," *Proceedings of Northeast American Institute for Decision Sciences*, Philadelphia, Pennsylvania, April.

Laurel, Brenda K. (1986) "Interface as mimesis," in Stephen W. Draper and Donald A. Norman (eds), *User Centered System Design*, Lawrence Erlbaum, Hillsdale, New Jersey, pp. 67–86.

Lee, Jae K., and Hurst, E. Gerald, Jr (1983) "Supporting goal setting to solve typical semi-structured problems," Working Paper 83-10-02, Department of Decision Sciences, the Wharton School, University of Pennsylvania.

Lee, Jae K., Hurst, E. Gerald, Jr, and Lee, Jae Sik (1985) "The third generation multiple criteria Decision Support Systems," Working Paper 85-04-04, Department of Decision Sciences, the Wharton School, University of Pennsylvania.

Lerch, F. Javier, and Mantei, Marilyn M. (1984) "A framework for computer support in managerial decision making," in Leslie Maggi, John Leslie King, and Kenneth L. Kraemer (eds), *Proceedings of the Fifth International Conference on Information Systems*, Tucson, Arizona, 28–30 Nov., pp. 129–139.

Liang, Ting-peng, and Jones, Christopher V. (1987) "Design of a self-evolving Decision Support System," *Journal of Management Information Systems*, **4**(1) (Summer), 59–82.

Lindberg, Lars-Ake, and Brehmer, Berndt (1977) "Subjects' selection of feedback information in an inductive inference task," Umeå Psychological Reports, University of Umeå, no. 122.

Little, John D. C. (1970) "Models and managers: the concept of a decision calculus," *Management Science*, **16**(8) (Apr.), B466–B485.

Lopes, Lola L. (1983) "Pattern, pattern—who's got the pattern?" *Journal of Forecasting*, **2**(3) (Sept.), 269–272.

Luconi, Fred L., Malone, Thomas W., and Scott Morton, Michael S. (1986) "Expert Systems: the next challenge," *Sloan Management Review*, **27**(4) (Summer), 3–14.

MacCrimmon, Kenneth R. (1973) "An overview of multiple objective decision making," in James L. Cochrane and Milan Zeleny (eds), *Multiple Criteria Decision Making*, University of South Carolina Press, Columbia, South Carolina, pp. 18–44.

Makridakis, Spyros, and Hibon, Michele (1979) "Accuracy of forecasting: an empirical investigation," *Journal of the Royal Statistical Society*, Series A, **142**(2), pp. 97–145.

Makridakis, S., Andersen, A., Carbone, R., Fildes, R., Hibon, M., Lewandowski, R., Newton, J., Parzen, E., and Winkler, R. (1982) "The accuracy of extrapolation (time series) methods: results of a forecasting competition," *Journal of Forecasting*, **1**(2) (June), 111–153.

Malone, Thomas W., and Crowston, Kevin (1990) "What is coordination theory and how can it help design cooperative work systems?" *Proceedings of the Conference on Computer-Supported Cooperative Work*, Los Angeles, California, 7–10 Oct., pp. 357–370.

Manheim, Marvin L. (1988) "An architecture for active DSS," in Benn R. Konsynski (ed.), *Proceedings of the Twenty-First Annual Hawaii International Conference on System Sciences*, Vol. III, pp. 356–365.

March, James G., and Simon, Herbert A. (1958) *Organizations*, John Wiley & Sons, New York.

Markus, M. Lynne (1984) *Systems in Organizations: Bugs and Features*, Ballinger, Cambridge, Massachusetts.

Markus, M. Lynne, and Robey, Daniel (1988) "Information technology and organizational change: causal structure in theory and research," *Management Science*, **34**(5) (May), 583–598.

Mason, Richard O., and Mitroff, Ian G. (1973) "A program for research on Management Information Systems," *Management Science*, **19**(5) (Jan.), 475–487.

Mason, Richard O., and Moskowitz, Herbert (1972) "Conservatism in information processing: implications for Management Information Systems," *Decision Sciences*, **3**(4) (Oct.), 35–54.

McCosh, Andrew M., and Scott Morton, Michael S. (1978) *Management Decision Support Systems*, Halsted Press/John Wiley & Sons, New York.

McGrath, Joseph E. (1984) *Groups: Interaction and Performance*, Prentice-Hall, Englewood Cliffs, New Jersey.

Meador, Charles L., and Ness, David N. (1974) "Decision Support Systems: an application to corporate planning," *Sloan Management Review*, **15**(2) (Winter), 51–68.

Meador, C. Lawrence, Keen, Peter G. W., and Guyote, Martin J. (1986) "Personal computers and distributed decision support," in Ralph J. Sprague, Jr, and Hugh J. Watson (eds), *Decision Support Systems: Putting Theory into Practice*, Prentice-Hall, Englewood Cliffs, New Jersey, pp. 162–170.

Mintzberg, Henry, Raisinghani, Duru, and Theoret, André (1976) "The structure of unstructured decision processes," *Administrative Science Quarterly*, **21**(2) (June), 246–275.

Mittman, Brian S., and Moore, Jeffery H. (1984) "Senior management computer use: implications for DSS design and goals," in Robert W. Zmud (ed.), *DSS-84 Transactions*, Dallas, Texas, 1–4 Apr., pp. 42–49.

Montgomery, H., and Svenson, O. (1976) "On decision rules and information processing strategies for choices among multiattribute alternatives," *Scandinavian Journal of Psychology*, **17**(4), 283–291.

Moore, Jeffrey H., and Chang, Michael G. (1983) "Meta-design considerations in building DSS," in John L. Bennett (ed.), *Building Decision Support Systems*, Addison-Wesley, Reading, Massachusetts, pp. 173–204.

Nelson, R. Ryan, and Cheney, Paul H. (1987) "Training end users: an exploratory study," *MIS Quarterly*, **11**(4) (Dec.), 547–559.

Ness, David N. (1975) "Interactive systems: theories of design," *Joint Wharton/ONR Conference—Interactive Information and Decision Support Systems*, Department of Decision Sciences, the Wharton School, University of Pennsylvania, November.

Newell, Allen, and Simon, Herbert A. (1972) *Human Problem Solving*, Prentice-Hall, Englewood Cliffs, New Jersey.

Nunamaker, Jay F., Jr (1989) "Group Decision Support Systems (GDSS): present and future," *Proceedings of the Twenty-Second Annual Hawaii International Conference on System Sciences*, pp. 6–16.

Payne, John W. (1982) "Contingent decision behavior," *Psychological Bulletin*, **92**(2), 382–402.

Payne, John W., Braunstein, Myron L., and Carroll, John S. (1978) "Exploring predecisional behavior: an alternative approach to decision research," *Organizational Behavior and Human Performance*, **22**, 17–44.

Phillips, Lawrence D. (1984) "Decision support for managers," In Harry J. Otway and Malcolm Peltu (eds), *The Managerial Challenge of New Office Technology*, Butterworths, London.

Pitz, Gordon F. (1977) "Decision making and cognition," in Helmut Jungermann and Gerard de Zeeuw (eds), *Decision Making and Change in Human Affairs*, D. Reidel, Dordrecht, Holland, pp. 403-424.

Poole, Marshall Scott, and DeSanctis, Gerardine (1989) "Use of Group Decision Support Systems as an appropriation process," *Proceedings of the Twenty-Second Annual Hawaii International Conference on System Sciences*, vol. IV, pp. 149-157.

Poole, Marshall Scott, Holmes, Michael, and DeSanctis, Gerardine (1988) "Conflict management and Group Decision Support Systems," *Proceedings of the Second Conference on Computer-Supported Cooperative Work*, Portland, Oregon, 26-28 Sept., pp. 227-243.

Pounds, William P. (1969) "The process of problem finding," *Industrial Management Review*, **11**(1) (Fall), 1-19.

Reimann, Bernard C., and Waren, Allan D. (1985) "User-oriented criteria for the selection of DSS software," *Communications of the ACM*, **28**(2) (Feb.), 166-179.

Remus, William E., and Kottemann, Jeffrey (1986) "Toward intelligent Decision Support Systems: an artificially intelligent statistician," *MIS Quarterly*, **10**(4) (Dec.), 403-418.

Reneau, J. Hal, Wong-On-Wing, Bernard, and Pattison, Diane D. (1984) "Hypothesis confirming information search strategies and inquiry-type computerized Information Systems," unpublished working paper.

Robey, Daniel (1983) "Cognitive style and DSS design: a comment on Huber's paper," *Management Science*, **29**(5) (May), 580-582.

Rockart, John F., and DeLong, David W. (1988) *Executive Support Systems: The Emergence of Top Management Computer Use*, Dow Jones-Irwin, Homewood, Illinois.

Rockart, John F., and Flannery, Lauren S. (1983) "The management of end user computing," *Communications of the ACM*, **26**(10) (Oct.), 776-784.

Rockart, John F., and Treacy, Michael E. (1982) "The CEO goes on-line," *Harvard Business Review*, **60**(1) (Jan.-Feb.), 82-88.

Sage, Andrew P. (1981) "Behavioral and organizational considerations in the design of Information Systems and processes for planning and decision support," *IEEE Transactions on Systems, Man, and Cybernetics*, **SMC-11**(9) (Sept.), 640-678.

Schocken, Shimon (1985) "Probabilistic biases and computer-based debiasing mechanisms: an experimental design for the case of representativeness," unpublished manuscript.

Schoemaker, Paul J. (1980) *Experiments on Decisions Under Risk, The Expected Utility Hypothesis*, Martinus Nijhoff, Boston, Massachusetts.

Schultz, Randall L., and Ginzberg, Michael J. (eds) (1984) *Application of Management Sciences: Management Science Implementation* (Supplement 1), JAI Press, Greenwich, Connecticut.

Scott Morton, Michael S. (1971) *Management Decision Systems*, Division of Research, Graduate School of Business Administration, Harvard University, Boston, Massachusetts.

Scott Morton, Michael S. (1984) "The state of the art of research," in F. Warren McFarlan (ed.), *The Information Systems Research Challenge*, Harvard Business School Press, Boston, Massachusetts, pp. 13-41.

Sharda, Ramesh, Barr, Steve H., and McDonnell, James C. (1988) "Decision Support System effectiveness: a review and an empirical test," *Management Science*, **34**(2) (Feb.), 139-159.

Silver, Mark S. (1986) "Differential analysis for computer-based decision support," unpublished Ph.D. dissertation, the Wharton School, University of Pennsylvania, Philadelphia, Pennsylvania.

Silver, Mark S. (1988a) "User perceptions of Decision Support System restrictiveness: an experiment," *Journal of Management Information Systems*, **5**(1) (Summer), 51-65.

Silver, Mark S. (1988b) "On the restrictiveness of Decision Support Systems," in Ronald M. Lee, Andrew M. McCosh, and Piero Migliarese (eds), *Organizational Decision Support Systems, Proceedings of the IFIP WG 8.3 Working Conference*, Elsevier Science Publishers B.V. North-Holland, Como, Italy, June, pp. 259–270.

Silver, Mark S. (1988c) "Descriptive analysis for computer-based decision support," *Operations Research*, **36**(6) (Nov.–Dec.), 904–916.

Silver, Mark S. (1990) "Decision Support Systems: directed and nondirected change," *Information Systems Research*, **1**(1) (Jan.–Mar.), 47–70.

Silver, Mark S. (1991) "Decisional guidance for computer-based decision support," *Management Information Systems Quarterly*, **15**(1) (March).

Silver, Mark S., Boynton, Andrew C., Markus, M. Lynne, Nidumolu, Sarma, and Orlikowski, Wanda J. (1988) "Panel 1: Information system restrictiveness," in Janice I. DeGross and Margrethe H. Olson (eds), *Proceedings of the Ninth International Conference on Information Systems*, Minneapolis, Minnesota, 30 Nov.–3 Dec., p. 315.

Simon, Herbert A. (1955) "A behavioral model of rational choice," *Quarterly Journal of Economics*, **69**, 99–118.

Simon, Herbert A. (1972) "Theories of bounded rationality," in C. B. McGuire and R. Radner (eds), *Decision and Organization*, North-Holland, New York.

Simon, Herbert A. (1960) *The New Science of Management Decision*, Harper & Row, New York (revised edition, 1977).

Slovic, Paul, Fischhoff, Baruch, and Lichtenstein, Sarah (1977) "Behavioral Decision Theory," *Annual Review of Psychology*, **28**, 1–39.

Sprague, Ralph H., Jr (1980) "A framework for the development of Decision Support Systems," *MIS Quarterly*, **4**(4) (Dec.), 1–26.

Sprague, Ralph H., Jr, and Carlson, Eric D. (1982) *Building Effective Decision Support Systems*, Prentice-Hall, Englewood Cliffs, New Jersey.

Stabell, Charles B. (1974) "Individual differences in managerial decision-making processes: a study of conversational computer system usage," unpublished Ph.D. dissertation, Massachusetts Institute of Technology, Cambridge, Massachusetts.

Stabell, Charles B. (1975) "Design and implementation of DSS: some implications of a recent study," Research Paper Series No. 252, Graduate School of Business, Stanford University.

Stabell, Charles B. (1983) "A decision-oriented approach to building DSS," in John L. Bennett (ed.), *Building Decision Support Systems*, Addison-Wesley, Reading, Massachusetts, pp. 221–260.

Studer, R. (1983) "An adaptable user interface for Decision Support Systems," in H. K. Berg, W. E. Howden, R. R. Panko, and R. H. Sprague, Jr (eds), *Proceedings of the Sixteenth Annual Hawaii International Conference on System Sciences*, vol. I, pp. 490–499.

Stumpf, Stephen A., Zand, Dale E., and Freedman, Richard D. (1979) "Designing groups for judgmental decisions," *Academy of Management Review*, **4**(4) (Oct.), 589–600.

Swanson, E. Burton (1988) *Information System Implementation: Bridging the Gap Between Design and Utilization*, Irwin, Homewood, Illinois.

Taylor, Ronald N., and Benbasat, Izak (1980) "A critique of cognitive styles theory and research," *Proceedings of the First International Conference on Information Systems*, Philadelphia, Pennsylvania, 8–10 Dec., pp. 82–90.

Thompson, James D. (1967) *Organizations in Action*, McGraw-Hill, New York.

Todd, Peter, and Benbasat, Izak (1987) "Process tracing methods in Decision Support Systems research: exploring the black box," *MIS Quarterly*, **11**(4) (Dec.), 493–512.

Todd, Peter, and Benbasat, Izak (1988) "An experimental investigation of the impact of computer based decision aids on the process of preferential choice," Working Paper 88-MIS-026, University of British Columbia, Faculty of Commerce and Business Administration, June.

Turban, Efraim, and Watkins, Paul R. (1986) ''Integrating Expert Systems and Decision Support Systems,'' *MIS Quarterly*, **10**(2) (June), 121–136.

Tversky, Amos (1972) ''Elimination by aspects: a theory of choice,'' *Psychological Review*, **79**(4) (July), 281–299.

Tversky, Amos, and Kahneman, Daniel (1974) ''Judgment under uncertainty: heuristics and biases,'' *Science*, **185** (Sept.), 1124–1131.

Vroom, Victor H., and Yetton, Phillip W. (1973) *Leadership and Decision Making*, University of Pittsburgh Press, Pittsburgh, Pennsylvania.

Watson, Hugh J., and Hill, Marianne M. (1983) ''Decision Support Systems or what didn't happen with MIS,'' *Interfaces*, **3**(5) (Oct.), 81–88.

Watson, Richard T., DeSanctis, Gerardine, and Poole, Marshall Scott (1988) ''Using a GDSS to facilitate group consensus: some intended and unintended consequences,'' *MIS Quarterly*, **12**(3) (Sept.), 463–478.

Weber, E. Sue (1986) ''Systems to think with: a response to 'A vision for Decision Support Systems','' *Journal of Management Information Systems*, **2**(4) (Spring), 85–97.

Wedley, William C., and Field, Richard H. G. (1984) ''A predecision support system,'' *Academy of Management Review*, **9**(4) (Oct.), 696–703.

White, D. J. (1975) ''Coordinating paper: the nature of decision theory,'' in D. J. White and K. C. Bowen (eds), *The Role and Effectiveness of Theories of Decision in Practice*, Hodder & Stoughton, London, pp. 3–16.

Wright, William (1983) ''An empirical test of a Bayesian decision support procedure in a financial context,'' in Catherine A. Ross and E. Burton Swanson (eds), *Proceedings of the Fourth International Conference on Information Systems*, Houston, Texas, 15–17 Dec., pp. 241–249.

Young, Lawrence F. (1989) *Decision Support and Idea Processing Systems*, William C. Brown, Dubuque, Iowa.

Zachary, Wayne (1986) ''A cognitively based functional taxonomy of decision support techniques,'' *Human–Computer Interaction*, **2**, 25–63.

Zeleny, Milan (1982) *Multiple Criteria Decision Making*, McGraw-Hill, New York.

Zemsky, Robert, and Oedel, Penney (1983) *The Structure of College Choice*, College Entrance Examination Board, New York.

Zigurs, Ilze (1989) ''Interaction analysis in GDSS research: description of an experience and some recommendations,'' *Decision Support Systems*, **5**(2) (June), 233–241.

Zionts, Stanley, and Wallenius, Jyrki (1976) ''An interactive programming method for solving the multiple criteria problem,'' *Management Science*, **22**(6) (Feb.), 652–663.

Zmud, Robert W. (1979) ''Individual differences and MIS success: a review of the empirical literature,'' *Management Science*, **25**(10) (Oct.), 966–979.

Zmud, Robert W. (1983) *Information Systems in Organizations*, Scott, Foresman, Glenview, Illinois.

INDEX